PENGUIN BOOKS

WHY THE RECKLESS SURVIVE

Melvin Konner, Ph.D., M.D., is professor of anthropology and associate professor of psychiatry at Emory University. He is the author of *The Tangled Wing* and *Becoming a Doctor*, and coauthor of *The Paleolithic Prescription*. He has written frequently for *The New York Times*, the *Los Angeles Times*, and *The Sciences*.

WHY THE

RECKLESS

SURVIVE

. . . and Other Secrets of Human Nature

MELVIN KONNER

PENGUIN BOOKS

PENGUIN BOOKS
Published by the Penguin Group
Viking Penguin, a division of Penguin Books USA Inc.,
375 Hudson Street, New York, New York 10014, U.S.A.
Penguin Books Ltd, 27 Wrights Lane,
London W8 5TZ, England
Penguin Books Australia Ltd, Ringwood,
Victoria, Australia
Penguin Books Canada Ltd, 2801 John Street,
Markham, Ontario, Canada L3R 1B4
Penguin Books (N.Z.) Ltd, 182–190 Wairau Road,
Auckland 10, New Zealand

Penguin Books Ltd, Registered Offices:
Harmondsworth, Middlesex, England

First published in the United States of America by
Viking Penguin, a division of Penguin Books USA Inc., 1990
Published in Penguin Books 1991

10 9 8 7 6 5 4 3 2 1

"Genes and the Soul" as "Under the Influence" first appeared
in *Omni* and "The 'I' of the Storm" in the *Los Angeles Times
Magazine Good Health Supplement*. The remaining essays,
with the exception of "Nervous Energy" and the introduction,
were previously published in *The Sciences*,
Copyright © The New York Academy of Sciences, 1985,
1986, 1987, 1988, 1989, 1990.

THE LIBRARY OF CONGRESS HAS CATALOGUED THE HARDCOVER AS FOLLOWS:
Konner, Melvin.
Why the reckless survive — and other secrets of human nature/by
Melvin Konner.
p. cm.
ISBN 0–670–82936–6 (hc.)
ISBN 0 14 01.5289 X (pbk.)
1. Human behavior — Miscellanea. I. Title.
BF149.K76 1990
155.2'32 — dc20   89–40679

Printed in the United States of America

TO MARJORIE

ACKNOWLEDGMENTS

This book is in a sense a sequel to *The Tangled Wing: Biological Constraints on the Human Spirit*, which first appeared in 1982. I meant that book as an introduction to the science of human nature for the intelligent general reader. Back then, I might have put this last phrase in quotes, but the response to my book, both public and private, showed me that this is no euphemism, but a real and substantial category: people who, regardless of training, just plain love books. Not that they all loved *my* book, of course; but that they were able to enter into its realm of discourse without being intimidated by academic barriers to understanding.

This book, like that one, is designed to stand up to academic scrutiny without letting the general reader see the effort involved in gaining that legitimacy. Who is this general reader? Someone who loves to learn but does not want to feel quite like a pupil again. Someone who appreciates the subtleties of language but does not want to keep getting up to go to the dictionary. Someone who knows perfectly well that complex ideas can usually be expressed without gobbledygook. Someone who wants to feel that reading is conversation, not lecture or catechism. In retrospect, it seems odd that I should have doubted in the slightest the existence of such people, since I myself have been one since childhood.

The Tangled Wing set forth what I had learned about human nature until a decade ago, and in it I tried to acknowledge all who had helped me acquire that overview. Since its completion I have been to medical school, with its enormous fund of information and extraordinary clinical experiences; returned to anthropology after my M.D.; taught at Emory University for six years, including courses on human behavioral biology and human development through the life cycle; written a book about medical school; engaged in several scientific collaborations; spent a year at the Center for Advanced Study in the Behavioral Sciences; had a third child, a daughter; traveled to Germany and Israel, having what seemed to me profound experiences in both places; and had thousands of helpful conversations that advanced my systematic understanding of human nature.

Among those whose generosity with time and knowledge have helped to shape this book are the following: Walter Abelmann, Lauren Adamson, Roger Bakeman, H. Thomas Ballantine, Peggy Barlett, Ronald Barr, Joseph Beck, Kay Beck, Peter J. Brown, Michael Cantor, Stephan Chorover, Suzanne Corkin, Julian Davidson, Thomas Deeble, Carl Degler, Irven DeVore, Boyd Eaton, Daphne Eaton, Irenäus Eibl-Eibesfeldt, Marjorie Elias, Arthur Falek, Daniel Federman, Emmanuel Feldman, John Felstiner, Mary Felstiner, Norman Geschwind, Rene Girard, Joseph Glazer, Rachel Glazer, Avram Goldstein, Julian Gomez, Arnold Goodman, Robert Green, James Gustafson, Robert Hamerton-Kelly, Nancy Howell, Jeffrey Houpt, David Ingle, Kay Jamison, Jerome Kagan, Hazel Karp, Herbert Karp, Bettyann Kevles, Daniel Kevles, Bruce Knauft, Lawrence Konner, Ann Cale Kruger, Jane Lancaster, James T. Laney, Richard Lee, Robert Liebman, Gardiner Lindzey, Joseph Lipinski, Lorna Marshall, David Minter, !Xoma N!aiba, Robert Paul, Herbert Perluck, Robert Rose, Albert Rothenberg, Sandra Scarr, Bradd Shore, Marjorie Shostak, Elisabeth Sifton, Euclid O.

Smith, Stefan Stein, Sarah Steinhardt, John Stone, Sherry Turkle, Allison Williams, E. O. Wilson, Marian Wood, Carol Worthman.

These are the people whose intellectual friendship helped me add enough to my understanding of human nature to warrant another book. But the exact impetus for these essays came from a beautiful and intelligent magazine—it wins prizes frequently, so this is not merely my opinion—called *The Sciences*. It is the bimonthly magazine of the New York Academy of Sciences, but it is read far beyond the northeastern United States. From 1985 until the present, I have been a contributing editor, and have had the privilege of writing a regular column, "On Human Nature," where all but two of these essays were originally published. ("Nervous Energy" has at this writing been accepted for publication but not scheduled.)

My editors at *The Sciences* have been not just science journalists but literary professionals, and several have gone on to positions of great responsibility in the world of publishing. The majority of the essays were edited by Robert Wright (now at *The New Republic*) and Geoffrey Cowley (now at *Newsweek*), but some were edited by Mary Murray and Ed Dobb. Paul Libassi, the editor-in-chief for most of this period (now at *Reader's Digest*), also contributed in important ways. Others at the magazine who helped with meticulous fact-checking and additional editorial tasks include Pat Bontinen, Jane Bracciale, Art Charity, Jennifer Gilland, and David Kelly. Peter G. Brown, the new editor-in-chief, has helped with two of the essays.

I wish I could take credit for the titles, but as with most magazines, the author in this case could only propose, while the arcane, committee-based titling process did the disposing. Fortunately for me, that process usually tossed up something superior to the title I had thought of—including that of this book. I like the titles a lot, and I humbly thank whoever was responsible.

Two of the essays were published elsewhere than in *The Sciences*: "Genes and the Soul" in *Omni,* under the editorial hand of Murray Cox (the title there was "Under the Influence"); and "The 'I' of the Storm" in the *Los Angeles Times Magazine Good Health Supplement*, edited by Joel Greenberg. I thank them both. In 1989 and 1990 I was contributing regularly to the "Body and Mind" column of *The New York Times Magazine*, and although none of those essays is included here, my experience in working with Holcomb Noble, a superbly talented editor there, now shapes everything I write.

The compilation of the book required substantial recasting, the writing of an introduction, and the invention of a coherent whole. In this process the encouragement and editorial contribution of Dan Frank have been invaluable. My agent, Elaine Markson, has been an advocate and friend since long before this book was conceived, and I owe her a great deal. For technical assistance in the preparation of the manuscript, I thank Roger Devine at Viking and Debra Fey, Lauren Root, and Judy Robertson at Emory.

I cannot name the many patients and students who have played key roles in the growth of my understanding, but I am grateful to all of them. My wife, Marjorie Shostak, has tolerated my obsessive scribbling—"hypergraphia," the behavioral neurologists call it—for more years than I care to count any longer. My children—Susanna, Adam, and Sarah—have not only served as unendingly fascinating subjects for observation, but they have now begun to return the favor. Their candid observations of their father thus are now grist for his science-of-human-nature mill, making self-reflection through the prism of their childhood a new source of not-always-welcome data. As Sarah, the increasingly imperious three-year-old, said recently, "Papa, you have to put your book down now and play with me." Just so.

Atlanta, Georgia
March 1990

CONTENTS

INTRODUCTION

I.

In the eighteenth century Johann Wolfgang von Goethe, the great German poet and scientist, proposed that there is an archetypal form among plants, a sort of key to the very order of life itself. Indeed, he made his search for order a foil to that of Newton, which he considered too mechanical; Goethe thought that even the fundamental ordering principles of the universe might be biological, not physical.

Although he went too far with this, there is a sense in which the *Urpflanze*, Goethe's ultimate plant form, really does exist, and in which it has become, two centuries after he proposed it, as central to the enterprise of at least the life sciences as he believed it would be. It is not the form that appears in his idealized drawings of plants, but one much simpler and yet much more powerfully generative. It is an exceedingly long spiral shape, triply twisted upon itself according to firm and known laws. And it contains a code that, with only four elements, can specify every living thing in the whole world—past, present, and future.

The *Urpflanze* is, of course, DNA; and in the scientific unraveling of its beautiful form has come, and will continue to come, a sense of order and power in the realm of biology that even a mind like Goethe's could perhaps not have dreamed of.

How much of the realm of behavior will also come under the sway of its ordering power remains to be seen; but even the answer to this question will be largely provided by that power. Undoubtedly, it will include such things as conditioning, sensitive periods, psychological trauma, mental maps, and symbol systems, as well as love and cruelty—not to mention diet, infection, and injury.

But the way these things operate—within and against the constraints of the genes—to produce the unsettling complexity of human nature is much more uncertain than today's psychology and psychiatry textbooks allow; indeed, the mutual contradictions of those textbooks only serve to underscore the uncertainties. That the delineation of how the environment affects the individual, beyond the hoary pieties of plasticity, remains a task almost completely for the future—that we know so much less than we thought we knew—is perhaps the greatest discovery of the past twenty years.

Nevertheless, we do know some things.

II.

The fossil evidence for human evolution has accumulated steadily for over a century, and no one familiar with it doubts the reality and continuity of that evolution. New discoveries are made each year that change the details of the picture, and during the past two decades biochemical approaches have filled it in further. We don't need to follow each stroke, but we have to understand the general background of the human species and the rules of evolution as applied to behavior and reproduction.

All our nearest relatives, the monkeys and apes, are social animals with great learning capacity, and with the mother-offspring bond at the center of social life. This bond is always prolonged; development is slow and life is long. Laboratory and field studies alike demonstrate the capacity for complex social learning, including "cultural" transmission of social rank, tool-using techniques, and knowledge of food sources. Play—useless activity that looks like fun—is seen in all monkeys and apes, especially young ones, and aids learning. This reliance on the mother-infant bond and on play strengthens the pattern established by the early mammals and is a key to the evolution of the emotional parts of the brain.

Monkey and ape groups generally have a core of genetically related individuals with associated nonrelatives. Usually the core is a stable group of female relatives. Social support and generosity tend toward genetic relatives—but not exclusively. Individuals aid nonrelatives and can often expect reciprocal aid in return. Cooperation is ubiquitous, but so is competition, and one of the major purposes of cooperation is mutual defense against opponents within the group. Conflict is frequent and involves both sexes, but males do more of it than females.

"Personality" exists in wild monkeys and apes and includes types that would be considered pathological in humans, such as antisocial, isolative, phobic, or depressed individuals. Some patterns, such as severe depression (as in the case of an eight-year-old wild chimpanzee after the death of its mother), may make survival impossible. Others, however, such as extreme aggressiveness (as in the case of two female chimpanzees that systematically and repeatedly killed the infants of other females), may actually enhance reproduction for the abnormal individual. This does not mean we have to like it, or even that the individual performing it likes it. It may be psychically painful and morally abhorrent. But calling it maladaptive *because* we dislike it can mislead us badly.

Thus, the social world of our ancestors for roughly 40

million years. Against this background hominids (upright-walking apelike creatures—"humanoids" would not be an outrageous translation) evolved during the last few million years; our species within the last few hundred thousand; and, finally, truly modern *Homo sapiens*—us—within the last hundred thousand. Aside from growing intelligence—expanding brain size and greater complexity of stone tools and weapons—one hallmark of the transition to hominids was an increasing reliance on hunting, rare in monkeys and apes.

Among the most technologically primitive humans, hunting is always of major importance. Most stone tools that we have found were used in hunting or butchering, and the demands of this activity have always seemed central to the emergence of human intelligence and social organization. The stone used for this purpose had to be traded over long distances—implying complex social networks at least two million years ago. Even chimpanzees share meat after a kill (but not plant foods); and among human hunter-gatherers, departing from regulations for sharing meat may lead to a life-and-death conflict. Finally, with one impressive exception (the Agta of the Philippines, where women routinely hunt, and hunt well), all hunting-and-gathering societies on record have a division of labor by sex, with men doing almost all the hunting while women collect most of the vegetable foods. These features of society related to hunting were grafted on to an already complex social life characteristic of monkeys and apes.

Yet this traditional male view omits half the story. In many societies plant foods gathered by women make up more than half of the diet. These are shared with the immediate family, which is not true of any monkey or ape. Upright posture may originally have had more to do with the need for females to carry plant foods—and infants—to a base camp than with any advantage it conferred in hunting. And the first tools may have been digging sticks and carrying slings for plants or infants—nonstone tools that, however crucial, would not be preserved for posterity, and that would most likely have been invented by women.

The phrase "environment of evolutionary adaptedness" aptly describes the hunting-and-gathering way of life. This was the context for which natural selection prepared us, and from which we have departed only in the past ten thousand years—a short time in evolutionary terms. (The industrial revolution, in the same terms, happened only a moment ago.) Thus, most of human evolution and prehistory; we are, in effect, hunter-gatherers in business suits, propelling ourselves in metal boxes, through scores of stories, to the upper reaches of glass-and-steel structures that we arrogantly (and, in the end, rather pathetically) call skyscrapers.

I I I .

The mid-1970s saw the birth of a powerful new field of evolutionary study known as *sociobiology*. This novel set of principles has been quickly adopted by most naturalists, and has also influenced many anthropologists and psychologists. Briefly, the principles are these.

An organism is in essence a gene's way of making another gene. More strictly, it is a way found by thousands of genes, through transient or long-term cooperation, to make copies of themselves. As long as we admit that there can be no forces operating in nature other than physical and chemical ones, then continued membership in an ongoing stream of genetic material is the only goal served by any given gene. To the extent that a gene influences behavior, it can continue in the genetic stream only if it maintains or increases, through the behavior, the number of copies of itself in the gene pool of the next generation.

Genes spread by increasing reproductive success. Enhancing survival is only one way of doing this. Where the two goals are in conflict, as they often are, genes that enhance reproductive success will replace genes that enhance survival. The concept of fitness in evolutionary theory has no meaning except the relative frequency of genes. It is a tautological definition of reproductive success and has nothing necessarily in common with medical, social, or athletic definitions of fitness, all of which can be achieved without an increase, or even with a decrease, in technically defined reproductive fitness.

Fitness is best defined as *inclusive*. This means that genes tend to spread not only through the survival and reproduction of the individual carrying them but also through relatives who may be carrying the same gene through common descent. It is the concept introduced to account, using the algebra of evolutionary genetics, for the existence of altruism in animals, which previously seemed to be something that should be eliminated by natural selection. Hence the need for a newly defined process: *kin selection*.

If I die to save my identical twin, then the frequency of any gene that helped make me do that will (all else being equal) be unaffected by my death. In general terms, any genes leading me to sacrifice for a relative should be favored under conditions where the ratio of the relative's benefit to my cost exceeds the inverse of the degree of genetic relatedness. This concept has been invoked to explain the self-sacrifice of soldier ants for the colony, alarm calls of birds and ground squirrels, and nepotism in human beings, among many other phenomena. Other theories that have been brought to bear on the problem of altruism are reciprocal altruism and the prisoner's dilemma model of cooperation, which do not require that the individuals be related.

Sociobiology has also produced a theory of sex differences. Where the two sexes invest differently in the young, the sex that invests more will be the scarce resource over which the other sex competes. In fish with parental care, males frequently do more. In mammals and in most birds, females do more, but direct male care is very impressive in some species. Species in which males "father" a lot tend to be those in which male-female bonds are long-lasting, physical and behavioral distinction between the sexes is small, male competition for females is low, and differences among males in reproductive success are small.

These "pair-bonding" species, a category including eight thousand species of birds but only a minority of mammals, may be contrasted with "lek," or "tournament," species, so called because they have annual seasonal breeding "tournaments" in which males compete fiercely for females. These species often have specialized male organs for display or fighting (say, antlers or peacock feathers), little tendency to form pairs, low levels of "fathering," and some males with large numbers of offspring while others have few or none.

Human beings are near but not at the pair-bonding end of the continuum. Men are larger than women, mature more slowly, and exhibit peculiar displays of bodily hair. Women have done more child care than men in every human society on record. And polygyny, in which one man marries several women, is allowed or encouraged in most cultures in the anthropological record (708 of 849, or 83 percent), while the converse arrangement, polyandry, is rare (4 of 849); and a double standard of sexual restriction is found in the majority of societies. Still, men and women differ much less than the sexes in tournament species, and most human marriages have probably been monogamous at least in principle.

Sociobiological theory also has profound implications for the nature of the family. Generations of psychologists have presumed that evolution (or some very powerful force) must have intended the family to function more smoothly than it ordinarily does. A naive model of the nature of the family assumes that it is harmonious under ideal conditions, since that is allegedly how it was designed. But it was not so designed. Like the male-female pair, it is an association among individuals with partly distinct evolutionary purposes. Family members are often at odds with each other's ultimate (not merely temporary) purposes, and their relations are naturally conflictful rather than naturally harmonious. This conflict is not friction in what should or could be a smoothly functioning system but is intrinsic.

As for competition among unrelated individuals, it can be expected at times to be extreme. The belief that human beings are rare among animal species in that we kill our own kind is wrong, and more evidence to the contrary accumulates every year. Most animal species that have been observed long and carefully have been seen to exhibit violent conflict, including deadly conflict, in the wild.

In the past decade the application of sociobiological theory to primitive cultures has often seemed to bypass complex questions about society, culture, and the individual. For example, societies in which young men inherit from their mothers' brothers are more lax about the prevention of female adultery than are societies in which young men inherit from their fathers; in societies in which polygyny is allowed, wealthier and more influential men tend to have more wives (Asian and African despots, an unbelievable number); and in small-scale societies in which adoption of children is common, it tends to follow patterns predicted by genetic relatedness.

Yet none of these adaptations requires a simpleminded genetic explanation. Even in animal species it would be an underestimate to assume that similar adaptations are under similar genetic control. The wings of insects come from chest tissue, the wings of birds from forearm structures, the wings of bats from fingers, and the wings of humans from technology. These four adaptations to the problem of flight serve similar functions with very different mechanisms.

Sociobiology sometimes seems to imply that whatever is, is right. An extension of this fallacy would hold that the devastating blood disease sickle-cell anemia must be accepted because natural selection has maintained it—the genetic relatives of victims are more resistant to malaria—or that nearsightedness should not be corrected because natural selection in favor of sharp vision is thereby relaxed.

Human judgments about what is desirable must transcend any observations or explanations of what exists in nature, altbough they must take the facts of nature into account. Professionals who deal with mental suffering must define maladaptive behavior differently from the way evolutionists do. Still, the goals of reproduction and survival parallel those of mental health as Sigmund Freud independently defined them: *lieben und arbeiten,* to love and to work.

IV.

Although anthropology has focused on cross-cultural differences, there has always been an inevitable, even if tacit, complement: the discovery of features of human behavior that vary relatively little. This complementary concept of universals has at least five different meanings.

First, some behaviors, such as upright walking or smiling in greeting, are shown by all normal members of every known society. Second, some behaviors are universal within an age or sex class, such as the sucking reflex in all normal newborn infants, or the ejaculatory muscle contractions in all adult men. Third, there are statistical features that apply *on the average* to all populations but not all individuals, such as the sex difference in physical aggressiveness. Fourth, some universals are features of culture rather than of behavior, such as the taboos against incest and homicide, or the changeable but always present institution of marriage. Fifth and finally, there are characteristics that, although uncommon, are found at some low level in every human group, such as homicidal violence, thought disorder, depression, suicide, or incest.

The list of universals in these five categories is very long— much longer than most prominent anthropologists would have predicted. The search for societies without violence, or without gender differences that go beyond childbearing, or without mental illness, or even without the ability to make and use fire, has been a vain one. There is a large core of constant features; these demonstrate the reality of human nature and its validity as a scientific concept.

For example, in the realm of emotional development, Freud proposed a universal sequence that interacts with the family environment to produce enduring traits. Cross-cultural studies support only a few general elements of the scheme— infantile sexuality, attachment to a primary caretaker who is usually the mother, fundamental conflicts and jealousies within the family—but they have produced extensive evidence supporting some other possible universals of psychosocial growth, which can be plausibly related to underlying brain events.

These include becoming social, as heralded by smiling and eye contact, during the first four months of life; the emergence of strong attachments, as well as of fears of separation and of strangers, in the second half of the first year of life; the development of language during the second year and after; a sex difference in physical aggressiveness appearing in early and middle childhood, with males on the average showing more; and the growth of adult sexual motivation in adolescence.

Although their underlying biology is often unknown, these and other universals are maturational in essence, not just learned. They are a first approximation of the true structural basis of emotional development, which Freud was groping for with his bold pioneering theory.

V .

Within the last five years we have seen a new kind of inquiry in the study of human nature—the revolution in DNA technology, which is rapidly leading to a molecular genetics of brain, behavior, and mind. Its findings already range far beyond simple animal systems to the most complex function of the human mind, and from the beginning of life to senescence.

Some discoveries:

- A form of human gender ambiguity has been traced to an enzyme defect that blocks one normal form of testosterone; those affected appear female until puberty, when they become physically and *psychologically* male despite having been raised as girls.
- Huntington's disease, a brain disorder that appears in

the thirties or forties—sometimes beginning with emotional changes—is caused by a gene on the short arm of chromosome 4.

- Manic-depressive illness, a severe form of mental illness beginning in adulthood, including extreme mood swings and even psychotic thought, may be caused by a gene on the X chromosome.

- Alzheimer's disease, the most common form of late-life dementia, is caused in some families by a gene on chromosome 21, and the abnormal protein that causes the brain damage has been traced to the same part of the same chromosome.

- One form of schizophrenia, the most severe mental disorder, has been linked to a gene on chromosome 5.

These new discoveries remove any doubt about the fact that genes affect complex behavior. Soon we will be able to follow some biochemical pathways from the genes to the brain. That is decisive. Extreme skeptics will still claim that these findings have no bearing on the development of normal behavior, but they are fighting a hopeless holding action against the advance of knowledge. Of the hundred thousand or so genes in the human genome, the ones most easily identified would be the ones with the most devastating effects. But we *will* identify genes that affect *normal* human behavior, within at most one or two decades.

Such findings, though, will not be the end but the beginning of a scientific approach to human nature. In the absence of other treatments, few would argue that we should refrain from "gene surgery" for Huntington's disease. But even with manic-depressive illness there are serious ethical obstacles to tampering, because the same genes may produce desirable personality variations or even exceptional creativity as well as serious mental illness. With normal behavior the arguments for restraint would be still stronger.

Still, genetic technology will provide insights that will transform our philosophy of human nature. Already we have learned that mental and emotional functions can be damaged by specific genes, which can begin their effects at almost any stage of life. But we must progress beyond disease processes to certain distinctively human—genetically coded, wired-in—perceptions, thoughts, abilities, responses, and action patterns, as well as more treacherous realms like those of love, fear, sacrifice, selfishness, lust, and violence, which come most readily to the mind when the concept of human nature is invoked, to determine how much they are subject to the kinds of arguments applicable in the safer realms of disease.

To do this properly requires exploring the evolutionary origins of the pattern, cross-cultural variation in it, its physiology and development, and its genetics. Each has progressed so far in the last two decades as to render suspect any opinion on human nature that does not give clear evidence of having kept abreast of this progress. Unfortunately this suspicion applies to most accounts of human behavior and experience offered in recent years. But we can now lay the groundwork for a better one. The question will be: how does the environment interact with genetic predispositions and vulnerabilities?

One devastating form of mental retardation—phenylketonuria, or PKU—points the way. It is a fairly simple disorder with increasingly understood genetics, yet with an environmental trigger. It is solved through modification of one of the most mundane features of life: changing the diet blocks the impact of the gene. Drug treatments have also been tried, and one day "gene surgery" may be possible. At that point there will be a full spectrum of treatment possibilities—a showcase of the complex interactions of genes, bodily functions, and environment.

There will also be new discoveries about how environment influences brain and behavior. Recent research on brain development shows the great importance of competition among nerve cells and connections in the growing brain, and the process of selective pruning goes on after birth as well as before it. Some brain functions crucial to mental life even depend on complex changes in the chemical climate of the womb, under indirect, not direct, genetic control; these mechanisms of brain growth were not only unexplored but unsuspected until a few years ago.

VI.

If modern evolutionary principles are even partly correct—and the best current evidence on animal and human behavior insists that they are, and more than partly—then the fundamental metaphor of modern social science is in error.

That metaphor, as old as social science itself, claims that society is an organism, with individuals as cells, specialized subgroups of individuals as tissues or organs, and conflict as a transient aberration—pathology—the elimination of which restores the social organism to health. The basic weakness of the analogy is starkly exposed each time an individual or group departs from the society and joins or forms another—something the cells or organs of an animal cannot of course do; but in fact the weakness is evident in the ubiquity of social conflict even within the most interdependent social relationships. Such conflict is not inadvertent friction in a system that should, by design, function smoothly, but is inherent and inevitable, an expression of the conflict-ridden purposes of social life itself.

Looking inside the organism, we find that the motivational portions of the brain have functional characteristics relevant to the apparent inevitability of human dissatisfaction. Animal experiments on the hypothalamus suggest that motivation is to some extent nonspecific; the internal state is responsive to but not geared for the particular external circumstances. A continuum between attentiveness or alertness and intense arousal or "drive" states ensures that action will never be long delayed—but also that it will not always be appropriate; and, more important, that the organism's chronic internal state will be a vague mixture of anxiety and desire, best described perhaps by the phrase "I want," spoken with or without an object for the verb. This insight about the internal states of animals like ourselves fits well with the insights of sociobiology about conflict.

With these insights the view of life current in behavioral biology bears more resemblance to the view taken in time-honored traditions of the humanities than either does to the canons of social science. Henry James once described life as a "slow advance into enemy territory" and wrote, "Life *is*, in fact, a battle. Evil is insolent and strong; beauty enchanting, but rare; goodness very apt to be weak; folly very apt to be defiant; wickedness to carry the day; imbeciles to be in great places, people of sense in small, and mankind generally unhappy."

Similar sentiments have been common in the literary traditions of many societies, from the earliest religious and epic sagas to novels and plays completed this morning. Religious traditions also recognize the reality of a deeply, even tragically, flawed human nature, and most philosophers have shared this view. It would seem unlikely that Plato, Aristotle, Hillel, Augustine, Aquinas, Hobbes, Hume, Jefferson, Marx, and Nietzsche had much in common. Yet each had a firm concept of human nature in which animal instincts—selfishness, sex, violence—were seen to be struggling for supremacy against better human judgment supported by shared culture. Religious leaders exhort against flawed human nature, while literary artists seem satisfied to describe it. But both groups view it, sadly, as all too real, and their vivid classic observations of it fit well with Darwin's remark to the botanist Joseph Hooker: "What a book a Devil's Chaplain might write on the clumsy, wasteful, blundering low and horribly cruel works of nature!"

Of course, that nature also includes a built-in ethical component that derives the potential for responsibility, decency, love, even happiness from the animal necessity for cooperation and altruism. These capacities too are shared by many animals, and we can take heart from the fact that they are so widespread in nature. But for them to really prevail requires the kind of collective attention that is possible only in the framework of human culture. In this framework reflection on the outcomes of natural tendencies can restrain or modify those tendencies. Culture is full of deceptions, but it is much better than nothing, and with it we exceed the capabilities of any other animal for similar restraint.

The biological view of human nature provides many parallels with that of animal natures, and only a few clear distinctions. Traditionally and presently, distinctions between ourselves and animals have emphasized the primacy and complexity of human rational faculties. But in recent years the development of artificial intelligence has duplicated a surprising number of those same faculties, and people who think about this fact distinguish humans from machines by referring to the human emotional faculties—precisely those we share in common with animals.

It would seem that we are sorted to a pulp, caught in a vise made, on the one side, of the increasing power of evolutionary biology in explaining the emotions and, on the other, of the relentless duplication of human mental faculties by increasingly subtle and complex machines. So what is left of us?

What is left is that only we combine the emotions and the life-cycle drama of the animal world with a fully empowered reflective and communicative faculty. No other animal has that faculty, and no machine has an animal bodily life. Other animals can communicate, but they do not exchange views on the rightness or wrongness of their emotions. Machines can network and think, but they cannot ache with romantic longing or regret their fear of dying.

What religious people think of as the soul or spirit can perhaps be fairly said to consist of just this: the intelligence of an advanced machine in the mortal brain and body of an animal. And what we call culture is a collective way of using that intelligence to express and modify the emotions of that brain, the impulse and pain and exhilaration of that body. Both the intelligence and the impulse, the communicative ability and the pain, are components of human nature, and the way they interact is the unique feature of that nature. Without admitting the existence of human nature, without describing it as forthrightly and richly as possible, we will never fully exercise that crucial interaction, which alone holds the prospect of an admittedly limited, but absolutely imperative, transcendence.

TRANSCENDENTAL

MEDICATION

Dusk is closing. The horizon of the Kalahari Desert makes a distant, perfect circle, broken only by scrub bush and an occasional acacia. The human sounds of the evening meal are heard throughout the village camp, a rough ring of small grass shelters with a fire and a family in front of each. For some reason, on this night, there is an unusually high level of excitement among the people of the !Kung San band. Perhaps there is meat in the camp, or perhaps it is just the round moon rising. Perhaps someone has been ill—or maybe no one has. What is about to happen will benefit the healthy almost as much as the sick.

The women have talked among themselves and decided to try. They may have been prodded by the men, or they may have tested the men's interest with questions—or they may have just decided, simply and unilaterally. They begin to clap in complex rhythms and to sing in a strange yodeling style that bridges octaves gracefully, creating a mesmerizing array of sounds. Gradually, they collect into a circle around a fire. Emotionally and musically they echo one another's enthusiasm. Someone stokes the fire as the dusk turns to dark.

Two of the men sitting cross-legged in front of a hut poke each other and stir. "These women are really singing," says one. "But we men are worthless." They chuckle and then become more serious, although the joking will begin again as the night wears on. They strap dance rattles onto their lower legs and get the feel of the sound that bounces back when their feet slap the ground. "Look," one of the women says, smiling. "These things might become men tonight." The dancing begins as other men join in, tracing a circle around the singing women. The men's feet slam to the ground repetitively and solidly. That sound becomes orchestrated with the clapping and singing of the women, and the network of echoing enthusiasm widens.

A newborn baby wakes and cries, and is adjusted in the sling at her mother's side. A toddler stumbles over to his mother, leans against her, and stares, wide-eyed, at the dancers. A pretty young woman whispers something into the ear of the woman next to her; both of them glance at one of the men dancing and burst out laughing. The fire is stoked again, and it burns more brightly. None of this causes even a brief pause in the music.

Suddenly a man falls to the ground. Because he is in late middle age, the naive observer wants to rush to his aid, but for the same reason his !Kung companions are unconcerned. (They have been expecting someone to fall, and the older and wiser among them, because of their experience, are most susceptible.) He lies there for a time, moaning softly and trembling. Other men drift over to him and kneel. They rub him gently, then vigorously, as one of them lifts the fallen man onto his lap. Finally, the man comes to a semblance of his senses and gets to his feet. Now he is in another state entirely, still trembling and moaning but walking, fully charged with energy. He bends over one of the women in the circle and places his hands on her shoulders. The trembling intensifies, taking on the rhythm of his breathing. With each breath, the amplitude of his voice and the tremor of his arms increase until the crescendo ends with a piercing shriek: "Kow-hee-dee-dee!" He seems to relax momentarily, then moves on and repeats the ritual with each woman and child in the circle.

Meanwhile, the circle of singers has swelled, more men have joined the dancing, and other villagers, mostly children and adolescents, have formed a spectators' circle outside the inner two. One of the onlookers is a pregnant woman with a fever. The man in the healing trance goes to her for the laying on of hands, exerting himself at exceptional length and with exceptional vigor. At one point he pauses and stares out into the blackness, shouting almost hysterically, "You all! You all get out of here! You all get away from here!" Then he stares for a time into the void beyond the circle of spectators, before returning to the task of healing.

How does the healing trance come about? Could it actually confer any power to heal? And if so, how?

If Lorna Marshall, Richard Lee, and Richard Katz—three students of this ritual—could be at your elbow while you watched the !Kung dance, they might provide the following information. The trance and its power to heal are due in large part to the energy of the community. If the women sing and clap well, the men will dance well; if the sound of the dance rattles is good and someone begins to fall into a trance, the clapping and singing will rise to a new plane of excitement; if that plane is high enough and the men are sufficiently trusting of the women and of one another, several may enter deep and prolonged trances, and their healing power may last until after dawn.

The power itself, called *n/um*, is said to reside in the flanks of the abdomen, the pit of the stomach, or the base of the spine, and to boil up in a very painful way during the trance. The power to heal is not exactly the same as susceptibility to trances, but both are said to grow steadily during early adulthood and then diminish after middle or late middle age. A young man may have all the courage and energy he needs but, lacking experience and control, may be quite useless as a healer; an elder may have all the experience required, but his energy will not be what it was. (The parallel to the life cycle of male sexuality is striking, and, given the attitude of women to male trancers, perhaps significant.) As many as half of all men in the group can attain the healing power—an act of considerable courage, since the !Kung San believe that in a deep enough trance the soul may leave the body forever. The trance itself is at once exotically self-involved and heroically selfless. The individual is elevated in a way that is almost unique in this egalitarian culture, and yet his identity is dissolved; the ritual is of, by, and for the community.

If the dancer is experienced, his soul can travel great distances, to the world of the spirits and gods, and communicate with them about the illnesses and problems of the people. This marginal condition, between life and death, can be controlled only by the healer's own skill and by the vigorous ministrations of other healers. Their taking him in their arms, embracing him, and rubbing him with their sweat are considered lifesaving. In the process, the healing power can be transferred from an older, "big" healer to a novice; the novice places himself and his life in the hands of the older man, who must convey the power while protecting the novice from the grave dangers—both spiritual and real—that lie in wait.

In the active curing state, the healer "pulls" the illness (believed to consist of tiny objects) out of the patient and through his arms into his own body. With the climactic shriek he throws the illness out again into the sky (that inhuman world) from which it must have come. Since this ritual casts the community into what anthropologists call a "liminal" state—one in which the usual crucial boundaries between the phases of life, or even between life and death, are blurred—spirits may form a fourth circle behind the circle of spectators. Some of these spirits will often be the ones most responsible for the current illness, and their presence is considered a mockery of human suffering. Thus the healer in trance may address them directly, almost always in a berating rather than a conciliatory or supplicating tone.

The !Kung healing trance is one technique among many. Cultures of anthropological record abound with strange forms of altered states of consciousness and also with a prodigious variety of folk-healing systems. Few if any human groups have ignored the potential of our brains for generating experience detached from the everyday, and even fewer have failed to respond to injury and illness with some kind of healing strategy. In many cultures, as among the !Kung, the two are combined: cure is achieved through an actively sought, ritualized ecstasy.

Altered states of consciousness in primitive societies evoke both avid interest and smug derision, but in many cases the documentation is excellent, the altered state undeniably real. It is obvious to outside observers, sometimes using objective physiological measurements. It may be deliberately sought or inadvertent, dependent on or unrelated to drug ingestion or dietary manipulation, and with purposes as various as religious insight, sexual stimulation, ritual purification, clairvoyance, curiosity, relaxation, knowledge, fun, and healing—either of oneself or of others.

Altered states of consciousness and folk-healing systems thus overlap but are not the same sets of phenomena. The latter systems sometimes use pharmacological interventions that are effective—local anesthetics and digitalis are only two examples of modern drugs that were developed through imitation of successful folk practice. Many such systems of course also include practices that are of negligible value or even harmful. But they all have in common—and this is something they share with modern scientific medicine—a relationship between healer and victim that can affect the course of illness.

The behavioral and psychological features of this relationship—such elements as authority, trust, shared beliefs, teaching, nurturance, and kindness—significantly, and sometimes dramatically, promote healing and prevent recurrence. And these effects work in the modern research setting: counseling and psychotherapy speed recovery from surgery and heart attack and mitigate the suffering of patients receiving radiotherapy for cancer. Even a room with a view reduces the amount of pain medication requested by patients recovering from surgery.

Call it placebo if you like, but the human touch has a real and measurable effect. Some aspects of it appear to act directly, through neuroendocrine mechanisms, which, though poorly understood, clearly serve as intermediaries between mind and body. Meditation, for example, decreases heart rate and blood pressure and thus helps relieve hypertension, and there is recent evidence that psychological factors affect the immune system in various puzzling ways. On a more mundane level, the human touch can improve the patient's understanding of and compliance with medical advice—an area in which modern physicians have not exactly excelled.

In the 1970s, when I lived with the !Kung San in northwestern Botswana, along the fringe of the Kalahari Desert, I became an apprentice healer myself. The music created by the combined instruments of voice, clapping, and dance rattles struck me as being what used to be called psychedelic. Its eerie beauty seemed to bore into my skull, loosening the moorings of my mind. The dancing delivered a shock wave to the base of my head each time my heels hit the ground. This happened perhaps a hundred times a minute and lasted between two and ten hours. The effects on the brain and its blood vessels, and on the muscles of the head and neck, were direct and physical. Hyperventilation probably played a role, and perhaps smoke inhalation did as well. The sustained exertion may have lowered blood sugar, inducing light-headedness. And staring into the flames, while dancing those monotonous steps around and around the circle, seemed to have an effect all its own. ("Look not too long into the fire," warns Ishmael, the narrator of *Moby Dick*, for it may derange the mind.)

But more than any of these factors, what made it possible for me to enter into the trance (to the limited extent that I did) was trust. On the one night that was followed by a morning full of compliments, especially from the women, on how well I had done, I had it in the extreme—that "oceanic" feeling of oneness with the world, which Freud viewed as echoing our complete, blissful infant dependency. Whom did I trust? Everyone—the women; the other dancers, apprentices, and healers; the whole community—but especially my teacher, a man in his late forties (I was then twenty-six). He was not one of the most powerful healers, but he was strong enough to teach a novice like me. God, he explained, had strengthened his healing power (and given him his own dancing song) in a dream, during the course of a long illness. He was a well-respected leader in the community and, most important, he was my friend.

He had taught me many other things. He guided my first stumbling efforts to master the language, with its difficult clicks and musical tones, and he laughed at me only occasionally, and kindly. He showed me the elements of tracking, with its intricate process of reasoning. Once, while following the path of a wildebeest, he said, "No, I was wrong—the tracks are old." When I asked why he had changed his mind, we knelt down in the sand and he showed me tiny mouse tracks superimposed on one of the hoofprints of the large antelope. "Mice come out at night," he said. "The wildebeest must have been here long before dawn." Every day he opened my mind and heart to the strange subtleties of his distant, ancient world.

Over the two years during which we worked closely together, my regard and affection for him matured into love. He was sensitive, wise, loyal, witty, bright, vigorous, generous—in a word, the perfect father. During that night I committed myself entirely into his hands, much as a suggestible person might do with a hypnotist. And as I drifted into a mental world not quite like any other I have experienced (although it shared some features with states induced by alcohol or marijuana), my mind focused on him and on my feeling for him. I felt sure that he would take care of me. He left me to my own devices for hours, and then at last, when I most needed some human contact, he took my arms and draped me over his shoulders. We must have looked comical— a six-foot-tall white man slumped over a five-foot-high African hunter-gatherer—but to me it seemed one of the most important events of my long and eventful stay in Africa.

Yet the deep and all-encompassing sense of trust did not last the whole night through. I drifted into a delusion that something terrible was happening to my wife, who was back resting in our grass hut, a mile or so away. This idea arose from an almost completely irrational fear of the Kalahari and all the creatures in it, animal and human. I darted from the circle, jumped into a Jeep truck, and began to drive—a sort of technological American version of the inexperienced trancer's stunt of sprinting involuntarily into the bush. My trance was broken by the sound of the Jeep lodging itself on a tree stump, and I stumbled out in a dazed state to calculate the extent of the needed repairs.

What was happening in my mind and brain? No one can really say. We can guess that the cerebral cortex, which is centrally involved in logical thought, was dulled; but it is possible as well that selected parts of my brain were heightened in their functioning. Because of the trance's superficial resemblance to a seizure (in the falling phase) and, more important, because of the powerful shifts in emotion, we can presume the involvement of the limbic system—the structure, between the brain stem and the cortex, that mediates the emotions and has been implicated in epilepsy. Finally, we can be pretty sure that the trance involves some alteration of the brain stem's reticular activating system, which is the regulator of consciousness, ushering us from sleep to waking, from concentration to reverie. But this is all what mathematicians call "hand waving"—lines of argument so vague and sweeping as to satisfy no one.

So it is too soon to conclude that !Kung healing "works" (according to scientific standards), and too soon to give an adequate explanation of the trance itself. I suspect, though, that in the end we will have convincing evidence. In the meantime, we can give the !Kung credit for discovering a deeply insightful system of psychology, based on knowledge and methods as interesting as those of Western psychotherapies—and with at least equal symbolic richness. Consider the case of a young mother who had a serious bout with malaria in the wake of her middle-aged father's death. The healer in charge of her care entered a deep trance, during which, he later said, his soul left his body. Traveling the road to the spirit world, he caught up with her father, who held the daughter's soul in his arms. After much argument, the father was convinced that his daughter's need to remain on earth outweighed his own need for her and even his own considerable grief, so he returned her soul to the world of the living. A few days later, her fever and chills were gone.

Could the healer's report of his encounter with the father, related to the daughter, have influenced the course of her parasitic illness? Your guess is probably as good as mine. But mine is that the !Kung may have something to teach Western physicians about the psychological, and even spiritual, dimensions of illness and healing.

HANDS AND

MIND

On a clear spring afternoon in 1915, in the no-man's-land between the trenches at Marcheville, France, thousands were destroyed by machine-gun fire, among them Robert Hertz. Hertz, age thirty-three, was a second lieutenant in the French infantry, a husband, and the father of an infant son. He was also foremost among the pupils of Emile Durkheim—considered, in fact, most likely to succeed Durkheim as the reigning figure in French sociology. Nearly seventy years after Hertz's death, in November of 1984, Norman Geschwind, the reigning figure in the discipline of behavioral neurology—the analysis of behavior through the study of the brain—died of a heart attack. There is a kind of tragic symmetry in these untimely deaths, not just because each man was felled by a common killer of his day but because the two scholars had approached the same subject from opposite ends: through the study of culture, on the one hand, and of anatomy, on the other. Indeed, there is a kind of symmetry (or, really, a kind of asymmetry) about the subject itself, because theirs was the study of right and left.

Of the several important papers that Hertz had published by his early thirties, one was to prove of lasting influence: "La Prééminence de la main droite: Etude sur la polarité religieuse" (The Preeminence of the Right Hand: A Study in Religious Polarity). This essay was a reasoned yet impassioned look into the cross-cultural symbolism of right and left, symbolism that had imparted a near-universal and, in Hertz's view, illegitimate aura of superiority to the right hand and everything connected with it, however arbitrarily. He began by observing that in primitive thought dualities are not only commonplace but central—sacred and profane, noble and base, decent and sinister, cultivated and wild, high and low, light and dark, hot and cold, male and female. This observation has stood the test of time (although as Claude Lévi-Strauss and other modern anthropologists have pointed out, dualisms—in particular, good and evil, "we" and "they"—have been as characteristic of the primitives in the White House and the Kremlin as of the ones who rule greener jungles).

Hertz showed not only that right versus left was one of the main dualities in many cultures but also that it was consistently associated with these more abstract polarities. Moreover, value judgments were attached to the poles. "Right" in English, as in the French of his essay (*droit*), referred both to the dominant hand and to the rule of moral law. "Dexterity" and "rectitude" were other obvious linguistic associations of the dominant hand, while "sinister" and "gaucherie" were etymological tracings of the work of the inferior hand.

Such associations went way beyond the languages and cultures of Europe. In the Maori chiefdoms of New Zealand the right side was sacred, the left profane, that of the demons; the right was the side of life, the left of death. When a Maori priest initiated a young woman into the valued craft of weaving, using a ritually designed model loom, only the right of two posts on the loom was sacred, and only the right hand was allowed to touch the post, which would consecrate the acolyte to her art. As she wove, throughout her life, her right hand would hold the thread.

Examples multiplied. During ceremonies among the Wulwango—hunting-and-gathering aborigines of Australia—the right hand held a stick that signified strength and masculinity, the left another representing weakness and femininity. In the sign language of the North American Indians, the right hand could be used to symbolize bravery, power, virility, high, and "me," while the left signified death, destruction, burial, low, and "not me." Among the natives of the Guinea coast, the very touch of the left thumb to food was thought to introduce a lethal poison.

In the decades following Hertz's death, as his essay began to inspire field and historical studies, more polarities of the same type surfaced. Among the ancient Greeks, the Arabs, the Mapuche of Chile, the Toradja of the Celebes, and the Meru, Kaguru, Temne, Nyoro, and Gogo of various parts of Africa, "right" was associated with masculinity, strength, superiority, order, cleanliness, gift-giving, and goodness. In many cultures throughout the world, the right hand was reserved for eating, the left for activities at the other end of the gastrointestinal tract.

But these cross-cultural studies, while underscoring the universality of the right-left duality, did not invariably give right the superior aesthetic and moral color. Apparently Hertz had been unaware that the case of China introduced distinctive subtleties and a kind of balance that should have pleased him. In the yin-yang duality, yin signifies right and female, while yang signifies left and male. In various settings, traditional Chinese etiquette gave preference alternately to the right or left side, often according to quite complex rules.

Sometimes blood from the right arm was used to consecrate an oath, but on other occasions it was blood from the left ear. When expecting to be punished, one uncovered the right shoulder, but when attending a joyful gathering, the left.

Eating, as in many cultures, had to be done with the right hand, but beyond this rule were many intriguing variations. For example, in winter, which was the reign of yin, the belly of a fish was considered the most succulent part (yin being associated with "below"), and the fish was served with the belly facing right. But in summer, the reign of yang, quite different rules applied. Traditionally the Chinese had evidently developed a system of crossed and interlocking dichotomies that rose above the usual simple dualities. If humanity seemed condemned to follow symbolic polarities, they were not necessarily always simple ones.

Hertz's belief in the ubiquity of the right-sided bias led him to advance a bold but unlikely hypothesis about the origins of right-handedness. He began by citing the work of the great French neurologist Paul Broca, who had shown a half-century earlier that the speech faculties of the overwhelming majority of people are situated in the left hemisphere of the brain, which controls the right side of the body, while the right hemisphere controls the muscles on the left. Broca, to explain the preeminence of the right hand, asserted that the left hemisphere was by nature the dominant hemisphere.

Hertz did not deny the dominance of the left brain, but he advanced a "radical denial" of Broca's organic hypothesis. He speculated instead that the imposition of right-handedness on infants and young children was the *cause* of left-brain dominance in most people (a great majority, he believed) who are naturally ambidextrous but become right-handed through training. Hertz seemed to feel that his viewpoint was needed to redress the imbalance of centuries: "If the constraint of a mystical ideal has for centuries been able to make man into a unilateral being, physiologically mutilated, a liberated and foresighted society will strive to develop the energies dormant in our left side and in our right cerebral hemisphere, and to assure by an appropriate training a more harmonious development of the organism." This statement, from the closing passage of "La Prééminence de la main droite," is remarkable for having come decades before research would convincingly demonstrate the unique aesthetic, musical, and emotional sensitivity of the right, nondominant hemisphere of the brain—as opposed to the more analytical bent of the left hemisphere—and before some psychotherapists would on those grounds argue for hemispheric "balance" in much the same terms.

Norman Geschwind, in contrast, belonged squarely in Paul Broca's tradition; both were brilliant neurologists exploring the organic basis of mind. Geschwind began by studying "split brain" syndromes, in which the anatomic connection between the two sides of the brain was severed by disease, trauma, or surgery. This work helped lay the foundation for modern studies of the very different functions of the two sides of the brain. He wrote extensively on the aphasias and agnosias—disorders of language, writing, calculation and other aspects of higher mental function. His work in this area was helpful to philosophers in the ivory tower as well as clinical neurologists at the bedside.

The "two brains" were never far from Geschwind's mind. He viewed hemispheric specialization as the evolutionary novelty responsible for some of the most impressive features of the human mind, such as complex language and abstract thought. In 1968, he and another neurologist, Walter Levitsky, published a key paper in *Science* showing a consistent anatomical difference between hemispheres in the structure of the planum temporale, a part of the temporal lobe involved in speech perception.

Later, Geschwind and a number of younger colleagues became interested in a kind of epilepsy that seemed to result from damage to that lobe, a disorder characterized not only by seizures, often preceded by an "aura," or a sense of déjà vu, but also by an odd behavioral syndrome that affects the patient between seizures. It consists—with much variation—of unusually fervent religious conviction, reduced sexual interest, recurring anger, the production of voluminous amounts of writing, and a certain behavioral "stickiness"—a tendency to keep returning to the physician with minor questions.

The work of the neuropsychologists David Bear and Paul Fedio, inspired by Geschwind, has recently added detail to the once-vague picture of the syndrome: temporal-lobe epileptics whose seizures originated in the right hemisphere have largely emotional disturbances between seizures, while those with left-hemisphere seizures have more ideational aberrations.

The most original, and potentially the most broadly significant project of Geschwind's life was his final work on left-handedness. He had been interested in the phenomenon originally for the light it shed on the division of labor between the two hemispheres, but the subject eventually led him to a series of investigations ranging from immunology to anthropology to genetics and culminating in a fundamental challenge to some central dogmas of developmental biology.

Some characteristics, Geschwind noted, are passed on to offspring in ways that do not make sense in terms of Mendelian genetics; these traits are fundamentally different from blue eyes, or the ability to roll one's tongue into a U, in that the probability of a given child's inheriting them cannot be confidently predicted from the characteristics of parents and other relatives. Left-handedness is a prime example. Although it certainly runs in families, decades of study have failed to reveal the exact pattern of inheritance. Geschwind's eventual explanation of this fact was grounded in one of his characteristic offhand observations.

Beginning around 1980, he noticed that left-handedness tends to be associated with certain other traits, notably dyslexia and other learning disabilities, migraine headaches, and "autoimmune diseases," a category of illnesses, such as rheumatoid arthritis, caused by an immune system so indiscriminately active as to damage the body's organs.

Geschwind's explanation of this pattern was even bolder than his intuition of the associations themselves: all of these traits, he believed, are related to the influence of the male hormone testosterone on the development of fetal organs during pregnancy. Citing evidence from experiments with animals, he argued that testosterone slows the growth of the left cerebral hemisphere and that unusually large amounts of it permit dominance by the right hemisphere, and thus by the left hand. Hence the greater frequency of left-handedness in males than in females.

But how could testosterone be linked to migraines and learning disabilities? Really excessive or poorly timed release of the hormone, Geschwind thought, would alter brain growth and cause marked abnormalities of the left hemisphere—in the one case giving rise to periodic pain and in the other impairing the brain's ability to master such skills as reading. Such a structural abnormality had been observed during an autopsy on a dyslexic patient. And, since the incidence of dyslexia is four to eight times greater in boys than in girls, the idea that testosterone plays a role in it had an immediate plausibility.

Geschwind's theory about the link between testosterone and autoimmune diseases seemed even more farfetched at first, but it found experimental support. In rats and mice, testosterone slows the growth of the thymus gland, which appears to be responsible for the development of "self-recognition"—the ability of antibodies to distinguish between foreign matter, such as germs, and the body's own cells. Excessive amounts of testosterone in humans, then, might limit the immune system's ability to distinguish invader from ally, thus leaving the body exposed to autoimmune attacks. In a single stroke, Geschwind had provided a fairly plausible explanation for phenomena so diverse that no one had detected any connection among them.

What does Geschwind's writing have in common with Hertz's seminal essay, written more than half a century earlier? First, Geschwind's work, along with other research, confirmed Hertz's suspicion that the left-right dichotomy is to some extent a false one—and not just culturally but neurologically. Far from being a species of either-or individuals, with a vast majority of right-handers and a minority of equally immutable left-handers, we are in fact on a continuum between the two extremes, with an infinitude of ambidextrous grades. As a species, we certainly lean right, but the absolute left-hander is rare and the absolute right-hander not all that common. Geschwind would probably agree with Hertz that many individuals in the intermediate range are forced by training to abandon ambidexterity and are crowded onto one side of a very dubious dichotomy.

Of course, Geschwind's explanation of the origin of hemispheric dominance was biological, in contrast to Hertz's cultural determinism. But Geschwind, like Hertz, challenged genetic dogma, invoking a set of influences more complex than simple Mendelian heredity. If the difference between a left-hander and a right-hander lies partly in the level of testosterone during intrauterine life, then it is no wonder that we cannot discern a strict pattern of inheritance. Genes will still play a role, but so will the less predictable forces of the mother's hormone flux and her other contributions to fetal life and growth. Generalizing from this and other observations about intrauterine development, Geschwind theorized that many mysterious patterns of inheritance would come down to the physiological climate of the womb—itself determined partly by genes but also by the environment—and that classic Mendelian laws would explain, in the end, only a minority of hereditary traits.

At the time of his death, Geschwind was fifty-eight years old, a husband and father of three. At Harvard, he occupied the James Jackson Putnam chair in neurology, and he served as chief of the busy neurology department in Boston's Beth Israel Hospital—a vigorous clinician and teacher who intervened daily to improve the lives of patients and young physicians. He was on the verge of publishing a major series of papers on his theory of left-handedness. These appeared in the *Archives of Neurology* in 1985, written with Albert Galaburda, and in a jointly written book published in 1987. These writings will no doubt will have a major influence, and Galaburda—an outstanding research neurologist who co-discovered one developmental brain abnormality in dyslexia—will carry the work forward. Still, it is a great loss that Geschwind will not be here to parry the criticisms with his well-known eloquence and wit.

Geschwind claimed to dislike aphorisms, but he had some very fine ones. "There are no coincidences"—any seemingly odd association between disparate observations may pay off. "Don't standardize too quickly"—if you decide too soon what variables to measure, you may miss a valuable insight. "Abandon common sense"—unexpected explanations are often better. "Cultivate naivete"—too much formal knowledge prevents discovery. He did not suffer fools gladly, and he would not have wanted to be lumped with vague modern theorists of the duality of the brain. Yet perhaps this advice could be summarized as "Use your right hemisphere, not just your left."

CUISINE

SAUVAGE

In 1972, when I left the Kalahari Desert and the !Kung San bands that reside there, I had a vastly enriched comprehension of hunter-gatherer cultures, enough data for a doctoral dissertation, and a very enlightening sense of embarrassment. I had gone to Africa to pursue not only specific scientific goals but also some personal philosophic ones, among them the confirmation of a naive, almost Rousseauan vision of a rather noble savage. I expected to find, on the plains of Botswana, the beauty of the human spirit in "pure" form, unadulterated by the corrupting influences of civilization. The not-so-noble savages I had in fact encountered—and came to know so well, and in some instances to love—proved collectively capable of selfishness, greed, jealousy, envy, adultery, wife abuse, and frequent conflict ranging from petty squabbles to homicidal violence. Not that they were any worse than we are; they just weren't evidently better. Thus I learned a lesson that sooner or later impresses itself on almost every anthropologist: it is a risky business, at best, to project human ideals onto our evolutionary past. The noble savage does not exist and never did.

It was with a sense of irony, then, that a dozen years later I found myself under attack for supposedly having revived him. The episode had begun innocently enough. During the summer of 1983, I got a call from S. Boyd Eaton, an Atlanta radiologist and champion of preventive medicine who wanted to collaborate on a study of hunter-gatherer societies. Eaton, I soon discovered, believed that in the study of such societies were to be found critical insights into the human condition as well as, perhaps, the key to a comprehensive theory of human biology and behavior. That is not to say that he believed the myth of the noble savage. Rather, he simply subscribed to what anthropologists call the hunter-gatherer party line: regardless of whether ancient hunter-gatherer societies were in any sense noble, their genetic endowment was very similar to ours. This belief rests on the considerable body of evidence suggesting that 95 or 98 or 99 percent of human evolution—depending on what you want to call human—took place in societies sustained by hunting and gathering. Inasmuch as genetic change in the mere ten thousand years since the advent of agriculture has probably been trivial, the argument goes, we are in essence hunter-gatherers transplanted out of skins and huts into business suits and high-rise condominiums.

My once faithful adherence to that party line had been shaken in an oblique way by my experience in Africa. The trip to the Kalahari, after all, had been motivated by both my belief in the existence of the noble savage and my commitment to the hunter-gatherer hypothesis; the ensuing disillusionment had somewhat indiscriminately diluted both. But as I talked with Eaton, I regained some respect for the party line— enough, certainly, to proceed with our collaboration.

We set out to study the diet of ancient hunter-gatherer societies against the backdrop of recent research on nutrition. Using anthropological data on the remaining groups (including the !Kung San) as well as paleontological and archaeological findings about various hunter-gatherer societies that flourished between two million and ten thousand years ago, we proposed a model of what human beings ate during the better part of their evolution. Broadly similar theories had been advanced before, but we enjoyed the benefit of quite good numbers—credible data amassed over decades of modern research. Moreover, we added what proved to be a provocative comparison between our hypothesized Paleolithic diet and two other diets: that of the average American today, on the one hand, and that recommended by physicians and scientists, on the other.

The results were mostly as predicted but no less impressive for it. The Paleolithic diet consistently met or exceeded the standards being proposed for shifting the American diet toward a more healthful pattern. For example, the ratio of polyunsaturated to saturated fat consumed by the typical American is 0.44. It is now recommended that this ratio be moved closer to 1.00 to protect against atherosclerosis—the epidemic illness underlying most heart disease and strokes. In the paleolithic age, we estimated, this ratio was even higher— around 1.41. Sodium, a suspected cause of high blood pressure, is consumed by the average American at the rate of 2,300 to 6,900 milligrams per day, despite recommendations that the rate be cut to between 1,100 and 3,300. Our hunter-gatherer ancestors, it appears, consumed only about 690 milligrams of sodium per day. For fiber, which may protect against several diseases of the bowel, including cancer, the figures were 19.7 grams per day for Americans, 30 to 60 grams recommended, and over 100 grams estimated for Paleolithic people. The high level of fiber intake among hunter-gatherers also implies a low intake of sugars and other simple carbohydrates widely considered too common in the American diet. Once complex carbohydrates, such as those found in fruits and vegetables, are added, the percentage of daily calories derived from carbohydrates in the late Paleolithic period amounts to about the same as it does today. But the percentage of protein was much higher and the percentage of fat markedly lower. (Large quantities of fat are thought to contribute to cancer of the colon, breast, uterus, and prostate.)

The Paleolithic estimate corresponds to the typical American diet rather than to the nutritional ideal in one respect: cholesterol intake. Like the high Paleolithic protein level, this is due to heavy reliance on meat; cholesterol, being the major constituent of animal cell membranes, is abundant even in lean meats. Nonetheless, contemporary hunter-gatherers have extremely low levels of serum cholesterol, which reinforces the recent finding that the major dietary determinant of serum cholesterol is not, paradoxically, cholesterol but saturated fat.

Our paper concluded that there was an impressive convergence between the Paleolithic diet—the diet that evolution designed us to eat—and the generally healthful diet prescribed by modern nutritional science. "The diet of our remote ancestors," we wrote, "may be a reference standard for modern human nutrition and a model for defense against certain 'diseases of civilization.' "

In a burst of optimism, we sent the paper to the *New England Journal of Medicine*, arguably the most prestigious medical periodical in the world. To our pleasant surprise, the journal accepted the paper and published it on January 31, 1985, under the title "Paleolithic Nutrition: A Consideration of Its Nature and Current Implications." I knew that the health and medicine sections of many newspapers regularly report the journal's more arresting findings. Still, I was not prepared for the reaction that our rather offbeat paper (offbeat, at least, by the journal's standards) generated.

Days before we even saw the published paper, Eaton and I

began to receive telephone calls from an array of newspaper and broadcast journalists ranging from science reporters to food editors. Several reporters adopted the phrase "caveman diet" and went on to use it despite our insistence that it was not only misleading but it was also insulting to contemporary hunting-and-gathering peoples. A few representative headlines: "Cavemen Cooked Up a Healthy Diet" (*USA Today*); "Cave Man Takes a Healthy Bite Out of Today's 'Civilized' Diet" (*Atlanta Journal*); "Check Ads for Specials on Saber-toothed Tigers" (*Atlanta Constitution*). There were many amusing cartoons and drawings, but the graphics award surely must go to the *Fort Lauderdale News/Sun-Sentinel*, which ran a series of "Paleolithic" recipes accompanied by a color photograph of an actor grotesquely made up as a caveman—skins, club, tooth necklace, and all. Even distinguished journalistic institutions were not above this sort of humor. *The Washington Post*, after predicting the appearance of our book-to-be on the best-seller list, added, "Some day in the near future you'll look out at daybreak and see people all up and down your street come loping out of their homes wearing designer skins and wielding L. L. Bean stoneaxes while every dog, cat and squirrel in the neighborhood runs for cover."

Ellen Goodman, the much-loved syndicated columnist based at *The Boston Globe*, ridiculed us in an uncharacteristically harsh tone. Her piece was accompanied by an etching of savages dancing, captioned "Make mine mastodon." The column seemed marred by resentment—the resentment of a noncompliant patient sermonized yet again by high-minded, pesky physicians. "But I am convinced," she concluded, "that the average Paleolithic person was the very role model of good health when he died at the ripe old age of 32." We had made perfectly clear in our paper that Paleolithic people died much earlier than we do because of infectious diseases we have now conquered, while we die younger than we should because of diseases of civilization they (including the substantial minority who lived to ripe old ages) were protected from by their diet and life-style.

By and large, though, I got a good laugh out of the copy. I am enough of a writer to realize what a superb target our article made. Most of the jokes and cartoons were presented side by side with fairly serious summaries of the paper, and the pieces generally got the message across—and to a much larger audience than we could have reached without such help. (Fellow physicians and scientists had sent us scores of letters, the majority of them positive.) As Eaton pointed out after we had stopped laughing and finished licking our wounds, the attention to our ideas was what counted, and we had now become one more small force for preventive medicine in a sea of cultural forces aligned against it.

Needless to say, the critiques that appeared in the journal itself were more serious in intent than was the popular commentary. One reader pointed out that Paleolithic hunter-gatherers would likely have eaten honey—a challenge to our contention that their consumption of simple carbohydrates was meager. (In fact, the Pygmies of Zaire have recently been found to gorge themselves on caches of honey.) But we countered that there was no way our ancient ancestors could have consumed anywhere near the 108 pounds of sugar a year now eaten by the average American child, and that the archaeological record shows a massive increase in tooth decay accompanying the rising consumption of refined carbohydrates. Another critic questioned one of our basic premises—that there has been little genetic change since the hunting-gathering era. This is an important issue, and it calls for further research; but all studies of modern hunter-gatherers suggest an overwhleming genetic continuity between them and us.

For the present, then, our model of Paleolithic nutrition seems to have some claim on the truth. Still, the criticisms published by the journal were serious enough to lend weight to the barb thrown by *The New York Times*: "Did people of the early Stone Age eat more healthily than their urban successors? The issue is being vigorously chewed in the *New England Journal of Medicine*, and it tastes like the myth of the Noble Savage."

Undaunted, we went on with our research, joined by Marjorie Shostak, another anthropologist who had studied the !Kung. We broadened the perspective to include much more than diet: exercise, work, baby and child care, and even relations between the sexes. Eventually enough data accumulated for a book, *The Paleolithic Prescription*, published by Eaton, Shostak, and myself in 1988.

By this time many medical authorities had embraced our unorthodox approach, making the journalistic cavils seem less important. Our 1985 paper was made the basis of the keynote address, by physician Alexander Leaf, to the International Society of Clinical Nutrition in 1987. Another paper, "Stone Agers in the Fast Lane," also co-authored with Shostak, focused on physiology and disease patterns in primitive and civilized societies, showing the consequences of differences in life-style. It was published in the *American Journal of Medicine* in 1988 and became the subject of an extremely favorable editorial in the prestigious *American Journal of Cardiology*. So when our book came out at last, the jokes were muted and the reviews much more respectful than the editorials of 1985.

Had we indeed projected today's medical ideals onto our evolutionary past? I won't speak for Eaton or Shostak, but I know myself well enough to concede that possibility; I don't purport to be conscious of all my motivations, and it may well be that I was still inspired by the same naivete that drew me to the Kalahari as a student. But whatever the inspiration for our study, we took pains to conduct it by the rules. We spent months examining and reexamining our premises and the data collected by scores of anthropologists, and we were very hard on any interpretation that even hinted at romanticism. But a solid core of good data survived our harshest scrutiny, and the burden of proof now rests with those who doubt that the diet and exercise pattern of hunter-gatherers, whether recent or ancient, was qualitatively better than the average American's. Other differences in life-style are of uncertain importance, but some of them will certainly prove as illuminating as differences in diet have been.

A scientific hypothesis, after all, should be evaluated not on the basis of its author's motives but on the basis of its merits. It does not find its way into a respectable journal because it was nobly conceived or because it is guaranteed to be right, but because it is sufficiently supported by facts to warrant admission, at least temporarily, into the stream of scientific discourse. Scientists' motivations must come from somewhere, and the realities of research are such that the pure pursuit of truth is often asked to coexist with a certain amount of advocacy. The best we can hope is that the resulting discourse resembles the contending thoughts in a single, rather superior mind—contradiction progressing toward synthesis.

THE NURSING

KNOT

Some two hundred million years ago—give or take, say, twenty million—our ancestors, the early mammals, ushered a brand-new physiological function into the realm of vertebrate biology. Lactation, the production of milky fluids for sustenance of the young, is today viewed as a hallmark of the mammalian class, along with body hair, homeothermy (stabilization of body temperature—often called "warm-bloodedness"), and a well-developed limbic system—that amalgam of cerebral circuitry that plays a key role in emotion, learning, memory, and motivation. We think of these signal adaptations not only as the defining characteristics of mammals (the things we had to remember about them to pass high-school biology) but also as the key to our success. This was the secret code that somehow unlocked the potential of our ancestors, enabling them to achieve that vast evolutionary expansion known as adaptive radiation and, eventually, to leave the dinosaurs in the dust.

Of course, we have lately come to view dinosaurs as more dignified. New fossil discoveries and fresh analyses of existing evidence suggest that they too may have been warm-blooded and perhaps even cared for their young. Indeed, some paleontologists no longer attribute the extinction of the dinosaurs to the animals' inadequacies (a blame-the-victim notion that never did seem very polite) but rather to some catastrophe at the end of the Cretaceous period—perhaps the collision of an asteroid with the earth.

Be that as it may, the mammals *did* make it, and have now reigned supreme for more than sixty million years. They filled the earth with their kind and even resulted, ultimately, in us. This gives us a forgivable bias toward other mammals, and an intense curiosity about what our precursors did right.

The nursing knot sits tightly wound at the center of this puzzle, and it is a knot in two senses. The first and more obvious is that of a scientific-problem knot, being picked at by investigators of many stripes. How does nursing work? What are the relative roles of hormones and nerve circuits? What is the real nutritional value of mother's milk? Answers to these questions can partly explain how lactation helped fuel the mammals' rapid proliferation—and thus how it secured a place in our genetic endowment. But additional clues may come from examining the second, metaphoric nursing knot: like almost nothing else in the annals of vertebrate life, nursing ties two creatures into a critical dependency, a prolonged and almost constant mutual regulation that affects the physiology and behavior of mother and offspring alike. For the one, the rewards are physical pleasure, a salutary adjustment of fertility patterns, and that evolutionary sine qua non, transmission of the genes; for the other, the reward is life itself. Perhaps it is in this complex bond of mutual influence, more than in any nutritional benefit, that the evolutionary value of nursing is to be found.

I did not pay much attention to the nursing knot until I went to Africa. I had grown up in New York City during the forties and fifties, when nursing, having been firmly discouraged by pediatricians, was not exactly seen on every street corner. Many physicians had concluded that bottle-feeding—for humans, in any case—was medically superior for all concerned. American women abandoned breast feeding, in droves.

Meanwhile, despite the insistence of Freudians that an infant's lifelong sense of security is forged during its "oral" stage, behavioral scientists were accumulating evidence to the contrary. Most influential were Harry Harlow's demonstration that contact comfort—hugging and touching—mattered more to infant rhesus monkeys than did the source of food, at least in determining whom the infant would love; and Bettye Caldwell's review of a large literature on children, showing that there was no psychological difference, at any stage of life, between those who had been breast-fed and those who had been bottle-fed. Apparently it didn't much matter how you were fed as long as you got, first, enough nutrition to thrive and, second, enough love to keep you interested in life. It is not surprising, then, that when I went to northwestern Botswana in 1969 to study infants among the !Kung San hunter-gatherers, my infant-observation protocol—a kind of behavioral scientist's shorthand—did not even have a symbol for "nurse." This omission presented itself immediately as a glaring one. !Kung San toddlers, rarely separated from their mothers, would nurse several times an hour until at least age three, and in the absence of a younger sibling until age six. (One boy observed by another anthropologist, Patricia Draper, was his mother's coddled last child and would take an occasional suck until age eight, when the ridicule of playmates induced him to stop.) As for the infants, it was barely possible to squeeze in a fifteen-minute observation of their play habits between bouts of nursing, and I finally quit trying, and incorporated nursing into my records of play.

In this culture, nursing was central not only in the life of the infant but in that of the mother as well. It certainly was ubiquitous. Infants up to two years of age (at least) went to the breast an average of four times an hour for around two minutes each time, throughout their waking hours. There were some longer nursing sessions—ten minutes or more— and many shorter ones, even just a few seconds. The amount and frequency were slightly greater in earliest infancy but declined only slowly until age three or four, to be cut off early in the mother's next pregnancy. Virtually all children under three woke up at least once each night to nurse.

As for the mother, she could count on spending most of her life either nursing or pregnant, from her first fertile period, in her late teens, until her last, some time around age forty. Menstruation was not the more or less constant round common in the West but a relatively infrequent event, suppressed by nursing for nearly two years after each birth and then once again by the almost inevitable ensuing pregnancy. After adolescence a woman's breasts were no longer primarily objects of sexual attention; they would be freely accessible to a succession of insatiable little creatures—a situation made tolerable only by great forbearance and, presumably, quantities of love.

The milk was of high nutritional quality, especially compared with that of other populations in the developing world. Fat and protein content were high, with a balanced amino acid profile, reflecting the balanced hunter-gatherer diet. (Almost any molecule that circulates in blood can pass to milk.) Growth itself was more questionable. !Kung infants fell below the standard curve for American children's growth between six and twelve months of age—an age when supplementary feeding of infants was inadequate and mortality was very high, although not different from that of other populations in the developing world. Although young children did not complain of hunger, nor were there any clinical signs of malnutrition—it was a world of cheerful, active children, some of whom succumbed to infectious diseases—it was possible that toddlers were drawn back to the breast by hunger as well as by habit or by love.

As I discovered after returning from the field in 1971, virtually all hunter-gatherer societies that have been studied—particularly those in warmer climates—have or had nursing habits roughly similar to those of the !Kung. Indeed, such habits have been observed in many other nonindustrial small-scale societies. The continual breast-feeding of infants and toddlers seems to be a basic human pattern and thus offers a solution to a long-standing paradox.

In the early 1970s, the ethologist Nicholas Blurton Jones, of the University of California at Los Angeles, noticed that the higher primates—the monkeys and apes that are our closest relatives—share certain characteristics of lactation with mammals whose young remain in continuous contact with their mothers, clinging to them tenaciously or, perhaps, being carried around indulgently. The milk of these mammals is relatively watery, yet still adequate for its purpose; the young nurse frequently but suck slowly. On the other hand, mammals that leave their young in caches or nests—rabbits are an example—tend to nurse less frequently. (Among some tree shrews, at the extreme of this continuum, the mother shows up only once every forty-eight hours.) In contrast with "carrying" creatures, "caching" ones have rich, thick, fatty milk, and their young suck at a prodigious rate whenever given the chance.

There are many variations in the milk composition of mammals, but this cache-and-carry continuum seems to cut across them all—except, it has long seemed, in the case of our species: humans in industrialized societies space their nursing sessions at least several hours apart and deposit their young in cachelike cribs and playpens, yet they have thinnish milk and the infants have low sucking rates. But the intense nursing pattern of the !Kung began to make humans look more logical: we are by nature a carrying species and were urged into the cache mode only by the dictates of modern life, long after our basic genetic composition had settled in.

But the question remains: why did nursing arise in the first place? And what compelled humans, during our hunting-gathering past, to carry it to such an extreme? Nutrition and water balance, of course, are primary. But a more subtle, and fascinating, answer centers on the transfer of disease immunity. Human milk is dense with antibodies, and with each suck the infant also ingests millions of macrophages that can assault gut bacteria. This is not just general protection. The mother forms specific antibodies against germs to which she is exposed and transfers *those* antibodies to the infant—who has likely been exposed to the same germs and is therefore in need of exactly this protection. (It could even be argued that because of the exponential growth of bacteria in the gut, it was advantageous to deliver the macrophage-laden milk as often as every fifteen minutes to keep the child's gastro-intestinal tract under surveillance and control.)

Yet perhaps the most interesting evolutionary rationales for nursing have to do not with what is transmitted by the milk but with the act of nursing—its effect on the behavior of mother and offspring and on the family's reproductive future. Take, for example, protection through proximity. During higher-primate evolution, an infant separated from its mother was likely quite vulnerable to predation. Frequent nursing, then, may have been just one of evolution's tactics for keeping mother and infant together.

Most intriguing to me, it may also have been a kind of automatic family planning, a possibility suggested by the work of

Nancy Howell and Richard Lee of the University of Toronto. They have shown that the !Kung increase their numbers much more slowly than other third-world populations, at a rate just barely above zero population growth. Since mortality is not higher, the explanation must lie in the four-year !Kung birth interval—about twice as long as that found in most other parts of Africa.

In 1975, after my second trip to Botswana, Carol Worthman, now of Emory University, and I explored the possibility that the solution to this puzzle lay in the effect of frequent nursing on the hormonal system. We found that !Kung women, besides not menstruating for nearly two years after giving birth, had profoundly suppressed levels of estrogen and progesterone in their blood. We suspected that this was caused by the hormone prolactin, which inhibits the ovarian cycle while promoting milk production, and that frequent nursing stimulated the release of prolactin just often enough to preclude pregnancy. Later we measured prolactin directly, and found it in levels far above normal. Studies of frequently nursing American women, conducted by Judith Stern, of Rutgers University, and Seymour Reichlin and Talia Herman, of the Tufts–New England Medical Center, confirmed these hormonal consequences, under more carefully controlled conditions. In addition, laboratory studies of monkeys have shown that frequent nursing could interfere with reproduction by disrupting the secretion of gonadotrophic (ovary-stimulating) hormones from the pituitary gland, even without mediation by prolactin; this suggested a second mechanism linking frequent nursing to prolonged birth spacing.

Thus, it is possible that the mammals as they evolved discovered not only a strategy for infant nutrition and protection against disease and predators but also a means of regulating birth spacing to maximize the number of surviving offspring. (After all, the higher primates require an extraordinarily long period of parental nurturing and teaching, so an overabundance of offspring in an early hunter-gatherer society might have left them all ill equipped to face their environment.) This mechanism, though imperfect, operates almost everywhere in the developing world today; despite a widespread decline of breast-feeding, more births are still probably prevented by nursing than by any other means of contraception.

In an evolutionary sense, love and lactation arose in one great phylogenetic breath. The neuroanatomist Paul MacLean views the main accomplishment of the early mammals as the invention of the paleomammalian brain, including the limbic system, which arose during the reptilian phase of evolution but did not reach full flower until later, when nursing too had become a physiological necessity. MacLean and his colleagues have shown that the limbic system suffices to orchestrate the basic behaviors of mammalian motherhood; one can deprive a female hamster of the cerebral cortex (the *neo*mammalian brain) at birth, and still she will grow up capable of most functions in the reproductive realm, including courtship, sex, and parental care. In coordinating these functions, the limbic system likely mediates sensations that are the emotional precursors of what we call love.

It was on the foundation of love and lactation (as well as that of homeothermy) that the mammals would later build their great complex of vigorous activity, braininess, and learning. Is it farfetched, then, to read the three central achievements of the early mammals—homeothermy, lactation, and the development of the limbic system—as "warmth," "interdependency," and "emotion"? Perhaps? But such a reading at least raises a worthwhile question: once we have explained lactation in mechanistic terms—pinpointed its diverse contributions to the survival and transmission of the genes—what is left to say about its psychological effect, its relation to the organism's inner life? Sadly, very little, for the time being anyway. Science has still provided no solid evidence that nursing has a lasting effect within the individual human life cycle. In one recent study, Marjorie Elias, of Harvard University, compared intensively nursed infants with infants nursed much less frequently and weaned much earlier. Intensive nursing did postpone the resumption of menses after birth. But in a wide-ranging battery of tests of social, emotional, cognitive, and motor development, she found no major differences between the groups that could be attributed to nursing.

So are the arguments for breast-feeding entirely evolutionary and hence outmoded? Does nursing provide merely those things, such as nutrition, immunity, and birth-rate regulation, that we can now provide in other ways? I would be more inclined to think so were it not for an experience I have had too many times—telling a nursing mother there is no evidence that it matters, only to see a beatific, pitying smile that tells me I am an utter fool. Perhaps questioning the benefits of nursing is like saying there is no evidence that, on balance, sex has a positive permanent psychological effect on you—an observation that needs only the response "So what?"

Still, there is little basis for going to the opposite extreme and insisting that every mother nurse. Each case must be taken on its merits, and the costs of nursing to the mother and the family (for example, the loss of work) must be weighed against any benefits. For those who choose it—although they may only be bamboozled by a huge hormonal flux, controlled by a tiny tyrant—it certainly seems to have its own rewards. As for us outsiders, all we can do is stand back and contemplate what may be the most sybaritic of all the ancient mammalian pleasures.

NOT TO BE

For Hamlet, that slightly mad, too thoughtful hero (and possibly for Shakespeare, speaking through him), the central uncertainty of human existence was whether or not to be. The question strikes many of us as close to the heart of what it means to be human. Few, if any, nonhuman animals can *choose* not to be. When soldier ants sacrifice themselves for the good of the colony, their behavior is in some sense genetically mandated. Sociobiologists may say similar things about some self-destructive human behavior—that it is a form of self-sacrifice, produced by evolutionary forces much like those that act on the ants. The individual is lost, but the sacrifice saves others, some of whom are closely related to the altruist; thus the genes contributing to the self-sacrificial tendency (however small that contribution may be) are carried forward by the surviving relatives.

It may seem to be stretching this argument to subsume suicide within it, but consider the kamikaze pilot of the Second World War, or the more recent holy warrior for Islam and Khomeini. These men are heroic and suicidal both, and they certainly bring honor to their relatives. More ordinary suicides can also be rooted, at least partly, in the belief that someone close may benefit, and life-insurance policies take this possibility into account.

Notwithstanding the validity of these arguments, the fact

remains that some self-destructive human behavior, be it heroic or suicidal or even hedonistic, cannot benefit one's kin, and this sort of human sacrifice the Darwinians can only call "maladaptive." That is, it is being selected against; in theory, at least, the tides of evolutionary time will finally wash it away. Until then, it remains an integral part of our range of choices, enlarging, at once, our sense of the world as a dangerous place and our deepest sense of human freedom. In fact, in the post-Darwinian world, the hallmark of our species may be precisely this: we are the only animal that can consciously choose to be selected against. Perverse? Yes—but superbly and beautifully human.

Of course, to defy the logic of natural selection is not necessarily to defy biochemistry. Could it be that a question of such philosophic moment as Hamlet's hinges ultimately on chemical interactions, perhaps on the presence or absence of a single molecule? Such speculation would be a foray into territory that has proved itself treacherous. One molecule thought to be a clue to schizophrenia turned out to shed light only on the food served at the hospital whose patients were under study. A naturally occurring LSD-like substance that seemed at first to shed light on mental illness could not be detected in subsequent studies. So even the most biochemically inclined of psychiatrists—perhaps especially they—are skeptical of broad claims about the role of any one molecule. "Well," one can almost hear them saying, "we'll see whether it's replicable. There might be a piece of the truth here, but only a piece. For diagnostic purposes, I'll stick to the workhorses—symptoms, history, course of illness, possibly also drug response. As for a prediction of something like suicide . . ." The derisory smile would be sufficient to complete the sentence.

Yet some of the toughest-minded biologically inclined

psychiatrists are beginning to take note of a molecule in the cerebrospinal fluid. This fluid fills the spaces in and around the brain and spinal cord, cushioning against shock and serving as a receptacle for the brain's secreted and excreted substances—the important products and incidental by-products of innumerable chemical reactions. It may even be a sort of underground river for distant transport of substances among regions of the brain. But at the least it is a first-line filter, capable of catching (and concentrating) various brain chemicals before they are dispersed throughout the body.

The cerebrospinal fluid of people destined to take their lives, it appears, contains an unusually low concentration of a simple substance that goes by the rather rhythmic name five-hydroxy-indole acetic acid, or to its friends, 5-HIAA.

For many years, 5-HIAA has been known as the major metabolite, or breakdown product, of serotonin—one of the first chemical transmitters proved to have a functional role in the brain. Serotonin (also called five-hydroxytryptamine) is synthesized in certain brain cells and secreted across the synapse—the gap between the cells and the neurons they stimulate or inhibit. The action of serotonin on the receiving neuron's membrane is what causes the inhibition—hence the name neurotransmitter. Serotonin is thus a vital link in various neural circuits, circuits with both known and unknown functions.

As critical as it is to get that pulse of serotonin across the synapse, it is equally critical to remove it, and quickly. The precision of the nervous system's function depends as much on the brevity of the pulse as on its existence; it would not do to have even as useful a molecule as serotonin indolently hanging around, causing inhibition not explicitly called for by the neurons that secreted it. So it is removed by an enzymatic reaction that, in the process, produces 5-HIAA; and 5-HIAA thus becomes an indirect indicator of serotonin turnover and of the level of activity of serotonin neurons.

The link between 5-HIAA and suicide—now confirmed by a number of studies, including those of Marie Åsberg, of the Karolinska Institute in Stockholm, and Frederick Goodwin, of the National Institute of Mental Health, among others— could provide a much-needed tool in the assessment of suicide risk. All psychiatric patients who suffer from mood disorders, who become periodically depressed and perhaps periodically manic, are considered to be at significant risk of committing suicide. The clinical signs of depression, particularly if they include suicidal ideas, suffice to justify at least some precautions. But patients do not always tell doctors what they are thinking; moreover, conscious mental activity does not necessarily reflect all of the brain's inner workings. So a biochemical indicator may be more telling than the most heartfelt revelation.

Åsberg's initial discovery was that those depressed patients with high levels of 5-HIAA in their cerebrospinal fluid— whatever their clinical symptoms—were not really at risk of suicide; but if a patient was destined to commit suicide during the next year, the level of 5-HIAA was almost certain to be low. For example, in one of Åsberg's study groups, consisting of forty-six patients who had previously attempted suicide, six patients took their lives within a year. All six belonged to a subgroup of thirty patients whose 5-HIAA levels were below the average. For patients with 5-HIAA levels above the average, the risk of death within a year was zero, and it has been very near that in other, similar studies. (Some of these patients *attempted* suicide, but by drug overdose, a method known to have a much lower success rate than do violent methods and, it has been speculated, one often employed by patients whose true intent is something other than suicide.)

Never before has a biochemical measurement in psychiatry had anything like this degree of discriminatory power. If future studies show it to be reliable, it will have immense practical value, permitting the effective management of an important source of human suffering and sparing those not really at risk the annoying and unnecessary precautions. (Checks by nurses every five minutes and the prohibition of sharp objects are not only indignities but legally sanctioned infringements on freedom as well, and they may interfere with some forms of treatment.) Scientifically and philosophically, the implications are enormous: here is a molecule so small that it is dwarfed by even a single base pair of DNA, yet it may spell the difference between life and self-destruction.

The question, of course, is how. Subsequent studies have provided some clues. For example, individuals who do not have pronounced mood fluctuations but are at risk of suicide because of personality disorders—chronic maladaptations, as opposed to bouts of depression—can be divided into the same two groups: those with low 5-HIAA levels, who are at high risk of committing suicide, and those with high levels, who are not. This suggests that the significance of 5-HIAA relates fundamentally and directly to suicide rather than to any one type of depression that may in turn lead to suicide.

The biochemical mechanism underlying this relationship is not yet clear; however, there is evidence that supports the obvious interpretation—that serotonin neurons are for some reason less active in people inclined toward suicide. The brains of suicide victims, for example, have yielded evidence of low serotonin levels. In light of such findings, established facts about serotonin become more interesting: a high serotonin level makes an animal more tolerant of pain, and a level artificially lowered—say, through a diet deficient in serotonin precursors—makes it more sensitive.

More subtle in its implications, though equally intriguing, is the fact that high serotonin levels are associated with normal sleep. Sleep disorders frequently accompany psychiatric illnesses, and psychiatrists have speculated that the problem goes beyond the insomnia that naturally accompanies unusually persistent anxieties and fears: the idea is that sleep disturbances are a basic and revealing characteristic of such illnesses rather than a consequence of them. If so, it is tempting to wonder whether those who, like Hamlet, are drawn to "that sleep of death" may have had a troubled sleep in life.

But this is far afield, and undoubtedly what we have here is only a piece of the truth. Still, such a piece can become a handle on a larger truth. It turns out, for instance, that individuals with low levels of 5-HIAA (again, whether they are depressed or not) are more likely to commit not only suicide but also other violent acts. This suggests that, as psychodynamic theorists have often claimed, inwardly and outwardly directed violence may be two sides of the same coin, separate expressions of a single aggressive urge— Freud's death instinct, which, turned inside out, becomes homicide.

This brings us back to *Hamlet*—a play that, somewhat contrary to its most famous soliloquy, is not really about whether "to be or not to be" so much as whether to act or not to act. It is a deed of outward violence that the hero is headed for; the notion of finding in his own breast a sheath for his "bare bodkin" is only a brief byway. Given the right circumstances, it may be that some utterly simple brain process determines whether we will "take arms against a sea of troubles/ and by opposing end them," yet leaves open—perhaps to different biochemical influences—the question of whether to direct those arms against ourselves or against others.

But of course, it is not always advantageous to act. Procrastination has its time and place, and even in Hamlet's case it is not clear that he should have acted earlier than he did. Impulsiveness—certainly, at least, the sort that leads to homicide or suicide—is not a luxury we can casually indulge in. For Hamlet the lack of action was a source of constant anguish; but most of us can perhaps feel grateful for the restraining effect of a certain small molecule.

THE STRANGER

Could the fate of the earth hinge on an infant fear? This odd possibility, which once occupied my thoughts a good deal, came back to mind after a recent conversation. The answer turns on the continuity between certain reactions in early life and some at least superficially similar responses in adulthood.

As parents have long known, and despite the claims of some psychologists, the infant at birth is barely a social creature. You can tickle and coo and bounce and sing and make yourself ridiculous with all sorts of funny faces, and the baby will go on taking its own counsel, a little Eastern philosopher serenely detached from you. Yet by the third or fourth month, the same baby will be a lively companion, smiling back at your silly face and gazing into your eyes with those prolonged soupy looks that make life and diapers seem worthwhile. And still another profound change in sociability is coming. Frequently, it is first noticed by grandparents, who nowadays may see the baby for only a few days several times a year. The grandmother who visits at four or five months and again at nine or ten may be in for an unpleasant surprise: the baby who gazed and grinned and giggled a few months earlier now turns and squirms away, crying.

Fear of strangers, stranger anxiety, and eight-months anxiety are some of the names given to the result of this metamorphosis. In some infants, there is overt fear—immediate gaze aversion, withdrawal, and crying; in others, it is closer to wariness, a cautious dance that allows the stranger to hover on the edge of the circle of trust, eventually to be brought in. Some infants show neither fear nor wariness, but all become more discriminating.

Learning? Partly. But the old idea about fear—that it results from the pairing of pain with consistent stimuli until an association arises—certainly doesn't apply; few infants have had painful experiences with strangers. Still, a more fundamental kind of learning may be involved: coming to trust someone may automatically mean a mistrust of others. The circle which once opened broadly, encompassing virtually everyone, has steadily narrowed. People who are not well known, or at least not remembered, may, despite past intimacies, become personae non gratae.

Twenty years later, the circle of trust may have broadened, but it is unlikely ever to regain its former scope. Firmly ensconced in the adult's repertoire of social responses will be xenophobia—an almost reflexive fear, or even contempt, of strangers. Whether drawn along the axis of race, religion, or politics, the "we-they" dichotomy is a fundamental part of us. We partition society into insiders and outsiders, as if our minds insisted on dividing everything by two. Like the eight-month-old infant, we experience these polar categories so deeply that we resist, at least unconsciously, every rational attempt to see the world as complexly as it deserves to be seen. The psychoanalyst Erik Erikson coined the term "pseudo-speciation" to cover this ubiquitous piece of stubbornness. It is as if we rejected out of hand the notion of unity of the species, setting up in its place a thousand egregious dichotomies, reflecting one another harshly and repetitively, like images in a vast hall of mirrors.

If it seems natural that humans should so categorize the world, we need to look back on a time of life when we didn't. Something has changed in the baby's mind during the seventh, eighth, or ninth month. According to one older psycho-analytic idea, eight-months anxiety is evoked by a fantasy that the stranger might replace the mother. This theory now seems to have little to recommend it, but it is true that at around eight months, when the fear of strangers is activated, so is the fear of separation. Signs of attachment to the mother (or other primary caretaker) become manifest, and her departure evokes protest in infants who would not have been fazed when they were younger and more socially serene. Notwith-standing individual variation, the percentage of infants who cry when the mother leaves, or who show distress when a stranger appears, rises in all cultures between six and twelve months of age.

What seems to be happening—as indicated by other changes in behavior—is a metamorphosis in the emotional landscape: once flat and dull, it now becomes dramatically uneven. Among other changes, the familiar acquires a more positive affective valence, or emotional significance, and the strange acquires a more negative one. The fearful face that emerges during the second half-year of life as a frequent reaction to strangers varies little across cultures: the corners of the mouth are retracted and turned downward; the brows are raised and straightened as the skin between them is furrowed; the eyes widen.

The only facial expression often mistaken for fear is that of surprise, and this is one among many bits of evidence that there may be a continuum from attention, through surprise, to fear. Low-level electrical stimulation of the amygdala in the brain of a cat produces attentiveness, whereas turning up the current at exactly the same site produces fear. And a great deal of evidence from the study of infants indicates that a stimulus pattern partly but not completely different from familiar ones can elicit attention (as indicated by prolonged visual fixation, heart-rate deceleration, and other signs) in some situations and fear (crying, withdrawal) in others not very different. The suggestion is that our brains, even in infancy, are set up to notice discrepancy and to focus on it until it is assimilated— absorbed into a framework in which it begins to to make sense, to take its place among the already known. This may be the basis of all our learning about the world. But if the focusing does not produce assimilation, something may be wrong, and we had better shift gears from attention to fear.

Why does such discrimination not appear until six to nine months after birth? Neurology offers some clues. The brain doubles in volume during the first year of life, reaching about sixty percent of its adult size. Dendrites and axons (crucial protrusions of nerve cells) form and branch, connections among the cells appear in ever expanding numbers, and myelination (through which a tight fatty sheath forms around the axon, greatly improving the conductive properties of the nerve) occurs. Two of the more important pathways that begin to myelinate during the second half-year of life are the fornix and the mamillothalamic tract—parts of the limbic system, which plays a major role in the mediation of emotions.

One widely accepted notion is that the fornix—a massive bundle of fibers, about the size of the optic nerve—reports discrepancy from the hippocampus, where perceptual mismatches are detected, to the hypothalamus, which may be the seat of our emotions. There we assign the valence, the emotional significance, to the discrepancy. So, just as the infant is metamorphosing into a complex and rather intense emotional creature, the brain is changing in ways that could plausibly underlie this development.

It is a sad irony that "discrimination" means both sophisticated detection of variety in the world and invidious distinctions among human beings. Studies of prejudice among children show that awareness of racial and other ethnic differences begins in nursery school and increases steadily with age. It can sometimes be mitigated—through racial intermingling, among other experiences—but rarely if ever abolished. By adolescence, racial awareness is intense, and the tendency to remain with one's "own kind" is pronounced. The desire, during young adulthood and thereafter, to avoid association with people different from oneself occurs in all populations, in all social classes, in all countries. What was once fear is now closer to contempt, but the behavioral response of avoidance is similar, and the possibility of an underlying continuum of emotion—and of neurological substrate—is real.

During my years in Africa, I was struck deeply by the ubiquity of prejudice. The !Kung San—racially quite different from the neighboring Bantu peoples, who are larger and darker skinned—were objects of utter contempt. "Bloody Bushman" was one of the milder epithets. I could close my eyes and almost hear a white bigot reviling blacks.

Discrimination, of course, does not require marked racial differences. The !Kung were contemptuous of neighboring groups of !Kung with slightly different accents. And as I traveled through Africa, I found that what appeared to be strictly political conflicts almost always concealed ethnic ones. Today, in Zimbabwe, the conflict between Robert Mugabe and Joshua Nkomo, the leading political figures, is also a conflict between the Shona and the Ndebele, ancient tribal rivals. In Uganda, beneath the political complexities, the struggles are largely tribal, among the Ganda, the Acholi, and the Lango, who have been hostile toward one another for many generations.

It is no different outside Africa: Sikhs, Muslims, and Hindus in India; Sunni and Shiite Muslims in much of the Middle East; Jews and Arabs in Israel; Catholics and Protestants in Ireland; blacks and whites in America; ancient ethnic subgroups in almost every country of Eastern Europe; and Basque separatists in Spain. Again, as in Africa, the distinctions do not need to be major. As the hero says in Nikos Kazantzakis's novel *Zorba the Greek*, people will slaughter each other because the members of one group cross themselves with two fingers and the other with three. Ethnocentrism, the belief that your group is better than the other guy's—a relentless dichotomization of the human world— was not invented only by the Greeks with their barbarians or by the Jews with their Gentiles or by the Christians with their heathens but independently, again and again, by every population on the planet. About the Nuer, technologically primitive cattle herders of the Sudan, anthropologist E. E. Evans-Pritchard wrote words that would need only a little modification to be applicable anywhere in the world: "Either a man is a kinsman . . . or he is a person to whom you have no reciprocal obligations and whom you treat as a potential enemy."

The conversation that brought these thoughts to mind occurred at one of those stiff farewell dinners for graduating college seniors. At my table were several premedical students, a prelaw student, and a slight, pretty, dark-haired young woman who was going into hospital administration. Think-

ing this a rather serious occasion, I asked at one point—
keeping a more or less straight face—whether they had
developed a philosophy of life while in college. I tried to ask
it without losing my sense of humor. Most of the students
begged off. The future hospital administrator said that she
had majored in philosophy and had written a long paper
answering my question, but that it was too complex to
explain.

A while later, only picking at my pie, I could hear the !Kung
saying, "Are you a person who destroys food?" This is one of
their greatest insults. "Wouldn't it be great," I wondered
aloud, "if we could get this piece of pie to Africa, where
children are dying tonight of starvation?" The cliché seemed
acceptable in the circumstances.

Here the philosophy major and future hospital administrator broke in in ringing tones. "I don't have to worry about
that," she said brightly. "It relates to what I was trying to say
before. My philosophy is that you only have to worry about
people in your own society."

For once I was speechless. What I as an anthropologist think
of as a particularly unfortunate form of ignorance was being
advanced as a belief system. It had even been accepted as a
bachelor's thesis in philosophy. I wondered how, in her future
profession, she would draw the line at the hospital door.
Would a stray tourist be part of her society? An illegal alien?
A heroin addict? A convict? A recent legal immigrant who
spoke only Spanish? An impoverished African-American? A
Jewish refugee? Just where would she end her aloofness from
strangers?

We are all ethnocentric, all selfish, all busy with the
demands of our own lives, all fearful and contemptuous of
strangers. But some of us are at least struggling with our
selfishness, not dignifying it with the name of philosophy.

Perhaps we recognize in our reflexive contempt of strangers an insidious holdover of early childhood fears. Much of our tendency to ignore the suffering of strangers, especially distant ones, stems from a childish placement of them outside the circle of trust. There is at least a possibility that these undercurrents of fear primitively energize civil and international conflicts.

Neither in moral nor in practical terms can we ignore distant suffering, since the technology of delivery—of messages, wealth, explosives—has overtaken our ancient insular impulses. As the fundamental units of nations in conflict, we as individuals must bear the weight of scientific explanation in politics, just as the properties of the atom explain much about the behavior of gases. The way the brain handles emotion, and the way its capacity matures, are at the core of our predictable belligerence. As the cartoon character Pogo said, "We have met the enemy and he is us."

The universality of ethnocentrism gives it the aspect of a genetically based trait, and it has been hypothesized as such by many observers. Yet apart from the universality itself— always suggestive of a biological predisposition—there is little evidence one way or the other. Studies of infant twins suggest substantial genetic influence on the development and intensity of fear, but the links between this phenomenon and xenophobia in adults are conjectural.

Still, one can conceive of evolutionary scenarios in which the genetic roots of ethnocentrism would be adaptive (though, as always in these just-so stories, adaptation must be seen as selectively biased but morally neutral—sensitive to the calculus of survival and reproduction but numb to accompanying questions of right and wrong). Throughout our history, the attention-surprise-fear continuum must have served well as a mechanism for warily assimilating the new. For infants especially, flight to the mother at the sight or sound of something strange but *not* readily assimilated must have been an effective protection against danger. It is possible that this is the whole adaptive story—that the adult form of xenophobia is simply an epiphenomenon of the infant adaptation, that the advantages in infancy may have outweighed any disadvantages of adult intolerance.

But it is equally possible that the adult form was independently adaptive and, with a kind of morbid elegance, made use of an existing neurological mechanism well suited to its expression. As protohumans evolved, with their increasing sense of group identity and their willingness to behave, in concert, in ways specifically damaging to outsiders (one can see such tribal hostility even among chimpanzees), xenophobic responses must have grown in value on the evolutionary marketplace. Xenophobia in adjacent groups would have been mutually reinforcing, both in the short run (by eliciting hostile responses) and in the long run (by favoring the natural selection of underlying genetic dispositions). Increasingly, the risks inherent in dividing the world into "us" and "them" would have become preferable to the risks accompanying compromise. Add to this the general human tendency to perceive the world—inanimate, social, or spiritual—in terms of dualities, and you have a cognitive infrastructure on which ethnocentrism can readily build.

Sadly, the fear of strangers is not completely unfounded. When two enemies fear one another enough, they begin to behave in ways that threaten, and then it is difficult to separate the real from the imagined threat. In each society, the most articulate among the fearful, the most vigorous among the contemptuous, legitimize their counterparts in the other. Nationalism—which historian Arnold Toynbee called new wine in the old bottles of tribalism—becomes the norm.

Patriotism, not in the subtle version of well-informed national pride but in the crude version of bigotry, comes to be viewed as virtuous. And the limbic system's circuitry of fear and "discrimination," first activated at eight months of age, ignites now with the strange spark of international hatred, becoming the fuse of absolute disaster.

IN THE SISTERHOOD

OF SEDUCTION

Since the dawn of history, some men have been willing to pay women for their charms, and this has not by any means simply meant sex. Today in American cities, for instance, men pay women to take their clothes off and dance in intimate settings—"couch dancing," it's sometimes called—or to model lingerie; they pay pretty women as escorts to help them impress their colleagues, not always expecting sex, but at a minimum wanting stimulating companionship; they pay for "erotic massages," of course, but also for nonerotic ones, which they nevertheless may prefer to have done by women; and in the better hotels they pay stylishly dressed, attractive young women to shine their shoes—at rates about double the rates charged by men for the same task. They also spend many millions a month for erotic magazines—indirect payment for nude displays. And at a more pervasive cultural level, men are still expected to pay for most dates, as if they were paying for the companionship—in spite of the growing economic power of women.

Of course, payment for sex itself has been an integral part of life at least since urban civilization began. Early prostitution frequently went hand in hand with slavery; both were ubiquitous ancient institutions. Men ran those societies—as they have run virtually all civilizations—through a combination of violent force, economic manipulation, and religious terror. Yet although prostitution was surely enabled by male political and social domination, enterprising women, often past the age of selling their own bodies, have frequently played a major role.

This institution transcends most cultural and historical boundaries. The Rig-Veda describes "public women, open to the visits of all"—red clothing signaled their status—on the Indian peninsula three thousand years ago. Prostitution associated with temple cults was widespread in the ancient Near East, where women brought men and their money into the temples, and secular descendants of these religious brothels were officially approved and numerous in both Greece and Rome. The Great Wall of China by the third century B.C. was staffed all along its length by army prostitutes who also served as an auxiliary militia. Fifteen hundred years later, Marco Polo was deeply impressed by China's complex hierarchy of women of pleasure, reporting "a multitude of sinful women."

Yet medieval Europe was scarcely above criticism. In fifteenth-century France, at the height of Roman Catholic religious power, towns such as Dijon and Lyons had active brothels as well as private prostitutes, all but sanctioned by civil authority. Indeed, throughout the Middle Ages in Europe, clergymen were essential patrons of prostitutes in many areas. In Japan a vast, officially regulated district full of brothels, known as "the Floating World," was established in 1617. London at that time was densely populated with brothels too, and much later, in 1857, still had an estimated six thousand of them. The seaports of China at that time harbored enormous "Flower Boats" purveying sex, entertainment, and opium.

This of course is not just past history. In the United States in the 1940s, as studied by the Kinsey Report, about 70 percent of a cross section of men had been to prostitutes at some time in their lives—although only 3 or 4 percent of the total orgasmic outlet for men was estimated to come from these encounters. And in the 1970s prostitution was alive and well in spite of the sexual revolution, although the number of men who resorted to it were estimated to be only half that in Kinsey's time. At present, in Amsterdam and Brussels, women sit all night under red lights in shop windows, openly displaying what they have to sell.

Relationships with prostitutes, especially expensive ones, need not just mean sex. The client of an "escort service" that provides fully for sexual needs may nevertheless want and expect a dinner date first, with proper dress and suitable conversation. The patron of a brothel may expect a certain atmosphere of levity, with drink, display of scantily clad women, and entertaining repartee. Men may establish long-term relationships with particular women. Studies consistently suggest that kinky sex plays little role. And many a call girl has said that some of her sessions with clients have more in common with psychotherapy than with simple, straightforward sex-for-money.

Yet no institution in which men pay for the companionship of women is as curious as geisha. Its mere mention evokes exotic mystery. Here, it would seem, is an institution of women apparently devoted to the service and entertainment of men, yet embedded in a larger society in which—as in our own—the structure of male dominance is being eroded away. Geisha is intimate and suggestive, but explicit sex is not included. It is a highly ritualized and formal mode of life, yet one that continually raises moral suspicion.

Geisha arose out of legal prostitution—the so-called "Floating World"—by a most indirect route during the seventeenth century. The first geisha, oddly (and ironically) enough, were men—jesters and musicians in brothels. The term itself is rendered as "artist," although "artiste" would seem to be closer in connotation. The first record of a female geisha occurs in 1751, but they gained steadily in popularity, essentially replacing males by the turn of the nineteenth century. Although the prostitutes—*yujo*—served men sexually, they were otherwise rather dull; geisha, in contrast, were easy in social intercourse, clever, friendly, and entertaining—in a word, fun. They were officially forbidden to compete for customers with the prostitutes they worked with, and from that day to this the legal and cultural distinction between geisha and prostitution has been clear.

Before the First World War girls were brought into "the flower and willow world" at around twelve, an age when there could be no question of choice. After that point they would be very unlikely to be viewed as suitable wives—until, in a few cases, much later. Their own almost inevitable illegitimate children would be destined for other roles with limited social mobility.

Politically geisha were associated with both patriotism and modernism, a seeming contradiction. They were known for their loyalty to the emperor, and they consorted with men of power who supported him; in the 1930s, they were among the most visible of the reactionary antimodernist elite. Yet they had already come to be seen by other women as being in the vanguard of Western-inspired fashion; for example, they led a trend in the carrying of manufactured parasols, and another in accepting jazz music. At this time there were eighty thousand geisha in Japan; most men of prominence in the country frequented geisha, and many gave out public opinions about them.

A book of such opinions, *The Geisha Reader*, was published in 1935. In it businessmen, politicians, intellectuals, and other influential men gave "advice" to working geisha. "Anyone who thinks the occupation of geisha is a lowly one is mistaken," wrote a restaurateur. "Look at the word itself— a woman who lives by art. Think of this, you geisha, and take pride in yourselves. Don't fall in love with fickle characters. . . ." Another contributor, a poet, wrote, "There is much I have resented about Japan's feudal age, but in this case, I feel, the geisha of the past were more admirable than what we have now—they were not so quick to offer their bodies. Those geisha were creators of new forms of beauty, and they could match their customers in education, taste, and wit. Truly, they were 'comrades of the opposite sex' . . ." The collection left no doubt about who must determine what geisha would be, and why: men, of course, but yet not just *any* men. The institution of geisha owes almost as much, historically, to the unequal distribution of wealth and power among men as it does to their enduring oppression of women.

As the Second World War approached, geisha switched from being leaders of new fashion to being curators of tradition. Facing criticism for excessive modernism, and dependent on an increasingly conservative clientele, many reverted to the more reserved ways of their past. They became, almost deliberately, anachronistic. After 1947 the modal age of geisha rose from the mid-twenties to the late thirties. In the 1970s their number dwindled to seventeen thousand nationally, and recruitment of new *maiko*, or geisha-in-training, reached a critical stage of difficulty. Perhaps a small population of geisha will persist indefinitely, if only for nostalgic value. But in the long view of history we may see them as a vestige of the last phase of feudal and imperial life in Japan—two centuries of temporary holding action against the rising tide of modernization.

Much of what we know in America about geisha is due to the work of anthropologist Liza Dalby. The watchword of cultural anthropology has always been "participant observation": the ethnologist seeks insight by living with, eating with, even identifying with, the subjects under study. To be sure, scientific objectivity has been a steady beacon. However, it was a basic belief of the founders of the discipline that the study of human culture required an empathy with the humans in question. When the anthropologist considers the ancient Roman saying "Nothing human is alien to me," it is not from the armchair of the philosopher but from the grass-thatched hamlet in the jungle.

Still, the luminaries of cultural anthropology, for all their dedication to participant observation, have rarely if ever tried to *become* the subjects they were studying. They have eaten the exotic foods, mastered the strange languages, slept in the frail huts, clapped and sung and danced in the arcane and marvelous rituals, but they have always stopped short of changing their identity. Admitted misfits, in many cases, in their own home cultures, they have nonetheless not attempted to slough off the old skin and grow into some entirely new one.

Dalby—or, as she came to be called, Ichigiku—did. She presented herself, in the mid-1970s, as a *maiko* at a respected Kyoto geisha house, and was accepted as such by those in charge of her training. She took on, and yet did not, all aspects of that role, for a period of fourteen months. The contradiction, of course, lies in that length of stay. She was fluent in Japanese at the beginning, and she diligently trained in all the graces of geisha culture—dress, coiffure, bearing, conversation, dance, ritual service—and, more important, formed bonds with her teachers of a depth of emotion and character that went far beyond the merely professional. But she (and to her credit, they) knew that she was there to do a study and that she would complete her training not in their "flower and willow world" in Kyoto but at Stanford University in California. She became quite well known in Japan as the first Western woman to attempt to become a geisha. Her study combines the best of current anthropological method with an extraordinary degree of empathy.

Although they no longer work among prostitutes, geisha are free to develop (and sooner or later do) sexual relationships with customers of their choosing. *Maiko* were traditionally initiated in a complex process that included deflowering at the hands of a client. A mature geisha may have had a number of lovers and may eventually become the "kept woman" of one of them. In a few cases, marriage ensues. Thus, the air of sexual innuendo carefully cultivated at formal geisha banquets is due not only to a code of dress and posture, and to deftly rendered suggestive pleasantries, but to realistic, if distant, possibilities. Though some geisha, and some geisha houses, have rather loose reputations, there is no market transaction for sex and no overt quid pro quo; a knowledgeable man who merely wanted sex would not waste many hours in a geisha house.

What these men are looking for—and have been for two centuries—is sophisticated and entertaining feminine companionship outside the confines of their frequently dull marriages. From dress and hairstyle to musical performance and on to drunken flirtation, geisha have mastered a code replete with meaning for the men who buy their company. For example, they wear the traditional kimono, and are obviously more comfortable in it than are other Japanese women. It is *more* demure—less revealing—than the kimono other Japanese women wear on certain formal occasions; but by varying the width and stiffness of the sash geisha can convey clearly to the sophisticated client almost any degree of prudish or wanton intent. They learn to play the *shamisen*, a three-stringed, fretless, lutelike instrument specifically associated with geisha (geisha say, "If you have three strings, you can eat"), and to sing subtly suggestive or plainly erotic songs. In Dalby's translation:

> If it's a shallow river
> Lift your skirts up to your knees
> But as the water deepens
> Untie your sashes please.
>
> My body flesh and hair is
> Received from Mom and Dad
> But the one thing I don't show them
> I'll show to you, my lad.

Here is the essence of geisha culture and behavior: they are capable of the bold eroticism of the second stanza but also of the beautiful indirection of the first. The first stanza is in fact the refrain of the song, the symbolic note to which it keeps returning. Just as no mere wife could achieve the open suggestiveness of the verse, no conventional harlot could presume to the high style of the refrain. For this unique and sophisticated eroticism a man must go to geisha.

And there is more here than mere performance. Although geisha occasionally appear on stage, most of their entertaining is done at private parties and, as a result, is interactive. The geisha must assess a guest's willingness to join, however ineptly, in song, and make him feel artful. In conversation she must draw him out on subjects he would speak about with virtually no one else: memories of his own sexual and romantic education; exotic sexual techniques; and the looseness of certain geisha less discriminating than those among whom he is dining. If a guest becomes increasingly drunk, the geisha must both encourage and control the behavior exhibited by Japanese males under the influence: giggling, poking, slapstick rather than witty humor, lewdness—a general picture of boyish naughtiness and culturally sanctioned regression.

Geisha play a role that is not unfamiliar from other societies dominated by men: they are the women—actresses, singers, dancers, barmaids, cocktail waitresses, masseuses, courtesans, call girls—who, although not suitable as the mother of one's children, provide more interesting company than one's wife. Geisha institutionalizes this social role in a context specified by a dignified tradition. The women who choose it are almost always of an artistic bent, of higher than average intelligence, and willing to discipline themselves to learn and follow quite complex customs.

Above all, perhaps, and ironically, geisha are women who want autonomy from men. Without paying nearly as high a social price as a prostitute, a geisha liberates herself from the prospect of a life under the thumb of one man. She enters a sisterhood characterized by strong "family" ties (a "mother" and an "older sister" are assigned ceremoniously and with great and enduring seriousness), a family ruled, at least in the immediate sense, by women. The geisha will associate with interesting wealthy men, gain access to several channels of aesthetic expression, forge deep friendships with women, and have, more or less as she wants it, an outlet for her own sexuality. What others may gain from marriage—social status, financial security, a network of dependable "relatives," a sense of belonging—she will in large part acquire by membership in the culture of geisha. Quite telling in this connection is the story of a woman whose two daughters grew up to be a university professor and a geisha; the mother, who had wanted each of them to be—like herself—a good Japanese homemaker, was about equally disappointed in both. Or in the words of Kazue, a sixty-one-year-old geisha thinking back on her life, "My choice would be either to be born a man or be born a geisha." It is possible that in a society where women had equal rights the appeal of geisha would be nil.

Dalby conducted a questionnaire study which helped to support her view of geisha as a basically positive and viable life-style. But "thick description" remained her crucial anthropological tool. And in the following something more is in evidence, something that goes beyond sympathetic description:

> On one of those balmy late-April nights in 1978, a tendril of smoke drifted from the west bank of the Kamo River. Nobody noticed it issuing lazily from one of the closely spaced wooden buildings in the area where the geisha of Pontocho live and work. By four in the morning, a raging blaze had destroyed several houses. Distraught geisha clutched their cotton sleeping kimonos against the river breeze and splashed their roofs with buckets of river water in an effort to halt the spread of Japan's most feared natural catastrophe, fire. At daybreak, a dozen houses lay in smoldering ruins and one young geisha was dead.

Dalby could actually have been one of these distraught geisha clutching their kimonos. And when we learn that the dead young woman had been her own "older sister" in the fictive kinship order, the passage becomes a model of poignant understatement; it is all the more powerful for that, because it is evident that the sisterly feeling was real.

To the usual Western stereotype of servile entertainment for men, not far above prostitution—an image as enraging to feminists as it is titillating to male chauvinists—Dalby opposes mainly the sympathetic descriptive eye of the competent ethnologist guided by cultural relativism, the fundamental tenet of anthropology, according to which human cultures are neither good nor bad but various and valid. It is not, in this view, for us to judge, but to try in every possible way to see how this system works—what gives it its enduring cultural coherence. Yet we can still find the means to detach ourselves from admiration: the context of male chauvinism, the historical relationship to political reaction, the limited social options for geisha and their children, and, above everything, the need to be endlessly tolerant of the most obnoxious and spoiled behavior of men.

Dalby's geisha name, and those of her sisters, are descended from that of a founder named Ichiko, meaning "shamaness"—a woman who, in ancient Japan, entered a trance by dancing for the purpose of making magic. This is a perfect name, for if geisha are hypnotic to men, they also appear, in some ways, to hypnotize themselves—to dull their perceptions of the peripheral and ambiguous nature of their lives. Dalby's extraordinary empathy for her subjects makes us angry for them even as we admire them.

At this writing, a former geisha has just brought down a Japanese national government, sending the prime minister home in disgrace. In this, the most male-dominated of modern industrial states, the development came as an almost complete surprise. The facts were simple: he had developed a relationship with her, begun in the traditional way. He had eventually found cause to end it, but he had omitted the customary large sum of money expected as a departure gift. In understandable resentment, she made the affair public soon after he became prime minister.

The surprise lay in the public reaction. It was not, apparently, his failure to give the parting gift—a violation of old custom—that roused public ire. Rather, it was his participation in a part of the tradition itself: the accepted business relationship with a geisha had turned into an unacceptable "kept woman" relationship. He did not invent this arrangement—it has been a common outcome for geishas for generations. But suddenly the telephones of the ruling party were ringing off their hooks. And on the other end were thousands of Japanese women who had never made such calls before. Suddenly, around this scandal, women became organized as a political force to reckon with for the first time in Japanese history.

Will this end the ancient connection between sex and power? Sexism notwithstanding, it seems likely that men pay for women's favors—and have, in every culture, for millennia—not just because they have the power to do so but also because, for biological reasons, they want women's favors more than women want theirs. If this is so, then these exchanges are ineradicable. Even a world in which women earned more than men would leave some men scrimping and saving to buy sex or even company from some enterprising woman.

But the women of Japan, like their American counterparts in two recent cases of "womanizing" politicians, are drawing a new political line. *If you want our votes,* they are saying, *don't step across it. Don't use the power we have helped give you to buy or utilize or subjugate any of us. And this is not about prudishness—don't trivialize us with that old criticism. This is about respect.*

If, as is likely, women succeed—not just in Japan but eventually throughout the world—it will be perhaps the most fundamental change in politics since the dawn of our species, much more fundamental than power sharing by women, which actually harks back to our hunting-and-gathering ancestors. It will mean that one of the most predictable rewards of power for males, not only throughout the past of our own species but in our animal forebears too—the privilege of greater sexual access—will no longer be forthcoming.

This will change the character of men who seek political power, and eliminate what has in the past been one prominent group of them: those whose taste for power includes a taste for women. Perhaps, instead, they will try to become actors or musicians, for whom the sexual use of male power remains more acceptable. In any case, we can guess that there will be women politicians poised to take their roles as their peccadillos ease them out of politics. And those women—whom we are increasingly learning to see, on biological grounds, as the stronger sex—will probably have less trouble keeping their minds on the job.

THE RIDDLE

OF THE SMILE

Red deer stags signal their interest in females by prancing about with adolescent exuberance. Greylag geese challenge rivals by extending their necks and then duel until one "cries uncle" by lowering its head to the ground. The three-spined stickleback woos its consort with a zigzag dance and, having won her interest, swims toward his nest on the chance that she will follow. Herring gulls approach mating by bobbing their heads upward while uttering a soft, melodious call. All of these behaviors are fixed action patterns that serve the function of social display—acts of communication that have evolved by virtue of their contribution to survival and reproduction and that are, apparently, under strong genetic control. By contrast, most behaviors involved in human social rituals appear to be less a matter of genetic than of cultural inheritance. The handshake is not practiced everywhere. The curtsy came and went. And not even the most strident sociobiologist would argue that applause results from some genetic predisposition to clap the hands together.

But consider the smile. The subtlest play of the risorius—the facial muscle that governs the smile and that shares its etymology with the word risible—can spell the difference between the passing indifference of strangers and the flowering of lifelong romance, between peaceful coexistence and deadly violence; in an evolutionary sense, the most important things can easily hinge on it. It is difficult to believe that natural selection could have left so important a signal to the vagaries of individual learning. And, as far as we can tell, it did not. If there is one human social display that qualifies as a fixed action pattern, it is the tendency of people in certain well-defined situations to draw back the corners of their mouths and expose their teeth. Smiling, it appears, is something we are born to do.

The evidence for this assertion is diverse. First, there is the sheer universality of the smile. Film studies in remote areas of the world, mainly by the German ethologist Irenäus Eibl-Eibesfeldt, have shown smiling to be a consistent feature of greeting, often in combination with raising of the eyebrows. In France, Bali, and Samoa, among the !Kung of the Kalahari and the Waika of South America this complex motor action sequence runs like clockwork when people who enjoy each other come face to face. Not only the muscle contraction pattern but its interpretation by those who see it has been shown to be a cross-cultural constant.

Also pointing to a genetic underpinning of the smile are findings in psychology, zoology, and neurology. The smile appears with uncanny regularity in human infants; even blind and blind-and-deaf children begin smiling roughly on schedule—by about three months of age. Further, we see apparent precursors of the smile in the primates that are our nearest living relatives—a silent, bared-teeth grin in monkeys and a more recognizable smile in chimpanzees. Finally, the facial muscles behind the smile—the risorius, along with zygomaticus major and other, more delicate sheets of tissue—must contract in a precisely orchestrated concatenation to produce a genuine smile, implying the existence of a genetically determined central neural mechanism of great coordination.

(Consider the ease with which we detect hesitation, ambivalence, and, especially, fakery in a smile.)

But these strands of evidence, though converging on the conclusion that the smile is a legacy of natural selection, diverge over the question of just how it earned a place in our genetic heritage. There is general agreement on why greylag geese stretch their necks and why sticklebacks zig and zag, but isolating the evolutionary function of the smile is more difficult. Indeed, it sometimes seems that the more closely the smile is examined, the more enigmatic it becomes.

The first complication in the quest for a unified theory of smiling is that there are two kinds of smiles. It is possible to lose either the capacity to smile on command or the capacity to smile spontaneously in response to a joke or a friendly greeting without losing the other. Typically, the loss of smiling on command—what we might call the flight attendant's smile—is due to damage either in the part of the cerebral cortex that exerts motor control over the facial muscles or in the corticospinal tract, the stream of fibers connecting the cortex to the nerves governing those muscles. The loss of spontaneous smiling is somewhat more difficult to pin down neurologically, but recent studies of stroke victims have linked it to structures in the cerebral hemispheres, known collectively as the basal ganglia. This finding is consistent with the fact that Parkinson's disease, which affects primarily the basal ganglia, entails a masked-face syndrome—an emotional deadness of the face.

The evidence from comparative brain anatomy corroborates this clinical suggestion. Paul MacLean, an anatomist at the National Institute of Mental Health, and his colleagues have long maintained that the basal ganglia play a central and specific role in controlling fixed social displays in monkeys—

for example, eyebrow flashing or genital display. Damage to the internal portion of the globus pallidus ("the pale globe"), a major part of the basal ganglia, abolishes some species-typical social displays without causing any other losses.

This evidence has led to a redefinition of the basal ganglia as being in part a regulator of species-specific displays. Since nerve fibers serving the basal ganglia become fully functional during the first few months of life in humans, it is possible that they underlie the growth of social smiling.

Of course, not all smiling is social. Psychologists have identified something they call "the smile of recognitory assimilation." This smile occurs, beginning in later infancy, when a puzzling stimulus is absorbed into an existing mental framework. The relief of tension produces what may be an utterly private and yet rather satisfying grin.

Whatever the cerebral mechanisms that control the spontaneous smile, they are in place early in life. The sequence is present at birth although its social function is not. Even a premature infant of thirty weeks gestational age smiles winningly, but, like all newborns, does so almost exclusively during sleep. It used to be said that such smiles had something to do with "gas," until it was shown that—unlike, for example, belching or flatulence—they have no relationship to feeding. In fact, it is REM, or rapid-eye-movement sleep—the phase in which adult sleepers are often found to be dreaming—that sets the stage for these early smiles. Is it pleasant visions that set the smiles in motion? Unfathomable mysteries that suddenly become dreamily clear? Or merely some mechanical neural reflex in that primitive brain? We may never know. But what we do know is that newborn infants, premature or not, turn off this particular aspect of their charm more or less as soon as they open their eyes.

Not so the three-month-olds they will shortly become.

These creatures seem almost quintessentially social. Unless a three-month-old has indigestion or is otherwise indisposed, any halfway intelligent adult prepared to stoop to its level can easily elicit a smile. It is as if the infant's brain had matured to the point at which a semireflexive smile had clicked into use—but without any cultural context, or social discrimination, or hesitancy, or ambiguity. The smile seems automatic, almost like flinching from pain.

An analogy that is more than an analogy may help. Young frogs dart their tongues out at all small dark objects moving across their visual fields. Then, gradually, the response habituates—wanes selectively in the face of unpalatable results: after reaping too many flecks of dirt in the wind, and too many inedible insects, the tongue flick becomes rather finely tuned to the flies that constitute appropriate food. It would be inefficient for natural selection to wire in images of all the insects frogs eat, so the releasing stimulus—the visual pattern that evokes the reflexive tongue flick—is wired in crudely, painted in very broad strokes. Experience, mainly with things that don't taste good, leaves its mark beginning with the first flick and slowly fills in the details.

Similarly, the visual configuration that will evoke a smile from a four-month-old is very simple—an oval shape with two dark dots placed where eyes would be if the oval were a face. (Altered shapes—for example, an oval with the dots in the wrong place—will not work so well.) But over the course of several months, the infant becomes more discerning: the configuration has to be more similar to a real human face to earn a smile. It's as if there were some hard wiring designed to set the infant on a path, after which guidance is left to experience.

Experience will do more than direct the smile; it will also determine its frequency. Experiments have shown that infants who receive no social stimulation after smiling, such as an adult's approving gaze, will end up smiling less often, somewhat in the manner of rats that stop their barpressing after the rewards cease. And infants raised in environments with inadequate social stimulation, such as foundling homes, will smile much less at eight months or a year than will infants raised in middle-class homes. Nonetheless, the rise of social smiling by about three months of age is affected very little by learning. Maturation initiates, after which experience can differentiate.

The infant's smile, and the parents' responses to it, suggest a theory as to the evolutionary advantage that smiling confers. It appears to transform the infant's first, most fundamental relationship. Mothers say it is at this stage that they feel themselves to be dealing with another human being—that they are not mere attendants of a screeching diaper-soiling device but people involved in an intimate relationship: the infant has at last become a person. To be sure, the smile is not solely responsible for this change. Prolonged gaze contact is another of the infant's new capabilities, and it, too, evokes reverential, endless looks from the mother. And something that psychologists call contingent responsiveness—the infant's increasing sensitivity to the consequences of its acts, including a growing attentiveness to parents' reactions—also matures at around three months. But it is the smile that rewards the parent, the smile that decisively seals the emerging bond. Perhaps this is the evolutionary function of smiling—to help the baby wrap the mother around its little finger and thus receive the attention and nourishment needed to grow up and have babies of its own.

But this explanation raises as many questions as it answers.

If the purpose of smiling is infant-mother bonding, then why do adults continue to smile with such predictable frequency and in so many situations? And why does the smile's apparent phylogenetic precursor—the "smile" found in the primate species closest to us on the phylogenetic landscape—suggest an entirely different function?

In monkeys we find nothing quite like smiling. But J.A.R.A.M. Van Hooff, the Dutch ethologist, has traced the smile to other monkey signals, in particular the silent, bared-teeth grin. This expression, characterized by a liberal display of teeth, looks like a less comfortable, grimmer version of a smile (though that impression may just reflect my human bias). Usually, it occurs in the course of submissive behavior; a low-ranking monkey might flash it upon encountering the troop's dominant male. (This sort of grin is, of course, common in human hierarchies, too; an employee will often smile, sometimes uncomfortably, when passing the boss in the hall.) Our closest relatives, the chimpanzees (which in general exhibit a range of facial expressions very much like our own), have a look that resembles a smile more closely than does the monkeys' grin, and they, too, flash it as a sign of submission.

Could the smile, then, have arisen as a way to communicate status? That would certainly have made it a signal of some significance. Social hierarchies determine monkeys' access to food and other resources, and moving from one level to another within them typically entails much posturing and outright fighting. It is in the interest of any monkey likely to lose such fights to avoid them altogether; low status without bloodshed is evolutionarily advantageous—compared, at least, to low status with bloodshed. So the precursor of the smile, like other submissive signals, may simply mean something like "Don't bother attacking me, I am no threat to you. Let's not waste our time and energy fighting over what's already been decided."

This interpretation, however, like the theory of mother-infant bonding, soon encounters complications. In some monkey species, dominant males display the silent, bared-teeth grin to subordinates. And among chimpanzees, too, the smile occasionally appears without regard for status. Apparently, then, even among the lower primates, smiling can be more reciprocal, and more human, than a simple gesture of submission. It can mean "We are no threat to each other," which, I suppose, is a way of saying "We are friends." What is friendship, after all, if not—at least at first—the submission of two people to each other?

Already, our list of the smile's social functions has grown onerously long; a sign of submission or of benign dominance, a gesture of friendship, cement for the bond between parent and child. And what of its role in romance, and in childhood play? (A modified smile, known as a play face, appears during the play of young chimpanzees and is accompanied by sounds resembling laughter.) On what basis are we to choose from among the various explanations of the smile's existence? The answer, of course, is that we needn't. Evolution works too parsimoniously to assign only one function to each trait. Just as the canine tooth serves to kill, to consume, and to ward off, so the smile has come to perform a number of functions that help primates survive and reproduce.

Perhaps (as Van Hooff has argued) what was originally a sign of peaceful submission was adopted by high-ranking primates as a gesture of benign dominance to discourage fighting. After all, as soon as a chimpanzee has scaled the social hierarchy, it is in its interest to minimize challenges.

Once the meaning of the smile was established—"I am no threat to you"—it was a natural candidate for other functions. Thus, the same signal, occurring between male and female during sexual arousal, could exert a critical influence. And a similar signal might prevent the useful exercise of rough-and-tumble play from degenerating into costly fighting. Once smiling had acquired a positive emotional value, its expression by infants charmed mothers—all the more reason for babies to practice it often in the company of adults.

Of course, this is only a just-so story—one of many evolutionary scenarios that would fit the uneven body of evidence now available. The point is that there is an abundance of evolutionary explanations for the smile, not a shortage of them. And their unifying thread is that the smile began as an act of communication, as did the stickleback's mating swim and the greylag's neck extension.

Yet the smile has a subtlety, a multiplicity of meaning—an ambiguity—that is quintessentially human. Indeed, its mode of expression, its context, and its shades of meaning are shifting even now. During the past ten years, the hearing-impaired have had their lives transformed by the use of teletype devices that permit communication by telephone, and a new set of signals has arisen. One of these is the appearance of the word "smiles" as a sort of punctuation. It means "I am smiling as I write this." Without it, the same text might have a meaning different from—even the opposite of—what was intended. Indeed, it often appears after words that could otherwise create mistrust or distance between the speakers.

Thus, this phylogenetically ancient, maturationally guided, neurologically based motor-action pattern surfaces, completely transformed, not only in language but in writing, and on one of the most modern of all human machines. Is this a tribute to the ability of humans to emancipate their signals from the constraints imposed on the other animals? Or is it the opposite—a demonstration that there is no escape from our higher-primate heritage, even while we communicate through telephone wires? It is, in all likelihood, both.

BIRTH RITES

A woman in her early thirties, pregnant for the first time, is well into her ninth month and rather tired of waiting. She wants to spend a day or two relaxing with her husband in the mountains, three hours from the hospital, and they ask their midwife for permission. Although the woman is, in the terminology of obstetrics, an "elderly primigravida"—she is having her first baby after thirty—she is healthy, and the pregnancy has gone well. There is little chance that a first labor would have progressed very far within three hours of the first clear signs, so permission is cheerfully granted.

The couple considers childbirth a natural process and has gone to a midwife in reaction against its "medicalization." The midwife will deliver their baby in a hospital, with a fully prepared obstetric surgeon just down the hall, but the surgeon will not be called unless needed. Otherwise labor and delivery will go as the pregnancy has gone: with respect for the risks, with, as doctors say, "a careful, watchful-waiting pose," but with strict avoidance of unnecessary medical meddling.

They stay on a gentle nonworking farm in the rolling foothills of the Green Mountains, brushed now, in early fall, with the oranges, reds, and purples of a gathering wave of change. A good omen appears: in the afternoon light, near the

99

pond, a Canada goose with five goslings toddles imperturbably through the green and yellow grass. Later that day, the woman has a cramp or two, but she recognizes them as Braxton Hicks contractions, the classic false alarms of the latter part of pregnancy; the uterus is flexing its powerful muscle in preparation for the main event. They cook a meal, take some playful photographs in a mirror (in one, the pregnant belly disappears behind the man, and the woman looks as she did nine months earlier), and talk about the future.

At eight the next morning, the cramps begin in earnest. Even the first one doesn't seem like a false alarm, and by the third (they are equally spaced, twenty minutes apart) the man and woman get into their car and are on their way. There is a bad moment in a gas station when the gas cap is stuck (it would be funny if this were a movie), and the contractions are increasingly painful all the way home. Still, the breathless arrival at the hospital doesn't impress anyone. Examination reveals a typically slow first labor, with only a centimeter and a half or so—one finger—of dilation. The midwife shows them into the birthing room and notes that there is medicine on hand for pain. She seems to be preparing them for a long haul.

The midwife, as always, offers the medication apologetically. All her patients are people like these, dedicated to natural childbirth. They have attended classes that blur the colossal distinction between the role of the man and that of the woman; thus, "they" have exercised, been taught to breathe rhythmically (one way during the contractions, another way between them), learned that conquering pain is a matter of mind over body, and all in all come to mistrust the intervention of obstetricians as intrusive and self-serving. In medical terms, they view pregnancy and childbirth as physiological, not pathological.

The distinction is an interesting one. "It's physiological" is a phrase physicians reserve for what they think of as normal functions, even though patients may not: the growing pains in the joints of teenagers; the bulky stools of a high-fiber diet; the occasional extra beat, then pause, that feels disturbingly like a heart malfunction. Much is implied by the phrase: "This is not a symptom of illness," "Let nature take its course," "Stop worrying and learn to live with it." Only when the phrase "It's pathological" is invoked can the power of medicine—with all its attendant risks—be brought to bear on the process.

The couple waits for nature to take its course. Dilation progresses by millimeters. Contractions get longer, stronger, and closer together. After nightfall, fatigue sets in, and there is little sign of progress. There is back labor—pain referred from the uterus to the lower back, much like the left-arm pain in a heart attack—and the man presses on the sore spot, as instructed, with all his might, but to no avail. The breathing exercises increasingly seem to him a paltry device. One A.M., two, three. Dilation has progressed only five or six centimeters. The pain is tremendous. Medication is offered and refused again and again. No monitor is attached to the fetal scalp to ensure that the baby is weathering this assault in good condition—"obtrusive technology." Instead, a stethoscope is pressed against the mother's belly. Finally, one concession is made: the obstetrician, invited in for a consultation, advises rupturing the membranes, and the advice is taken. Fluid gushes from the uterus, and the baby's head, pressing directly against the cervix, can now be more effective in stretching it.

The pain becomes worse. The man has long since decided that medication is in order, but his wife continues to refuse. Since the cervix appears to be stretching lopsidedly, the woman changes position, which finally seems to accelerate labor. When the head crowns, it looks so purple and misshapen that the husband is sure it is malformed. (He smiles bravely, conscious of the need to protect his wife from the bad news.) But at six-thirty, after more than twenty-two hours of labor, as the sun comes up over the river near the hospital, a perfect baby girl is born, introduced to her mother (who is now grinning instead of cursing), and put to the breast.

Although it was eight or ten hours longer than the average for a first labor, the ordeal was not beyond the acceptable range, and no decision made by the midwife or the obstetrician was objectionable. Yet in many hospitals, medication would have been virtually forced on the laboring woman. In most large hospitals, electronic fetal scalp monitoring would have been performed, to make sure that the fetus was not suffering from oxygen deprivation or some other complication. And some physicians would have done a cesarean section, lest prolonged labor injure mother or child. This was a marginal case; it turned out well, but it needn't have.

The various risks that this couple averted are summed up in a venerable epigram of obstetrics: childbirth may be physiological for the species, but it's damned near pathological for the individual. In other words, childbirth, seen from an evolutionary perspective, is a normal, clearly essential process, but for the mother it can be painful, sometimes traumatic, even fatal. In this paradox lies the tension between the old-fashioned approach, with the attendant needles and drugs, and the newer, low-technology approach, with its abiding faith in nature. And in it lies the question of whether the return to "natural" childbirth has been carried too far.

Viviparity—the bearing of live young instead of the laying of eggs—is not limited to or universal among mammals, but they have carried it to its highest form of development. We think of the bearing of live young as being close to the essence of "mammalness," and as a trait that goes well with the mammalian invention of lactation. These characteristics of the early mammals set the stage for great advances in the complexity of maternal behavior and in the quality of the mother-infant relationship. And in a wide variety of mammals—rats, cats, goats, monkeys, and many others—the onset of that relationship occurs in the immediate aftermath of birth.

Watching dogs and cats give birth seems to underscore its naturalness. Rarely does the mother need assistance, and the same is true for nearly all other mammals. Among many primates, though, things are more difficult, partly because evolution has endowed them with such large brains. (Primates typically have a brain-to-body weight ratio of 12 percent at birth, as against 6 percent for other mammals.) The problem is not just that large brains mean large skulls, which pass through the birth canal only with difficulty, but that larger and more complex brains—and, indeed, larger and more complex infants—call for a longer gestation period. The longer gestation proceeds, the larger and more complex the young can get—but the more difficult it can be to get them born.

The sophistication of the mammalian placenta, and the biological intimacy of the connection between mother and fetus, increase as gestation progresses. In monkeys, the placental tissue (genetically a part of the fetus) so thoroughly invades the maternal domain that part of the uterine wall itself must be sacrificed in the afterbirth. Some mother and infant monkeys die as a result of this kind of disproportion— heads that are too big for birth canals.

The great apes—chimpanzees, gorillas, and orangutans—suffer much lower rates of this kind of disproportion, and birth for them is usually easy. They hold their infants, greet them, put them to the breast and begin to forge the most advanced form of that peculiar mammalian invention, the mother-infant bond—most advanced, that is, except for the human version. And, incidentally, they frequently eat the placenta, a behavior that appears to have important consequences: estrogen and progesterone, placental hormones, may play a role in returning the reproductive organ to pre-pregnant condition and even, perhaps, in promoting lactation and maternal behavior.

Why do the great apes have it so easy? They expel the fetus at a relatively early stage in its development and thus avoid the squeeze faced by monkeys, albeit at the expense of having a more fragile infant to care for. But the apes in this sense are an evolutionary island. The hominids, our post-ape ancestors, seem to have followed the monkey model; their rise was associated with an incredibly rapid advance in brain size, much of it achieved in the womb. To further complicate matters, those ancestors began to walk upright, so that the pelvis was being selected for weight bearing: it became shorter and stubbier, and the birth canal narrower and less pliant, while the fetal head became larger. For a time, it appears, this tension between the anatomy of mother and of child was eased in the manner of the great apes: fetuses were expelled proportionately earlier. But that trend could go only so far, and it never compensated fully for the growth in head size. We have ended up with an uneasy balance—a newborn infant of questionable viability and an unprecedentedly difficult birth, longer and riskier even than that of monkeys.

Still, for millions of years, we have managed to get ourselves born. Strategies have varied from one human society to the next. Frequently, birth is assisted, sometimes by an expert, a woman who, after attending many births, becomes the equivalent of a midwife, but sometimes only by an older female relative, and sometimes by someone in between—a grandmother or aunt with considerable experience. Such approaches have been found in societies as diverse as the Jicarilla Apache and the Zuni of the American Southwest, the Mansi of Siberia, and the Bang Chan of Southeast Asia, among others. Among the Siriono of the Amazon, many relatives might crowd into the labor room.

But not so the !Kung San, hunter-gatherers of northwestern Botswana, whose birth practices were studied by Marjorie Shostak in the 1970s. While nearly all !Kung women are assisted by female relatives for the first birth, thereafter they are expected to try to go it largely alone, and by the fifth or sixth child most give birth entirely alone. The !Kung insist that a major cause of difficulty in childbirth is fear; for this reason, perhaps (though there probably are others), they have demanded of themselves a truly extraordinary courage.

The !Kung and other primitive peoples have had to accept levels of infant and maternal mortality that we neither can nor should tolerate. Yet until quite recently we had to as well. During the nineteenth century, in Europe and the United States, most babies were delivered at home by midwives, and though tragic outcomes were less frequent than among the !Kung, the difference was not great. Into this ancient tradition stepped obstetrical physicians, who began to take deliveries away from midwives and bring laboring women into hospitals, where they could be efficiently followed. The results were disastrous. Obstetricians created hospital epidemics of childbed fever by unknowingly carrying microbes from bed to bed. During the 1840s, in the predawn light of the germ theory, two physicians—Ignaz Philipp Semmel-weis, in Austria, and Oliver Wendell Holmes, in the United States—announced, correctly, the cause of the disease; they were widely ridiculed.

Of course, their viewpoint eventually won the day: precautions were taken, death rates declined, and by the early twentieth century, obstetricians had largely taken over from midwives the management of childbirth. Many deliveries took place at home as late as the 1930s, and these had a high rate of success; but that was in all likelihood because they were of lower risk than those that came into the hospital. Antiseptic procedures, pain medication, the availability of transfusions, resuscitation, and cesarean section—these and other assets gradually made the hospital obstetrics ward the safest place to have a baby. Mortality rates declined to levels undreamed of by earlier generations.

By mid-century, American obstetricians were fully and firmly in charge of childbirth. They were overwhelmingly male, and they had intervened decisively in a process once controlled by women. They had begun by eliminating midwives and had ended up largely eliminating the mother herself. The popularity of twilight sleep—analgesia, induced by morphine, and depression of the cerebral cortex, induced by scopolamine—enabled most women to enter a pleasant, dreamlike state and emerge from it no longer pregnant, with the baby somewhere out of sight. They usually had no memory of the experience. Consciousness during childbirth, the rejection of pain medication, the presence of husbands in the delivery room, home births: these were strictly forbidden. They were considered not quaint but stupid and dangerous. Cesarean section became a common response to complications. The hormone oxytocin was intravenously infused to speed up or initiate labor (and labor was induced for the convenience not only of parents but also of doctors, sometimes merely to avoid weekend deliveries). Even breastfeeding was discouraged. The process of having a baby had been completely medicalized. Childbirth was considered unquestionably pathological, and as such was nobody's business but the doctor's. Technology—or so it was thought—had virtually nullified the ancient curse of Eve.

But by the late 1960s, the physician's authority was under fire. Good scientific evidence was accumulating about the disadvantages of delivery medications; some babies appeared drowsy for days after birth under anesthesia. And if the anesthesia was turning out to be a bad idea, what about induced labor? What about the obligatory insertion of an intravenous line in case blood transfusion or medication was necessary? And the shaving of the pubic area? The stirrups confining the woman to one, standard posture? The cutting of the threshold of the vagina, known as episiotomy? The separation of the baby from the mother right after birth? The exclusion of the father from the delivery room? And was the steady growth in the number of cesarean sections really warranted? The very success of modern obstetrics in reducing mortality had made such questions possible.

Grantley Dick Read, a British obstetrician, had advanced the concept of childbirth without fear, through psychological preparation—the concept to be picked up by Lamaze and others. "Fear," he wrote, "is in some way the chief pain-producing agent in otherwise normal labor." This sounded remarkably like the statements of !Kung and other "primitive" women, and seemed to support their tactics for the control of fear. It also raised questions about certain medical procedures that seemed likely to *increase* fear, at least for some women.

An alternative-childbirth movement arose. Women began

to pressure obstetricians for change. They wanted to be fully awake. They resented drugs that might make their infants groggy. They wanted some say in deciding on the posture they would assume during the ordeal. They wanted a husband or a friend with them in that cold white room full of strangers. They wanted to look into their babies' eyes after birth, to hold them, to put them to the breast. There were even recipes for placenta casserole being passed around, recalling the original meaning of "placenta": a circular cake.

Most obstetricians considered these trends ill advised, and they resisted them as long as they could. But some women would not take no for an answer: they simply refused to come to a hospital when labor began. Midwifery and home birth were starting to take hold again. It was as if the medicalization of childbirth had finally gone too far, and human nature itself had risen in protest. A threshold had been crossed beyond which even a further reduction of mortality could not persuade mothers, fathers—families—to relinquish any more of this dangerous but crucial rite of passage.

Today, the natural childbirth revolution has achieved many of its goals, and in some sectors of society, at least, its tenets are the new gospel. Laboring women are no longer assaulted by medical technology. They are fully conscious during childbirth, and many of them love it—at least in retrospect. Nature, not convenience, determines the onset of labor. Medications are minimized and designed to avoid infant sedation. Fathers or other companions are encouraged to stay in the delivery room, and evidence suggests that their presence shortens labor. In some hospitals, birthing rooms— with pretty wallpaper, ordinary furniture, a picture or two brought in by the patient, and an assiduous avoidance of chrome and tile—are available as a substitute for the surgical delivery suite. Highly trained nurse-midwives work under the watchful eyes of obstetricians (many of whom, now, are women). Babies are presented to their mothers almost as soon as they are born, and some researchers feel that this enriches the mother-infant relationship, especially when that relationship is at risk—when the mother is poor or in her early teens, for example. Vaginal birth by a woman who has previously had cesarean delivery—once unheard of—now is not uncommon in major medical centers.

All this is well and good, but there remain reasons for caution. The first is that, like any revolution, natural childbirth has its excesses and its ideologues. There are those who insist on home birth, for example, and this simply is dangerous. In one study, 20 percent of normal pregnancies resulted in unpredictable high-risk births. And women who refuse to undergo episiotomy risk tearing tissue all the way from the vagina to the rectum during birth. As for fetal monitoring: though its usefulness has not been proved (it is not clear that what the monitor discerns are signs of real distress), the fear that it is cruel to the infant is unfounded; the pinprick of a fetal monitor, amid the brutal pressure of the uterus, is probably all but imperceptible.

More questionable, perhaps, than any single practice favored by the natural-childbirth school is the dogma that sometimes emanated from it. In some circles, women are ashamed to ask for painkillers of any kind, even in the most dire circumstances. Aside from the needless suffering that such asceticism sometimes entails, there is the risk that extreme pain could throw the woman into panic. Rejection of an intravenous line may stall treatment of complications such as profuse bleeding. Even if most births are more physiological than pathological, pathology is never far away, and it often appears on short notice. Obstetricians are justifiably proud of their accomplishments in reducing unnecessary risk. Ironically, it was only because they were so successful in reducing mortality that such a happily regressive movement could arise at all.

But if the revolution in childbirth has gone too far in some circles, it has not even reached others. All along, it has been primarily an upper-middle-class phenomenon, and its benefits remain inequitably distributed. For example, electronic fetal scalp monitoring is insisted upon in many American centers, despite new research suggesting that old-fashioned listening in with a stethoscope is adequate, while the scalp monitor may introduce infection. Epidural anesthesia—the injection of local anesthetic into the sac surrounding the lower spine—has become very common since the demise of twilight sleep. But some argue that it slows down labor, which then has to be speeded up with the use of oxytocin, which in turn leads to other complications—a cascade of untoward events in a process that could have been left alone.

Rates of cesarean section have gone as high as 25 percent, and some obstetricians insist that such rates reduce mortality. But outside the United States—in Dublin, for example—a greater decrease in mortality was achieved over the same time period without an increase in the section rate. As for the routine placement of an intravenous line in every laboring woman, many obstetricians with wide experience and good judgment now feel that such a line can be placed after a risk makes itself known.

Yet even as some women reject all sorts of medical intervention, others blindly obey instructions, unaware that they have some say in the matter. Whatever its shortcomings and excesses, the return of natural childbirth is helping to give women a greater sense of their options. It has been basically good and probably inevitable—our evolutionary heritage reasserting itself after a hundred years of growing technological intervention.

I was the father in that twenty-two-hour birth, and it scared the living daylights out of me. Still, I would not have missed it for the world—and neither (or so she insists) would my wife. Later, as a medical student, I delivered thirty-six babies. Nearly all of them were born to conscious mothers, in the presence of fathers or other helpers. And as I gazed across the site of what had been such intense pain—at the father, holding the baby I had handed him; at the mother, face to face with that baby for the first time—the smiles on their faces said as much as any obstetrics text. To be sure, the rite of passage we have evolved in the 1980s has its idiosyncrasies—as what ritual shouldn't? It belongs to our optimistic, overly romantic culture. But it also has something in common with the rites of passage in any number of ancestral human societies. And it echoes, too, certain rhythms of reproduction that must have surrounded the first live-born young as they wriggled out of the wombs of early mammals two hundred million years ago.

LOVE AMONG
THE ROBOTS

When I was a boy of sixteen or so, an episode of "The Twilight Zone" changed my view of life. Since I was a serious student, thoughtful and deeply religious, this rather unconventional source of a world view takes some explaining.

The show's plot was simple: In some future society, a man has been exiled, after committing unnamed political offenses, to solitary imprisonment on an asteroid. Once a year he is visited by a supply ship, whose captain takes pity on him and one year brings him a present in a very large box. On opening the box after the ship has gone, the hero reacts with disgust: it is a female robot, a mere mechanical substitute for genuine companionship. The robot, however—portrayed by an appealing actress—is remarkably lifelike and, after some fumbling and learning, appears completely human. In seeming (being?) palpably hurt by his rejections, she wins his first attention. One thing leads to another on this desolate orbiting rock, and by the supply ship's next visit, they have formed what must be construed as a powerful bond of affection. If the word has any meaning at all, they *love* each other.

The next year, the captain brings undreamed-of news: the winds of political change have blown a breath of amnesty from one end of the galaxy to the other. The hero can return home at last—but the captain is brought up short by the hero's use of the word "we." He is smack up against his weight limit and, having failed to think of the android, has room for only one passenger. When reason fails to disabuse the hero of his sentimental attachment to the machine (the argument goes on painfully in the presence of this third party, who bears an expression of tragic apprehension), the captain resorts to his ray gun, shooting the seeming woman in the face. The wound reveals a tangle of wiring and circuitry, and the robot's voice, repeatedly calling the hero's name, runs down like a record player with its plug suddenly pulled.

As I recall the final moments of this denouement, no tears were shed, and it appeared (though this was left to the viewer's imagination) that the hero would be brought to his senses and sent home to freedom a sadder but wiser man. But to me this was murder, not only unpunished but condoned, and I could not get it out of my mind. With all the intensity of adolescent idealism, I worked the issue through in my mind and a few days later gave up my belief in the insubstantiality of the soul. By virtue of her animated responses, her full range of thought and feeling, and, above all, her trust in and love for the hero—not to mention his for her—the android was human and had as much of a "soul" as any person, regardless of whether the hardware within was carbon or silicon. Or, to put it another, more distressing way, a human being could have no more of a soul than she.

In the years since I was so shaken by this fiction it has come a long way toward fact. Artificial intelligence, then an obscure undertaking confined to a few university campuses, is now a large commercial enterprise, and, according to its enthusiastic practitioners, such as Marvin Minsky, machines of the future not only will perform bigger calculations than humans ever could but also will make scientific discoveries, form medical and legal judgments, perform psychotherapy, and compose beautiful music and poetry.

I suppose this prospect should be easier for me to accept now than it was thirty years ago. But in a way it is more unsettling than ever. For a decade or so, the relentless depredations of sociobiology—like the Freudian ones of an earlier era—have eroded, it seems, the very basis of the human spirit. The most cherished differences between humans and animals have been swept aside, one after another: motherly love, altruism, cooperation, and sacrifice are now seen as mere adaptations—genetically programmed strategies for survival that we share with many other species. All that has been left to us after this beastly onslaught is rational thought; we are animals, yes, but thinking animals, and no other configuration of matter on Earth can rival us in this domain. But now even rational thought is being taken over—lock, stock, and memory board—by computers. The turf separating animal and machine is shrinking, and it is only human to wonder whether there will always be a place for us, and us alone, to stand.

The question of whether machines will ever be able to think is, in artificial intelligence—or AI—circles, commonly cast in terms of the Turing test, devised by the British computer scientist Alan M. Turing, who died in 1954. Turing imagined an "imitation game," in which a human interrogator communicates with two unseen people—a man and a woman—via teletype. The interrogator can ask any question he likes, the goal being to determine which is the man and which the woman. The catch is that the man will be trying to deceive him and is free to lie egregiously—claiming, for example, to have long, elaborately styled hair. The woman, Turing wrote, "can add such things as 'I am the woman, don't listen to him!' to her answers, but it will avail nothing as the man can make similar remarks." The questions that fascinated Turing were: What will happen when a machine replaces the man? Will the human interrogator err as often as before? "These questions," he wrote, "replace our original, 'Can machines think?' "

The idiosyncrasies of this game may have had special significance to Turing, who was a homosexual, at a time when male homosexuality was a crime. (Some observers have attributed his death—an apparent suicide, involving a cyanide-laced apple—to harassment by the British government, which he had served nobly in the Second World War, breaking a critical and supposedly impregnable German code.) But the game can be recast so that it does not revolve around gender, and these days it usually is: a machine that could pass the Turing test is now defined as one that would fool a human interrogator into believing that it, too, is human.

The belief that someday a computer will pass this test—an article of faith for Minsky and like-minded computer scientists—has not gone unchallenged, of course. Humanists decry the claim that machines might think as people do, even as AI researchers try to develop machines that will decry the decrying humanists. The humanists' case rests, first of all, on what might be called the intuitional fallacy. This argument, as commonly stated, is that computers will never be able to do everything humans do, because computers rely exclusively on rules, whereas people act intuitionally, with a keen but unspecifiable sort of inference from experience. Thus, no machine will ever beat a world champion at chess, and no computer will ever be a good physician.

Understandably confused about what intuition might be, programmers have leaned on the words "from experience" and tried to design expert systems that learn from their mistakes. Thus a checker-playing program that learns can beat world champions at least occasionally. A similar chess-playing program beat the British international master David

Levy one and a half games out of five in 1984, leading Levy to conclude that "having played the thing now, my feeling is that a human world chess champion losing to a computer program . . . is a lot farther away than I thought." But Levy is by profession almost as much a computer expert as he is a chess master. Thus his game against the machine is unfairly informed by a profound knowledge of how the machine thinks. More to the point, however, the program beat him at least once, and similar programs are getting better all the time. For example, "Deep Thought," a program developed in 1988, can defeat all but the top one hundred grand masters in the world.

Sometimes the humanists invoke a special pleading that borders on petulance. Hubert Dreyfus, a philosopher at the University of California at Berkeley, has written about the "failures" of expert systems. For example, a program known as INTERNIST-1 makes medical diagnoses. Given laboratory test data from real case histories, Dreyfus has noted, it missed eighteen of forty-three diagnoses, while a team of clinicians at Massachusetts General Hospital missed a mere fifteen, and a committee of medical experts only eight.

So if you get yourself a committee of medical experts to agonize over the data as doctors rarely would, you get slightly fewer that half as many errors as with the machine; while if you settle for a team of clinicians at one of America's best teaching hospitals, you better the program's error rate by something like 17 percent. It doesn't take much experience in clinical medicine to surmise that INTERNIST-1 would probably outperform a large minority (at least) of American physicians, to say nothing of lesser-trained physicians in some parts of the world—and this at the very dawn of the use of such systems. Thus, Minsky and his colleagues properly brush aside the intuitional fallacy with allusions to the future.

This aspect of what computers can't now do is technically, but not philosophically or scientifically, interesting.

The second argument humanists make, which might be called the intentional fallacy, is philosophically interesting but far from decisive. It amounts to a rejection of the Turing test. The contention is that even if computers are someday able to accomplish the same intellectual tasks as humans, "thought" will not be the right word for the information processing behind their performance. The philosopher John Searle advanced this position in a 1980 paper, published in the journal *Behavioral and Brain Sciences* with simultaneous replies by the great and near-great of artificial intelligence and cognitive science, and with Searle's replies to the replies.

Searle's paper begins with his "Chinese room" argument: Imagine a room with no windows or doors, only a mail slot. Suppose you passed a story written in Chinese into the room, then passed in questions about the story, also in Chinese. Twenty minutes later, perfectly sensible, well-crafted answers come out of the slot, again in Chinese, suggesting that something in the room understands Chinese. But, said Searle, it might be that within the room was Searle himself, who understands no Chinese but was merely following rules he had been given for converting some kinds of foreign squiggles into other kinds. Thus, nowhere in the room is there true understanding of Chinese, even though the room behaved as if there were.

Among the criticisms of this argument that Searle did not convincingly answer are psychologist Bruce Bridgeman's— that not even humans are fully aware of the mental operations underlying conscious thought; computer scientist Douglas R. Hofstader's—that the man in the Chinese room is functionally no more sophisticated than a few neurons, and that such a system could not possibly pull off anything so complex and subtle as language translation; and philosopher Richard Rorty's—that if the system really *could* pass this variant of the Turing test, it *would* understand Chinese, since a truly scientific definition of "understanding" must be stated in strictly behavioral terms. Further, there is the behaviorist criticism (which Searle also answers unconvincingly): our skepticism that this system has a mind implies a skepticism of other minds in general) including human ones; if we can't infer thought from behavior, we must spend our lives wondering whether anyone on the planet other than ourselves is truly conscious. This is something that few of us see a compelling reason to do.

These criticisms, taken together, suggest that the Chinese room argument is specious. But even if they did not, Searle himself has acknowledged a loophole in his argument, one that is frequently overlooked in discussions of it. He believes that mind is a kind of insubstantial secretion of the brain and emanates from our neurochemistry, as dependent on physiology as is the milk from a mother's mammary glands. A mechanical system could have mind, he concedes, if it precisely simulated the physical processes of the brain.

But how do we know that brain biochemistry is important? True, milk can only be simulated through biochemistry; but walking can be simulated without it. Is the act of thought more like milk production or walking? On this question turns the issue of whether programmed computers will one day have minds—an issue that, as AI enthusiasts point out, must be resolved empirically, not philosophically.

But even if AI doesn't work, machine minds will still be possible. This is a point frequently missed in discussions of Searle. He is not ruling out artificial intelligence in the broadest plain-English sense of mechanical minds. He is only ruling out minds supplied to machines by programs.

This is not, of course, the only approach being tried. Roboticists take an entirely different approach to simulating a mind. Consider, for instance, a system known as WISARD, described by Igor Aleksander and Piers Burnett in *Reinventing Man*. Rather than asking, as typical AI does, "How can we program a machine with rules that will simulate mind?," this approach—"millennial robotics"—asks, "How can we build a machine that will have a mind without the addition of a program?" By posing the problem as an engineering one rather than a programming one—hardware rather than software—it puts itself squarely in a realm where even a skeptic like Searle will not object. The machine will have senses and active limbs and will react to the world as, say, an infant or an animal does. But most important, it will learn from experience, in ways designed to produce it all; growth of mind, intuition, intention, whatever in human thought seems most human, and without benefit of programs—except, of course, for the ones it gives itself.

Enter the humanists' third argument, which AI enthusiasts might call the emotional fallacy, except that it isn't really a fallacy. This is the one presented by Sherry Turkle, an MIT sociologist also trained as a clinical psychologist, in *The Second Self: Computers and the Human Spirit*. The book is based on years of fieldwork among MIT computer hackers, AI experts and their groupies, and ordinary children playing computer games. Beginning in the late 1970s, when the age of personal computers was colorfully dawning, Turkle examined people's relationships with computers, in the twin senses of interaction and comparison. As she shows, these twins are Siamese: interaction with a computer involves an assessment, if unconscious, of how it compares to us, and comparison assumes some relationship (the Turing test, after all, implies as much).

Among Turkle's findings is that whether a machine can pass the Turing test depends on the mind of the beholder. To one five-year-old encountering it for the first time, Texas Instruments' Speak & Spell toy was alive. Other children, not convinced but clearly uneasy, took special delight in "killing" it by taking out the batteries—as if reaffirming their own uniqueness. Much more at ease with the idea of an animate machine were the hackers—college-age people, usually men, who work, live, eat, sleep, and breathe computers. Hackers articulate frankly the satisfactions of their relationships with computers: complete devotion, predictability, and control— the kinds of things another person could never provide. As hackers themselves seem to recognize, their spirits have found in the computer a sort of superperson cut from the cloth of fantasy. The computer has in a sense passed the Turing test as posed by some of their most fundamental human needs.

But hackers are the exceptions. Most people feel the need to defend themselves from the computer's insult to their humanity. They do so, usually, by defining themselves in opposition to it: sure, the machine can play a dazzling game of chess, but only humans enjoy winning; it can diagnose illness, but only humans fear making a fatal mistake; it may have thought, but only humans have feelings. As Turkle realized, this is but a variation on the game of defining humans in opposition to animals. "In the presence of the computer, people's thoughts turn to their feelings," she wrote; and, "Where we once were rational animals, now we are feeling computers, emotional machines."

We have come full circle, and our identity crisis remains unresolved. We say we are rational animals, but other animals have the same vivid array of motives and feelings. The process of definition-by-exclusion would seem to have left us sorted to a pulp.

Of course, we are not. It is the intersection of the sets that makes us human—the tiny corner of the diagram where animal motives overlap with mechanical rationality. It is the inner argument between the ache of sexual desire and the thought of ultimate consequence that produces the lover's plaint; the climbing of animal fear on the latticework of symbol that makes possible the comfort of ritual; the bubbling of the consciousness of our own mortality through everyday sensual experience that gives rise to the human sense of beauty.

Consider the example given by the computer scientist Joseph Weizenbaum, in *Computer Power and Human Reason*, of what computers can't simulate: the wordless communion that a mother and father share as they stand over their sleeping child's bed. Contained in their glances is the shared love growing out of the three relationships; the subtle memories of the sex that engendered the bonds; the life histories of the man and the woman, the events of their own childhoods echoing ineffably through the sleeper, the cascade of family dramas falling for generations; and, above all, the man's and the woman's sense of their own, and their child's, mortality—the fear, the grief, the intensified love of the things of this world.

Could computers simulate—perhaps even experience—this tragic sense of life? Simulate, possibly. But to experience it they would have to participate in a fully human life cycle. They would have to be born, grow, surrender themselves to some kind of family life, confront the demands of maturity, reproduce, age, and, especially, be conscious of the prospect of their dying. Not to mention their having to experience the aches and pains, the shivers and sweats, the hormonal flux, the sludge of fatigue, the neuronal dropout, and the nine-hundred-and-some-odd other natural shocks that flesh is heir to. As Turkle put it, "A being that is not born of a mother, that does not feel the vulnerability of childhood, a being that does not know sexuality or anticipate death, this being is alien."

But how well will Turkle's comforting contention fare in the future, when computers compose plainly good poems? In considering how we would respond to such poems, recall our response to the nice abstract paintings composed a few years ago by a chimpanzee. We were curious about them, admired them, even paid a good price for them, but we knew they were not real paintings. A machine much simpler than the simplest of computers could produce abstract paintings, some of which would be pleasing to the eye. But, like the chimp ones, they would not be real. Real paintings come out of human experience, respond to human traditions, are informed by human expectations even when they violate them.

Or consider poems written by children. These are often freer, more engaging, and lovelier than any the same child will be capable of writing when grown. So why don't we admire them the way we would similar ones written by adults? Because it it precisely the grown-upness of its source that makes the freedom and grace of a poem so admirable. A good poem by an adult is a communication from a person who, like the rest of us, has been ambushed by life but who has miraculously escaped the loss of the gracefulness that came easily in childhood—or, perhaps, has found an artful way to recover it. In this sense a "good" poem by a computer would be of no more interest than the tragic drama typed by the random key strokes of the proverbial roomful of monkeys—except, of course, for its value as scientific curiosity.

So what will it be like when computers are—as they will surely be—vastly smarter than we are in many ways? We will ask them, I think, to speculate about the influences of

Shakespeare on Shelley, or maybe even expect them to suggest such a study; but we will not curl up near the fire with a slim volume of verse they have written. We will go to them for most sorts of medical diagnoses, maybe even for surgery. But, at our bedside, while we are dying, we will want someone who knows that he or she will also, someday, die. Computers will be, perhaps, like the gods of ancient Greece: incredibly powerful and even capable of many human emotions—but, because of their immortality, ineligible for admission into that warm circle of sympathy reserved exclusively for humans.

And what of the murdered android I mooned over at sixteen? I doubt that any robot could simulate emotion well enough to pass my ultimate Turing test: does this machine have a tragic sense of life? Of course, my feelings toward her would not be irrelevant; relationships help define people, and the question of what constitutes murder hinges partly on how the murderer violates the relationship as he himself perceives it. Nonetheless, I would steel myself and apply my ultimate test; if she failed, even I might draw my ray gun.

WHY THE RECKLESS

SURVIVE

In a recent election Massachusetts rescinded its seat-belt law. As a result some hundreds of citizens of that commonwealth have in the past year gone slamming into windshields instead of getting a pain in the neck from the shoulder belt. Quite a few are unnecessarily brain-damaged or dead. Such laws in fact make a difference. Americans in general use seat belts at a rate of about 20 percent; but in Texas, where failure to wear one can cost you not only your life but also fifty dollars, nearly seven people in ten wear them habitually—a fivefold increase since the law was passed in 1985. Having lived in Massachusetts for fifteen years, I considered it—wrongly, perhaps—the most sensible state in the union, so I was rather amazed by its recent collective decision.

But I shouldn't have been. All I needed to do was to look at my own behavior. I have, while coauthoring a book on health, sat at my word processor at three a.m. guzzling coffee and gobbling Oreo cookies by the dozen, pecking solemnly away about our need to take better care of ourselves. I could almost feel the fat from the cookies sinking into the arteries of my brain, the coffee laying the groundwork for future cardiac arrhythmias.

Why can't we follow our own advice, or others', even when we know it's right? Is it the heedless child in us, or the perverse, destructive teenager, or only the antiauthoritarian, freedom-loving adult that says, *I will do as I please, thank you?* Or could it be that there is something inevitable—even something good—about the taking of all these chances?

People don't think clearly about risk. This is no mere insult, but a conclusion that emerges from attempts by behavioral scientists to understand how people make decisions. In part these studies were sparked by the unprecedented demand for risk reduction that has emerged in recent years. How many cases of cancer do people consider acceptable nationally as a result of the widespread use of a food additive or an industrial chemical? None. How many accidents or near-accidents at nuclear power plants? None. How many airline crashes per decade? Basically, none.

We may consider the change good: doesn't it reflect a healthy increase in awareness of real risks? But consider that this is the same American public that, after years of education, wears seat belts at the rate of 20 percent and has reduced its cigarette smoking only somewhat. The widespread success of lotteries alone shows that people do not think or act rationally, even in their own self-interest.

So we ignore some risks and overestimate others. The conundrum for an evolutionist is simple. Natural selection should have relentlessly culled systematic biases in decision making, producing a rational organism that hews to the order of real cost-benefit analysis—an organism that behaves efficiently to minimize those ratios. How can evolution, with its supposedly relentless winnowing out of error, have preserved this bewildering array of dangerous habits?

We are highly sensitive to certain dangers. A Harris poll conducted in 1980 showed that 78 percent of the American public (as opposed to roughly half of business and government leaders) thought that risks in general were greater than they had been twenty years before. The greatest perceived risks were in the areas of crime and personal safety, international and domestic political stability, energy sources, and "the chemicals we use." Comfortable majorities of the general public (but only small minorities of the leadership groups) agreed with the statements "Society has only perceived the tip of the iceberg with regard to the risks associated with modern technology" and "Unless technological development is restrained, the overall safety of society will be jeopardized significantly in the next twenty years."

But the logic of our concerns is problematic. People are willing to pay indirectly large sums of money to reduce the risk of a nuclear accident or a cancer death from a chemical to levels they consider acceptably low. But they will not pay a much smaller amount for air bags in automobiles, that, inflating on impact, will save many more lives; and they will not stop smoking, although this risk-reducing measure would actually save money, both immediately and in the long term.

Apparently, irrational factors are at work. But before we consider them, and why we may be subject to them, it is worth looking at the realities of risk. John Urquhart and Klaus Heilmann, both physicians, have reviewed some of these realities in their book *Riskwatch: The Odds of Life*. There is a genuine hierarchy of danger. For example, the number of deaths linked to cigarette smoking in the United States is equivalent to three jumbo jets full of passengers crashing daily, day in and day out. We have fifty thousand traffic fatalities a year—almost the number of deaths we suffered during our entire involvement in Vietnam. Half involve drunk drivers, and a large proportion would be prevented by seat belts or air bags.

Yet neither of these sources of risk evokes the interest—indeed the fear—shown in response to possible nuclear accidents, or to toxic-shock syndrome caused by tampons, or even to homicide, all (for most of us) trivial risks by comparison to smoking or driving. If you tremble when you strap yourself into the seat of an airliner, you ought to really shudder when you climb onto your bicycle, since that is much more dangerous as a regular activity. As for homicide, the people most afraid of it are the ones least likely to be victimized. And the millions of women who stopped taking birth-control pills because of the risk of death from stroke did so in response to an annual probability of dying equal to about one fourth their routine risk of death in an automobile.

Urquhart and Heilmann deal with this quirkiness in our response to risk by developing a Safety-Degree Scale analogous to the Richter scale for earthquake severity. The units are logarithms of the cohort size necessary for one death to occur. Thus lightning, which kills fewer than one person per million exposed, has a safety degree of more than six, while motorcycling, which kills one in a thousand, has a safety degree of three; motorcycling is three orders of magnitude more dangerous. But they aren't perceived in that relation. In general, people will accept one to two orders of magnitude more danger in voluntary risks than they will in involuntary ones. And that is only one aspect of the quirkiness. Risks that result in many deaths at once will be perceived as worse than probabilistically equal risks that kill in a more distributed way. And any bad outcome that is reported unexpectedly—especially if its shock value is exploited—increases fear.

Chronic departures from rationality have been the subject of a major line of thought in economics, in which the most distinguished name is Herbert Simon's. Simon, a winner of the Nobel Memorial prize in economics, has for years criticized and occasionally ridiculed the economic decision theory known as subjective expected utility, or SEU. According to this classic approach, individuals face their life choices with full knowledge of the probability and value of all possible outcomes, and furthermore they possess an unambiguous value scale to measure utility—in plain English, they know a great deal, in advance, about the consequences of their choices, and, more important, they know what they want. In the real world, Simon points out, no such knowledge exists. Whether in the choices of executives or in those of consumers, knowledge is imperfect and values (at least to some extent) indeterminate and mercurial.

A similar point was demonstrated in laboratory experiments by psychologists Amos Tversky and Daniel Kahnemann, in which people are shown to be rather feeble in their abilities to choose among various outcomes. They are readily confused by differences in the language in which a problem is posed. In one study, Tversky and Kahnemann asked physicians to choose among possible programs to combat a hypothetical disease that was on the verge of killing six hundred people. The physicians favored a program guaranteed to save *two hundred lives* over one that had a one-third probability of saving everyone and a two-thirds probability of saving no one. Yet a second group of physicians favored the riskier program over one described as resulting in exactly *four hundred deaths*. They were, of course, rejecting the same alternative the previous group had chosen. The only difference was that it was now being described in terms of victims rather than survivors. Human decision making is rife with such framing errors, and analyzing them has become a cottage industry.

At least equally interesting is a new psychological view— advanced by Lola Lopes among others—that certain "errors" may not be errors at all. Lottery players can be shown to be irrational by multiplying the prize by the probability of winning, and comparing that number to the cost of the ticket. But that does not take into account the subjective value placed on becoming rich, or the fact that this may be someone's only chance for that outcome. Nor, of course, does it consider the thrill of playing.

But another aspect of this behavior clearly is irrational: people—especially, but not only, compulsive gamblers—have unrealistically high expectations of winning. On the average, in the larger game of life, they also have unrealistically high expectations of protection against losing. Linda Perloff and others have shown that people—average people—think that they will live longer than average, that they will have fewer diseases than average, and even that their marriages will last longer than average. Since average people are likely to have average rates of disease, death, and divorce, they are (in these studies) underestimating their risks—a tendency Lionel Tiger has summarized as a ubiquitous, biologically based human propensity to unwarranted optimism.

While these results fit well with the prevalence of risky behavior, they seem to contradict the findings about people's *over*estimate of the risk of violent crime, or terrorist attacks, or airline crashes, or nuclear-plant accidents. Part of this is resolvable by reference to the principle that risks beyond our control are more frightening than those we consider ourselves in charge of. So we drink and drive, and buckle the seat belt behind us, and light up another cigarette, on the strength of the illusion that to *these* risks at least, we are invulnerable; and we cancel the trip to Europe on the one-in-a-million chance of an Arab terrorist attack.

Three patterns, then, emerge in our misestimates. First, we prefer voluntary risks to involuntary ones—or, put another way, risks that we feel we have some control over to those that we feel we don't. By the way we drive and react to cues on the road, we think, we reduce our risk to such a low level that seat belts add little protection. But in the case of the terrorist attack or the nuclear-plant accident, we feel we have no handle on the risks. (We seem especially to resent and fear risks that are imposed on us by others, especially if for their own benefit. If I want to smoke myself to death, we seem to say, it's my own business; but if some company is trying to put something over on me with asbestos or nerve gas, I'll be furious.)

Second, we prefer familiar risks to strange ones. The homicide during a mugging, or the airliner hijacked in Athens, or the nerve gas leaking from an armed forces train, get our attention and so loom much larger in our calculations than they should in terms of real risk. Third, deaths that come in bunches—the jumbo-jet crash of the disaster movie—are more frightening than those that come in a steady trickle, even though the latter may add up to more risk when the counting is done. This principle may be related in some way to the common framing error in which people in Tversky and Kahnemann's studies will act more strongly to prevent two hundred deaths in six hundred people than they will to guarantee four hundred survivors from the same group. Framing the risk in terms of death rather than survival biases judgment.

But there is yet another, more interesting complication. "The general public," "average people," "human" rational or irrational behavior—these categories obscure the simple fact that people differ in these matters.

Average people knowingly push their cholesterol levels upward, but only a third pay essentially no attention to doctors' orders when it comes to modifying their behavior (smoking, or eating a risky diet) in the setting of an established illness worsened by that behavior. Average people leave their seat belts unbuckled, but only some people ride motorcycles, and fewer still race or do stunts with them. Average people play lotteries, friendly poker, and church bingo, but an estimated one to four million Americans are pathological gamblers, relentlessly destroying their lives and the lives of those close to them by compulsively taking outrageous financial risks.

Psychologists have only begun to address these individual differences, but several different lines of research suggest that there is such a thing as a risk-taking or sensation-seeking personality. For example, studies of alcohol, tobacco, and caffeine abuse have found these three forms of excess to be correlated, and also to be related to various other measures of risk taking.

For many years psychologist Marvin Zuckerman, of the University of Delaware, and his colleagues have been using the Sensation Seeking Scale, a questionnaire designed to address these issues directly. Empirically, the questions fall along four dimensions: *thrill and adventure seeking*, related to interest in physical risk taking, as in skydiving and mountain climbing; *experience seeking*, reflecting a wider disposition to try new things, in art, music, travel, friendship, or even drugs; *disinhibition*, the hedonistic pursuit of pleasure through activities like social drinking, partying, sex, and gambling; and *boredom susceptibility*, an aversion to routine work and dull people.

At least the first three of these factors have held up in many samples, of both sexes and various ages, in England and America, but there are systematic differences. Males always exceed females, and sensation seeking in general declines in both sexes with age. There is strongly suggestive evidence of a genetic predisposition: 233 pairs of identical twins had a correlation of 0.60 in sensation seeking, while 138 nonidentical-twin pairs had a corresponding correlation of only 0.21.

More interesting than these conventional calculations is a series of studies showing that sensation seeking, as measured by the questionnaire, has significant physiological correlates. For example, heart-rate change in reaction to novelty is greater in sensation-seekers, as is brain-wave response to increasingly intense stimulation. The activity of monoamine oxidase (MAO), an enzyme that breaks down certain neuro-transmitters (the chemicals that transmit signals between brain cells), is another correlate. Sensation seekers have less MAO activity, suggesting that neurotransmitters that might be viewed as stimulants may persist longer in their brains. Finally, the sex hormones, testosterone and estrogen, show higher levels in sensation seekers.

But in addition this paper-and-pencil test score correlates with real behavior. High scorers engage in more frequent, more promiscuous, and more unusual sex; consume more drugs, alcohol, cigarettes, and even spicy food; volunteer more for experiments and other unusual activities; gamble more; and court more physical danger. In the realm of the abnormal, the measure is correlated with hypomania, and in the realm of the criminal, with psychopathy.

In other words, something measured by this test has both biological and practical significance. Furthermore, independent studies by Frank Farley and his colleagues at the University of Wisconsin, using a different instrument and a somewhat distinct measure they call thrill seeking, have confirmed and extended these findings. For example, in prison populations fighting and escape attempts are higher in those who score high on thrill seeking. But Farley also emphasizes positive outcomes—a well-established correlation between sensation seeking and the extraverted personality underscores the possibility that some such people are well primed for leadership.

We can now return to the main question: how could all this irrationality have been left untouched by natural selection? Herbert Simon, in an accessible, even lyrical, summary of his thought, the 1983 book *Reason in Human Affairs*, surprised some of us in anthropology and biology who are more or less constantly railing against the un-Darwinian musings of social scientists. He shows a quite incisive understanding of Darwin's theories and of very recent significant refinements of them.

But my own anthropological heart was most warmed by passages such as this one: "If this [situation] is not wholly descriptive of the world we live in today . . . it certainly describes the world in which human rationality evolved: the world of the cavemen's ancestors, and of the cavemen themselves. In that world . . . periodically action had to be taken to deal with hunger, or to flee danger, or to secure protection against the coming winter. Rationality could focus on dealing with one or a few problems at a time. . . ." The appeal to the world of our ancestors, the hunters and gatherers, is as explicit as I could wish. As Simon recognizes, this is the world in which our rationality, limited as it is, evolved. It could not be much better now than it needed to be then, because less perfect rationality would not have been selected against; and we, the descendants of those hunters and gatherers, would have inherited their imperfections.

The result is what Simon calls "bounded rationality"—a seat-of-the-pants, day-by-day sort of problem solving that, far from pretending to assess all possible outcomes against a clear spectrum of values, attempts no more than to get by. "Putting out fires" is another way of describing it; and it follows directly from the concept of economic behavior that made Simon famous: "satisficing," the notion that people are just trying to solve the problem at hand in a way that is "good enough"—his practical answer to those too-optimistic constructions of economists, "maximizing" and "optimizing."

Simon has perceived that the basic human environment did not call for optimal decision making, in the modern risk-benefit sense of the phrase; thus our imperfection, this "bounded rationality." But this does not explain the systematic departures from rationality—the preference for "controllable" or familiar rather than "uncontrollable" or strange risks, or the particular fear attached to large disasters. And it does not explain, especially, the sense of invulnerability of risk takers. Certain kinds of recklessness are easy to handle by looking at the specific evolutionary provenance of certain motives. Kristin Luker, a sociologist at the University of California at San Diego, studied contraceptive risk taking and uncovered what often seemed an unconscious desire for a baby. It is no challenge to reconcile this with evolutionary theory; a Darwinian couple ought to take such risks right and left. Sexual indiscretions in general could be covered by a similar line of argument: sexy sensation seekers perpetuate their genes. Slightly more interesting are the specific risks involved in certain human culinary preferences. We overdo it on fats and sweets because our ancestors were rewarded for such excesses with that inch of insulation needed to carry them through shortages. Death by atherosclerosis may be a pervasive threat today, but for most of the past three million years it was a consummation devoutly to be wished.

But we are still far from the comprehensive explanation of recklessness we need. For this we must look to the darker side of human nature, as expressed in that same ancestral environment. Martin Daly and Margo Wilson, both psychologists at McMaster University in Ontario, explore this matter directly in a book called *Homicide*. Although their analysis is restricted to only one highly dramatic form of risk taking, it is paradigmatic of the problem.

Homicides occur in all human societies, and a frequent cause is a quarrel over something seemingly trivial—an insult, a misunderstanding, a disagreement about a fact neither combatant cares about. Of course, these conflicts are never *really* trivial; they are about status and honor—which in practical terms means whether and how much you can be pushed around. And on this will depend your access to food, land, women (the participants are almost always male)—in short, most of what matters in life and in natural selection. In societies where heads are hunted or coups counted, the process is more formalized, but the principle is similar.

If you simulate, as Daly and Wilson do, a series of fights in which individuals with different risk propensities—low, medium, and high—encounter each other, the high-risk individuals invariably have the highest mortality. But any assumption that winning increases Darwinian fitness—virtually certain to be correct in most environments—leads to predominance of high- or medium-risk individuals. Their candles burn at both ends, but they leave more genes.

The underlying assumption is that the environment is a dangerous one, but this assumption is sensible. The environments of our ancestors must have been full of danger. "Nothing ventured, nothing gained" must have been a cardinal rule; and yet venturing meant exposure to grave risk: fire, heights, cold, hunger, predators, human enemies. And all this risk has to be seen against a background of mortality from causes outside of human control—especially disease. With an average life expectancy at birth of thirty years, with a constant high probability of dying from pneumonia or malaria—the marginal utility, in economic terms, of strict avoidance of danger would have been much lower than it is now, perhaps negligible. In Oscar Lewis's studies of the Mexican "culture of poverty" and in Eliot Liebow's studies of poor black street-corner men, the point is clearly made: the failure of such people to plan for the future is not irrational—they live for the day because they know that they have no future.

To die, in Darwinian terms, is not to lose the game. Individuals risk or sacrifice their lives for their kin. Sacrifice for offspring is ubiquitous in the animal world, and the examples of maternal defense of the young in mammals and male death in the act of copulation in insects have become familiar. But great risks are taken and sacrifices made for other relatives as well. Consider the evisceration of the worker honeybee in the act of stinging an intruder and the alarm call of a bird or ground squirrel, calling the predator's attention to itself while warning its relatives. During our own evolution small, kin-based groups might have gained much from having a minority of reckless sensation seekers in the ranks—people who wouldn't hesitate to snatch a child from a pack of wild dogs or to fight an approaching grass fire with a counterfire.

In any case, both sensation seekers and people in general should have taken their risks selectively. They may have found it advantageous to take risks with the seemingly controllable and familiar, even while exaggerating the risk of the unknown, and hedging it around with all sorts of taboo and ritual. It is difficult to imagine a successful encounter with a volcano, but an early human would have had at least a fighting chance against a lion. And we, their descendants, fear toxic nuclear waste but leave our seat belts unbuckled.

Why can't we adjust our personal behavior to our modern middle-class spectrum of risks? Because we are just not built to cut it that finely. We are not designed for perfectly rational calculations, or to calibrate such relatively unimpressive risks.

For many of us, life seems compromised by such calculations; they too have a cost—in effort, in freedom, in self-image, in fun. And the fun is not incidental. It is evolution's way of telling us what we were designed for.

Sensation seeking fulfills two of the three cardinal criteria for evolution by natural selection: it varies in the population, and the varieties are to some extent inheritable. In any situation in which the varieties give rise in addition to different numbers of offspring, evolution will occur. The notion that riskier types, because they suffer higher mortality, must slowly disappear is certainly wrong for many environments, and it may still be wrong even for ours.

Ideally, of course, one would want a human organism that could take the risks that—despite the dangers—enhance fitness, and leave aside the risks that don't. But life and evolution are not that perfect. The result of the vastly long evolutionary balancing act is a most imperfect organism. The various forms of personal risk taking often hang together; you probably can't be the sort of person who makes sure to maintain perfectly safe and healthy habits, and yet reflexively take the risks needed to ensure survival and reproductive success in the basic human environment. If you are designed, emotionally, for survival and reproduction, then you are not designed for perfect safety.

So when my father buckles his seat belt behind him, and my brother keeps on smoking, and my friend rides her motorcycle to work every day, it isn't because, or only because, they somewhat underestimate the risks. My father wants the full sense of competence and freedom that he has always had in driving, since long before seat belts were dreamed of. My brother wants the sense of calm that comes out of the cigarette. My friend wants to hear the roar of the Harley and feel the wind in her hair. And they want the risk, because risk taking, for them, is part of being alive.

As for me, when I avoid those risks, I feel safe and virtuous but perhaps a little cramped. And I suspect that, like many people who watch their diet carefully—despite the lapses—and exercise more or less scrupulously and buckle up religiously, I am a little obsessed with immortality, with the prospect of controlling that which cannot be controlled. I know I am doing the sensible thing—my behavior matches, most of the time, the spectrum of real probabilities. But against what scale of value? I sometimes think that the more reckless among us may have something to teach the careful about the sort of immortality that comes from living fully every day.

THE MANY FACES

OF MADNESS

Drawn and tense, his limbs twitching nervously, a man of about twenty-five appears in the emergency clinic of a big-city hospital, accompanied by his mother. It is July, the month when hordes of medical students are suddenly transformed into doctors (or so their patients are told), and one of these—call him Dr. Newbody—approaches the pair. "He's gettin' bad again," the woman explains. Dr. Newbody asks some questions, realizes he may have a very crazy patient on his hands, and does what any red-blooded American intern would do: he runs off to find the patient's record, hoping for some clue about how to respond.

As he flips through the files, finding nothing, he hears a commotion behind him and turns to find his patient standing in the center of the crowded waiting room, pointing at people and shouting. "Devil is here! Devil is here everywhere! Coming to get me! Krishnabuddhajesus! Coming to gemme now-now-now-now!" As the tirade becomes incomprehensible, a couple of nurses converge on the patient. "This boy needs some vitamin H," one of them says, referring to haloperidol, a drug used to bring psychotic breaks under control. Dr. Newbody nods nervously (the nurse knows a lot more than he does) and helps restrain the patient while she injects the drug into his buttock. A few moments later, four security guards pin the young man to the floor while the drug mounts toward his brain and slowly begins to calm him.

Dr. Newbody, feeling courageous but confused, finally finds the hospital record, which reveals that the patient has been through at least six similar episodes in recent years. Since being diagnosed as schizophrenic, at age seventeen, he has been treated with a variety of neuroleptic drugs, including chlorpromazine, the prototype of the class. These have helped stabilize his mind but recently have begun to take a toll on his nervous system, causing occasional muscle convulsions and paralysis. The psychotic breaks, referred to in the record as "acute schizophrenic attacks" or "acute paranoid reactions," usually have occurred when he cut back on his medicine or neglected to take it at all. At least six psychiatrists have offered the same diagnosis over the years—each calling the young man's affliction a classic case of "remitting," or "fluctuating," schizophrenia—and Dr. Newbody, not a psychiatrist himself, sees no reason to question their judgment. So he scribbles a note in the patient's record and prescribes more of the same treatment, presuming that the attending psychiatrist will find the whole matter routine.

Not Dr. Baffler, who happens to be on duty that night. Has the patient really had periods of *complete* remission? he asks, perusing the young man's chart. Has he had periods of depression? And what about his family history? Is there any record of depression or alcoholism among his close relatives? Any suicide attempts? Affirmative answers to these questions convince Dr. Baffler this is not schizophrenia at all, but mania. The patient needs to be stabilized, yes; but he should then be hospitalized for a trial on lithium, the accepted treatment for manic-depressive illness and a far less danger- ous drug than those the man has been receiving.

What is Dr. Newbody to make of all this? Dr. Baffler could

be incompetent, of course. Or he could be European (schizophrenia has always been defined more narrowly on that side of the Atlantic). Or he may have studied under Michael A. Taylor and Richard Abrams, psychiatrists now based at the Chicago Medical School. For the past fifteen years or so, Taylor and Abrams have been chipping away at the broad, American definition of schizophrenia, asserting that it has become an all-purpose diagnosis—an official-sounding term for a lot of disorders, many of which no one really understands.

American psychiatrists tend to think of schizophrenia as the cancer of mental illness—as an organic disorder, or perhaps a group of closely related ones, whose devastating symptoms may all be vanquished once the underlying cause (presumably genetic) is identified. So it is hardly surprising that Taylor and Abrams's critique, developed in a series of papers during the mid-1970s, remains a source of bitter contention. If they are right, the nearly two million Americans diagnosed as schizophrenics do not share a uniform brain disorder; there is no single solution to their problems; and many of those receiving neuroleptic drugs might derive equal benefit from less noxious treatments.

Today's broad categories of psychotic illness can be traced at least to 1899, when the German physician Emil Kraepelin distinguished what had been termed "dementia praecox," or premature dementia—a thought disorder that leads inevitably to complete incompetence—from manic-depressive psychosis, a *mood* disorder that, however severe, is usually not degenerative. The meticulous classification of bodily illnesses had brought new rigor to surgery and internal medicine during the nineteenth century, and Kraepelin sensed the possibility of making psychiatry equally scientific. Identifying various forms of mental illness would, he hoped, lead to an understanding of their causes and eventually to effective treatments.

Twelve years later, a Swiss psychiatrist named Eugen Bleuler used the general term "schizophrenia"—literally, a psychic splitting—to describe any severe disintegration of thought or dysfunction of thought from emotion. Bleuler's schizophrenia, like Kraepelin's dementia praecox, was set apart from manic-depressive illness. But whereas Kraepelin had based the distinction largely on the course of illness (dementia praecox was degenerative, manic depression episodic), Bleuler emphasized the nature of the symptoms. His schizophrenia came in four varieties—paranoid, catatonic, hebephrenic, and simple—but was always "cool," or cognitive, at root. Manic-depressive illness, on the other hand, was affective, its disordered thought emotional, or "warm." The implication was that schizophrenia was in essence a thought disorder, involving the emotions only secondarily; while manic-depressive illness was mainly a mood disorder, affecting thought processes only secondarily.

Bleuler's notion of schizophrenia had important implications. Kraepelin had assumed that dementia praecox, with its cruelly predictable course, was a unified disease with a single biological cause. Bleuler's schizophrenia, by contrast, was no more than a syndrome, a set of symptoms that might have any number of causes. It was not even clear that the cause or causes were biological. Indeed, Bleuler allowed that the disorder might be purely psychic in origin.

It is perhaps no coincidence that Bleuler's terminology gained currency just as Sigmund Freud was conceiving his revolutionary psychology. Freud recently had proposed a talking cure for the treatment of hysteria and had gone on to devise a system for exploring not only the neurotic, or mildly disturbed, personality but also its near cousin, the normal psyche. Interpretation of dreams, jokes, slips of the tongue, childhood sexuality, and other everyday exotica had become grist for the mill of his psychoanalysis.

The limitations of the approach were not, just at that moment, uppermost in his mind. Thus it was with a certain amount of confidence that he set about to psychoanalyze a man he had never met nor ever had any contact with—the distinguished jurist Daniel Schreber, who had written a memoir of his own paranoid psychosis. Freud analyzed Schreber's elaborate delusional system using his own almost comparably baroque theory and, in circular fashion, found in Schreber's book both a source and a confirmation of a specific psychoanalytic theory of the development of paranoid psychosis.

It is impossible to say just what Schreber had, but it is certainly possible that it would now be called schizophrenia. (Some psychiatrists would probably classify it as an affective disorder, others as a paranoid psychosis.) In any case, he ended his days in a mental hospital and, like most psychotics since, would probably have been helped rather little by psychoanalysis even if it had been tried on him.

Freud, to his credit, was pessimistic about the power of psychoanalysis to alleviate psychoses, the complete breaks with reality that had concerned Kraepelin and Bleuler. But a number of his intellectual descendants—including Carl Jung, Melanie Klein, and Harry Stack Sullivan, who himself spent time in a mental hospital after a psychotic break—believed such treatment was possible. In any event, psychoanalysis became such a powerful force that virtually all mental disorders were for a time discussed in its terms.

Then, during the early 1950s, two French psychiatrists, Jean Delay and Pierre Deniker, discovered the effects of the drug chlorpromazine on psychotic patients, and psychiatry entered a new era. With this treatment, hundreds of thousands of chronically hospitalized patients were able to return to the community and take up lives that, if not productive or pleasant, were at least somewhat independent. Just how the drug worked remains unclear, but its very effectiveness confirmed that schizophrenic psychosis is biological at root and not simply an exaggerated neurosis to be mastered through self-scrutiny.

Over the past thirty years, dozens of antischizophrenic drugs have been developed, all of which share the effect of blocking the brain's use of the neurotransmitter dopamine. And experiments have confirmed the relationship between the drugs' dopamine-suppressing tendencies and their clinical effectiveness—suggesting, if not confirming, that excessive dopamine activity is a factor in schizophrenia. Further evidence of a connection has come from the discovery that sufferers of Parkinson's disease, a condition associated with *insufficient* dopamine production, sometimes develop hallucinations or delusions when receiving the dopamine *enhancer* L-dopa.

These observations hardly add up to a causal explanation of schizophrenia (it is unknown, for example, whether the problem involves excessive production of dopamine, an abnormality in the cellular structures that absorb it, or some other defect altogether), but the dopamine theory ascended steadily. The road to a Kraepelinian understanding of schizophrenia began to seem like a royal highway, and the castle at the end of the road looked as if it would bear the emblem of the chemical structure of dopamine as a coat of arms.

Unfortunately there was a rut in the road that also involved dopamine. Patients treated for many years with this class of drugs began to develop tardive dyskinesias, movement disorders that can be severe and disabling. Since Parkinson's disease had been identified during the early sixties as in essence a dopamine-deficiency disease, and since there were immediate side effects of antipsychotic drugs that resembled Parkinson's, it was logical that years of dopamine blockade might have some disabling effect on movement. Ironically, it seemed to result from overcompensation of the dopamine system, and it could be temporarily suppressed by increasing the same drug that had caused it. But this was a paltry stopgap measure in an overwhelmingly tragic process.

Even if skeptical of this specific theory, most American psychiatrists concluded that schizophrenia is a biochemical entity. It became respectable to say that, at least for psychotic patients, the main function of psychotherapy was to ensure that the patient takes the drugs. And scientifically talented medical students with an interest in brain research began to choose psychiatry as a promising career path to the Nobel prize—a completely improbable notion a few years earlier.

Two further developments helped bolster this view. First, during the late 1950s, the German psychiatrist Kurt Schneider developed a clinical formula for determining whether a person is in fact schizophrenic. According to Schneider, anyone experiencing certain "first-rank symptoms"—"voices heard arguing" or "commenting on one's actions," "diffusion of thought," "delusional perception," or any feelings, impulses, or actions that result from the imagined influence of others—could be termed schizophrenic, as a "decisive clinical diagnosis," regardless of his case history, as long as he was not suffering from some known organic brain disorder, such as epilepsy. Schneider's permissive definition was widely adopted in the United States, and the identification of first-rank symptoms was seen as another step toward the goal of making schizophrenia as coherent and real as other medical entities. It also had the effect of discouraging the diagnosis of manic-depressive illness, which, it was felt, could be eliminated from consideration if first-rank symptoms were present.

The second development was the appearance of numerous studies suggesting that schizophrenia, or at least a susceptibility to it, could be inherited. The most elegant of these was reported in a 1968 monograph by Seymour S. Kety, a psychiatrist at the National Institute of Mental Health (and later with Harvard University and McLean Hospital, in Boston). Working out of Denmark, a country noted for its meticulous epidemiological records, Kety identified a group of adult psychotics—schizophrenics, under the broad, Schneiderian definition—who had been adopted during infancy and raised away from their kin. He then surveyed the subjects' relatives, both biological and adoptive, and found that the biological relatives suffered higher rates of schizophrenia than did the adoptive relatives or the general population. In short, schizophrenia seemed to run in families, even dispersed families.

These ideas never caught on in Europe to the extent that they did in the United States. European psychiatrists had no quarrel with the notion that mental illness might be heritable, but they still thought of schizophrenia as a quite rare disease, for they had never given up Kraepelin's system of classification for Bleuler's. They tended to restrict the term "schizophrenia" to chronic thought disorders, and to diagnose acute, *non*degenerative psychoses as manic-depressive illness. This bit of semantics had broad implications; as diagnosis differed, so did therapy. British and Continental psychiatrists often gave their patients lithium, which, despite possible adverse side effects, does not cause tardive dyskinesia, the severe nerve disorder associated with dopamine blockers.

Lithium, the third smallest element in the periodic table, administered in ionized form as a salt, had as powerful a long-term effect on manic-depressive illness—MDI—as dopamine blockers had on schizophrenia. It was serendipitously found in 1949 (as would be the case a few years later with chlorpromazine) to have behavioral effects, by John Cade, a physician who published his observations in the *Medical Journal of Australia*.

It gradually began to be studied in clinical trials. Like the dopamine-receptor blockers, it helped during the break itself and later, in the prevention of recurrences. Its mode of action remains unknown but is thought to depend on lithium's privileged access to ionic membrane channels in nerve axons. Its drawback was a narrow range of nontoxic therapeutic effectiveness, often requiring a month or more of hospitalization to get the right blood level, with some serious side effects in patients who exceeded that level substantially. These immediate drawbacks, as well as ordinary resistance to change, prevented lithium from coming into widespread use in the United States until the 1970s and reinforced the American tendency to diagnose much more schizophrenia than mania.

The stage was thus set for the publication of Taylor and Abrams's extraordinary series of papers. Beginning in 1973, they conducted a number of ground-breaking studies and reviewed the research of others in relation to one hypothesis: that American psychiatrists overdiagnose schizophrenia by a large margin and underdiagnose manic-depressive illness with comparable frequency. In fact, when Taylor and Abrams reexamined patients previously diagnosed as schizophrenic on the basis of first-rank symptoms, taking into account family history, course of illness, and response to different drugs—all mainstays of diagnosis in other medical specialities—they found that many (from 20 to 50 percent in different studies) looked like classic cases of manic-depressive illness and responded well to lithium treatment.

By 1978, Taylor and Abrams were pointing out with some urgency that they were talking about more than a diagnostic label. "Patients who receive a diagnosis of schizophrenia when in fact they have another condition (e.g., affective disorder)," they wrote in the *American Journal of Psychiatry*, "may be subjected erroneously and unnecessarily to chronic administration of neuroleptic drugs, with their high risk of permanent neurologic damage," and may be "deprived of appropriate treatment with lithium."

Other research psychiatrists—notably Harrison G. Pope and Joseph F. Lipinski, who were based, like Seymour Kety, at Harvard's McLean Hospital—had by now come to share Taylor and Abrams's view. In a paper published in the *Archives of General Psychiatry*, in 1978, Pope and Lipinski seconded the opinion that the tendency to diagnose severe mental disorders as schizophrenia could be exposing "large numbers of patients to increased social stigma, inferior treatment, and potentially irreversible neurological damage." They went on to argue in other papers that schizoaffective disorder—the term that American psychiatrists had been applying to patients who qualified as schizophrenics on the basis of first-rank symptoms but who also showed signs of manic-depressive illness—was essentially meaningless. "Since course, family history, and treatment response do not distinguish schizoaffective disorder . . . from manic disorder," they wrote in 1980, "there would seem to be no adequate reason on clinical grounds to make the former diagnosis. Such a diagnosis can only lead to confusion."

Eventually, these arguments persuaded the American Psychiatric Association to narrow its definition of schizophrenia.

The new designation, adopted in 1980, does not automatically exclude all disorders with an affective component (as Taylor and Abrams would), but it restricts the diagnosis to chronic, unremitting illnesses and excludes acute, or fluctuating, ones.

Having made these gains in the debate over what constitutes schizophrenia, the revisionists went on to challenge the contention that it runs in families. In a study published in 1982, Pope and Lipinski, as well as others, reviewed the family histories of the thirty-nine definite schizophrenics admitted to their research ward between 1974 and 1977— patients who suffered chronic, nonaffective psychoses and thus could not possibly be manic-depressives—and found not a single case of schizophrenia among two hundred of the patients' close relatives. And the next year, Abrams and Taylor reported similar results, concluding that "if familial transmission of narrowly defined schizophrenia occurs, it is either limited to a sub-group yet to be defined" or simply "weak."

In a letter to the *American Journal of Psychiatry* in January 1983, Pope, Lipinski, and two other colleagues went so far as to refer to schizophrenia as a "chronic idiopathic psychosis"—"idiopathic" being basically medical jargon for "Huh?" The implication was that it was not a real illness at all but a ragbag of anatomically subtle organic brain disorders.

Needless to say, these claims were met with criticism and counterevidence. In June of 1983, Kety mounted a spirited defense of his original study, arguing in the *American Journal of Psychiatry* that by excluding disorders with affective symptoms from the spectrum of those they were willing to call schizophrenia, his critics were diluting the trend he had identified. He rejected the notion that so-called schizoaffective patients are really manics, saying many are in fact clinically indistinguishable from definite schizophrenics, and he stood by his finding that the biological relatives of schizophrenics are at significantly higher risk than the rest of the population. If no concentration of mental illness was evident in the small, restrictive groups the newcomers had studied, he said, one could draw two alternative conclusions: that schizophrenia is indeed "a rare disorder with no evidence for familial or genetic transmission"—or that the researchers themselves "arbitrarily narrowed the definition of schizophrenia to the point where it is no longer particularly valid or useful."

Today, the debate over Michael Taylor's prophetic question "Is schizophrenia a syndrome representing a group of illnesses . . . or is it a specific disease with a defined onset, clinical picture, and natural history?" continues unabated, each camp accusing the other of ignoring sound evidence in order to defend a prejudice. Some studies—including one led by Kenneth Kendler, of the Medical College of Virginia; another by Peter McGuffin, now at the University of Wales in Cardiff; and a third by Samuel Guze, of Washington University in Saint Louis—have continued to find evidence of a genetic basis for schizophrenia, suggesting that it is in fact a disease and not just a ragbag of symptoms.

Meanwhile, the dopamine theory has received new support. Dean Wong and Henry Wagner of the Johns Hopkins School of Medicine have shown an increase in a subclass of dopamine receptors in the brains of schizophrenics, including those never treated with drugs. This is the first convincing direct demonstration that something may actually be awry in the brain's handling of dopamine, and could favor the idea of a genetically caused, unified disorder.

Others, such as Daniel Weinberger of the National Institute

of Mental Health, have demonstrated a variety of subtle alterations of brain structure and function using new techniques of brain imaging. Cerebral ventricles are enlarged, limbic-system structures are reduced, and blood flow to the frontal lobes is lower in schizophrenics. But these findings are so subtle that they would be considered by neuroradiologists to be part of the normal range. And in any case, they may support Pope and Lipinski's "chronic idiopathic psychosis" as much as they do a reified schizophrenia.

But other recent findings—the demonstration, for instance, that some forms of the disorder are associated with a genetic defect on chromosome 5, while others are not—suggest that even if schizophrenia is genetic at root, it may not be a single disease. Similarly, some, but not all, forms of manic-depressive illness are associated with a gene on the X chromosome.

If both schizophrenia and manic-depressive illness are eventually found to comprise a number of identifiable illnesses, the current debate over diagnostic labels may seem rather silly in retrospect. It has had important benefits, of course. As the definition of schizophrenia has narrowed, American psychiatric practice has shifted markedly toward the European model, with more diagnosis of manic-depressive illness and less of schizophrenia. As a result, it is becoming the rule among psychiatrists recently trained in this country that every patient with a fluctuating psychosis, with some features of manic-depressive illness, or with a family history of affective disorders deserves a trial on lithium or some other mood-altering drug. Only if these prove inadequate should the patient resort exclusively to dopamine blockers, which, however appropriately used, still pose a grave risk of neurological damage.

With that resolved, though, there is little to be gained from further debate over the merits of a diagnostic label. But also at stake is our notion of how human nature—the human mind—breaks down. It has been said that pain of the mind is greater than that of the body. The most severe mental pain takes essentially two forms: disordered thought and disordered mood. Kraepelin and many psychiatrists since have believed that these can be separated. Perhaps the greatest lesson of the current controversy is that often they cannot.

We may discover that what we now call schizophrenia and manic-depressive disorder are in fact, say, seven different genetic defects, each producing a biochemically different mental illness, and that some forms of these disorders have no genetic component at all. How all these afflictions are grouped—whether we call four of them schizophrenias and three manias, or vice versa—will not matter much.

If schizophrenia is the cancer of mental illness, then it may, like cancer, be protean. Cancers share a few general attributes—they all cause cells to grow uncontrollably, and many of them respond to the same crudely effective treatments—but beyond that they are extremely varied. It is only by bearing down on the various forms of cancer that researchers have begun to understand their different causes—recognizing, for example, that retinoblastoma is likely genetic in origin; that the vast majority of lung cancers result from cigarette smoking; that cervical cancer may stem from the papilloma virus, which is also responsible for genital warts. Fortunately for the science of oncology, few ideological voices have been raised to complicate the search for such truths, though they surely could have been. Perhaps psychiatry will have come of age when its practitioners achieve a similar consensus on what is really worth arguing about.

FALSE IDYLLS

It was more than two hundred years ago that the British philosopher David Hume calmly dismissed the romance of exotic places: "Should a traveller, returning from a far country," he wrote in *An Enquiry Concerning Human Understanding*, "bring us an account of men . . . wholly different from any with whom we were ever acquainted; men . . . who were entirely divested of avarice, ambition, or revenge; who knew no pleasure but friendship, generosity, and public spirit; we should immediately, from these circumstances, detect the falsehood, and prove him a liar, with the same certainty as if he had stuffed his narration with stories of centaurs and dragons, miracles and prodigies."

Centaurs and dragons were already child's play in 1748, and they're all but forgotten today. Yet we have never quite outgrown the idea that somewhere, there are people living in perfect harmony with nature and one another, and that we might do the same were it not for the corrupting influences of Western culture. Recall, for example, Margaret Mead's characterizations of life in Samoa. Mead left Manhattan in 1925 hoping not only to advance the new science of human nature being founded by Franz Boas, her teacher, but also to explore the South Sea idyll that had been popularized by the French Postimpressionist Paul Gauguin.

So far the idyll had always been a masculine one, and the

sultry, unadorned, seemingly uninhibited beauty of the women in Gauguin's paintings cannot have been irrelevant to the place's appeal. If Gauguin, still a junior executive in a Paris brokerage firm at thirty-three, could turn his back and go off to a new life, in a place of innocence and beauty—well, then, every broker in Europe could dream. Like the painter, Mead was especially interested in the island women; but whereas Gauguin was openly concerned with his own impressions of them, she would document *their* experience of growing up in paradise.

After completing her fieldwork, Mead returned home with the materials for *Coming of Age in Samoa*, perhaps the best-known work of popular anthropology ever written. Though the book described isolated instances of unhappiness, its overall theme was no disappointment to South Seas dreamers: aggression and competition, Mead implied, were virtually nonexistent. There was no stifling repression of sex or romance; free love was the norm. And adolescence— synonymous with stress and anguish throughout the Western world—was for island girls just a joyous coming of age.

Mead's characterization seemed to bear directly on the question of how narrowly biology circumscribes human behavior. For if, in some cultures, young people could sail through this period of surging hormones, bodily metamorphosis, and shifting social roles with nary a strong breeze, then it followed that the biological inevitability of adolescent *Sturm und Drang* must be greatly exaggerated by other cultures—including our own. Also, since this was a book about women, by a woman—and, at that, a courageous, adventurous one who could write like an angel—it began to redress the old androcentric bias, another form of biological determinism.

Coming of Age in Samoa—a tiny part of Mead's lifework,

really—was favorably received upon its publication, in 1928. But her characterization of Samoan life hasn't weathered the decades very well. Since the 1950s, various ethnographers, including Lowell Holmes, Paul Shankman, and Derek Freeman, author of the controversial *Margaret Mead and Samoa: The Making and Unmaking of an Anthropological Myth*, have published evidence of a Samoa far more complex, and less idyllic, than the one Mead described. Indeed, their data established that crimes of violence, including rape, are not uncommon; that adolescent males commit a disproportionate share of these crimes, just as they do in the industrialized West; that rank, prestige, and wealth are critical elements in the social system; that virginity is highly valued, at least among well-to-do girls (with suicide sometimes following the loss of it); and that, far from being perfectly calm, Samoan adolescence is subject to conflict, tension, and passionate outbursts of emotion.

As Bradd Shore, an anthropologist at Emory University, showed, the Samoan system is built from a set of fascinating tensions between the ideals, many of which Mead saw correctly, and the reality, which includes the things Freeman and others identified. "Contradiction is the stuff of life," Shore writes, and the truth of the Samoan social world is to be found in the interplay of "colliding impulses and incompatible values." He wisely asks, "Does the passive in us refute the aggressive, or our virtue refute our vice?" In short, Samoan life is not as different from our own as Mead, and many others, wanted to believe.

The Samoans are scarcely the only people ever to disappoint us this way. Again and again, ethnographers have discovered Eden in the outback, only to have the discovery foiled by better data. That the resident innocents are invariably found to possess a full complement of failings surely reveals something about the laws of human nature. Yet, for some reason, anthropologists persist in trying to find a place where the laws of human nature do not apply.

The fantasy of the noble savage can be traced back at least to the sixteenth-century French essayist Michel de Montaigne, who contrasted the "wholly noble and generous" ways of Brazilian cannibals with the relative barbarism of Renaissance Europeans. Among the primitives, he proclaimed,

> there is no sort of traffic, no knowledge of letters, no science of numbers, no name for a magistrate or for political superiority, no custom of servitude, no riches or poverty, no contracts, no successions, no partitions, no occupations but leisure ones, no care for any but common kinship, no clothes, no agriculture, no metal, no use of wine or wheat. The very words that signify lying, treachery, dissimulation, avarice, envy, belittling, pardon— unheard of.

However crude their lives, the cannibals were far from impoverished, he maintained, for "they still enjoy that natural abundance that provides them without toil and trouble . . . all necessary things. . . . They are still in that happy state of desiring only as much as their natural needs demand; anything beyond that is superfluous to them."

This sympathetic view, perverse though it must have seemed in 1580, went on to gain enormous influence, partly through the work of the eighteenth-century Swiss philosopher Jean-Jacques Rousseau. In *The Social Contract*, the *Second Discourse*, the *Essay on the Origin of Languages*, and other works, Rousseau advanced a view of the primitive that was concededly and explicitly more philosophic than factual. He put forth a set of distinctions, indeed oppositions, of a sort that has since been shown to be very widespread in human societies, distinctions that go to the heart of what people *mean* by culture: something that is opposed to nature. But he tried to build from them a complex moral philosophy. Being and seeming, happiness and unhappiness, speech and writing, poetry and prose, melody and harmony, sexual polyvalence and moral love—these are some of the oppositional pairs that modern scholars have found in Rousseau's work. In *Emile* an ideal childhood is imagined, in which nature is supposedly cultivated rather than repressed. Throughout, for Rousseau, what is primitive in human society and history is natural, and what is natural is certainly superior.

This view caught on not just among writers and philosophers but also among artists and composers. That it should eventually spill into science as well, and help spawn a discipline devoted to the observation of aboriginal societies, is therefore not surprising. What *is* surprising is that modern practitioners of that discipline can still believe so earnestly in paradise. I can't claim immunity; I once discovered Shangri-la myself, among the !Kung people of the Kalahari Desert.

When I traveled to Africa during the 1960s and '70s, with a team led by anthropologists Richard Lee and Irven DeVore, the !Kung had long been regarded as living embodiments of humanity's distant past. They were, after all, a society of hunter-gatherers—a surviving example of the kind of social group in which the human species is thought to have passed more than 90 percent of its history. Anthropologists thus assumed, reasonably enough, that the behavior of these unchanged few would shed light on humankind's evolutionary legacy. Yet, from the outset, some observers of the !Kung had been painting a suspiciously rosy picture of them.

The earliest studies, begun during the 1950s by Lorna Marshall, an anthropologist affiliated with Harvard's Peabody Museum, had produced valuable ethnographic data.

But the society those studies described was not unlike the one discovered by Margaret Mead in Samoa (or by overly credulous travelers in the fantasies ridiculed by David Hume). One member of Marshall's team, her daughter, Elizabeth Marshall Thomas, dubbed the !Kung "the harmless people" in a book by that title. And Marshall herself—despite having documented serious fights, as well as a fairly rigorous struggle for existence—concluded in *The !Kung of Nyae Nyae* that they "avoid arousing envy, jealousy, and ill will and, to a notable extent . . . achieve the comfort and security which they so desire in human relations."

The anthropologist Ashley Montagu, after reviewing the literature on the !Kung, had cast them in a still rosier light. Not only did he marvel at the gentleness of their child-rearing practices and at their ability to keep the peace by exchanging gifts and words rather than dispensing punishment; he also held up their ostensible pacifism as evidence that "no human being has ever been born with aggressive or hostile impulses, and [that] no one becomes hostile or aggressive without learning to do so." Montagu's reasoning was that there could be no exceptions to a universal law of human nature—that if one group of people were found to be utterly unaggressive, then aggressiveness could not possibly be an innate tendency. In two books, *Learning Non-Aggression: The Experience of Non-Literate Societies* and *The Nature of Human Aggression*, he based this claim partly on the case of the !Kung, despite mounting evidence (which he himself acknowledged in the second book) that they were perfectly capable of violence, and even homicide.

Marshall Sahlins, an anthropologist at the University of Chicago, had idealized another aspect of !Kung life, glossing over the group's typical Third World health conditions to depict it as "the original affluent society." Sahlins argued in

Stone Age Economics that the !Kung and other hunter-
gatherers, by desiring little, by limiting their accumulation of
surplus, and by pursuing mutual interdependence rather than
competition, had attained not just comfort but a sort of ideal
wealth—Montaigne's "happy state of desiring only as much
as their natural needs demand."

So my colleagues and I were not alone in our readiness to
romance the !Kung. In our studies, we documented (or
thought we did) a remarkable degree of economic and
political equality, including equality between the sexes. Like
Sahlins, we saw no evidence that the life of a hunter-gatherer
was one of deprivation. And, like Lorna Marshall, we
emphasized the idyllic nature of infancy and childhood. This
was the focus of my own work. Predictably, I determined that
the !Kung never physically punished their young, and I
accepted this as proof that children can be successfully raised
on nothing but tolerant, nurturing affection.

It was only as I followed the findings of my fellow field-
worker (and wife) Marjorie Shostak that I began to sense
something was wrong with these characterizations. She had
been encouraging individual members of the group—mostly
women in their middle or later years—to talk at length about
their lives. And these recollections (some stunning examples
of which were published in 1981 as *Nisa: The Life and Words
of a !Kung Woman*) created a picture of !Kung life somewhat
different from those painted by ethnographers. Many of the
women recalled being deprived of material things, including
food, and their emotional tone revealed more frustration and
anger than philosophical acceptance. Acts of violence were
reported with disturbing frequency, sexual jealousy being a
common incitement, and many of the women's stories suggested they were held to more exacting standards of marital
fidelity than their husbands were. Rape was not unheard of

among the !Kung, nor, it turned out, was the harsh punishment of children. One woman recalled being beaten as a girl for breaking a valued water container fashioned from the shell of an ostrich egg.

Of course, life-history interviews are not perfect windows onto other cultures: people are notoriously selective—even deceptive—in describing themselves, and individual recollections, no matter how accurate, may reveal little about a society's shared experiences. But subsequent studies, based on precise, quantitative methods, seemed to confirm the darker side of !Kung life. Data amassed by Edwin Wilmsen, of Boston University, for example, revealed a pattern of seasonal weight loss in some bands. And my own studies documented a decline in children's growth rates after the first six months of life. Likewise, statistics on illness and death collected by Nancy Howell, of the University of Toronto, hardly suggested an "affluent society." Life expectancy, it turned out, was only thirty years: half the children died before adulthood, and most adults succumbed to infections long before reaching old age.

Bearing down on the separate question of whether the !Kung were really as peaceful as conventional wisdom held, Richard Lee reconsidered their homicide rate, and again the data indicated that hunter-gatherer life was far from idyllic. In fact, Lee found that the !Kung's rate far exceeded that of the United States, unless the U.S. rate was raised to reflect vehicular homicides and deaths from the Vietnam War. Previous observers had apparently taken the small *number* of homicides committed by the !Kung from year to year, together with their espousal of nonviolence, as proof that they just weren't killers. But if a society consists of only a few hundred individuals, even infrequent killings can add up to a high per capita rate. Lee determined that within a population of fifteen hundred !Kung there had in fact been twenty-two killings over five decades—about five more than the same number of New Yorkers would have been expected to commit over the same period. (All the homicides were the work of men, interestingly, and most stemmed either from vendettas or from conflicts over women.)

Early reports of the !Kung's egalitarianism fared well during this period of reassessment; investigators continued to find that decisions were made collectively and that social and economic rank were of little consequence in daily life. But relations between the sexes turned out to be far more problematic. Shostak found, on the basis of interviews and direct observation, that !Kung women enjoy considerable independence—that, for example, they determine their own activities in the daily quest for food—but that the behavior of !Kung men is often dominating and coercive, sometimes even violent. It also became clear that the !Kung's traditional system of marriage—in which prepubescent girls are commonly wed to grown men (including a few men who already have wives)—is less than egalitarian. The age discrepancy gives husbands a certain authority over their young brides, and that imbalance can last for many years.

As for the harsh physical punishment of children, no ethnographer reported witnessing it firsthand. But I would no longer assume on that basis that !Kung children are never hit—not when there are !Kung adults who vividly remember it happening to them. A more plausible hypothesis is that corporal punishment, because it is rare, makes an especially durable impression on !Kung children, and that parents use it to precisely that end.

By the 1980s, then, our !Kung had gone the way of Mead's islanders; most of our sunny intuitions about human goodness and the state of nature were unsupportable. But even if the ideal society was not to be found in the Kalahari or the South Seas, might it not exist someplace else? The evidence is not encouraging. Consider, for example, what is known about one other culture, and one *non*human society, both once thought to embody, in some way, our lost innocence.

During the 1920s and 1930s, Ruth Benedict and Laura Thompson used the phrase "logico-aesthetic integration" to describe the remarkably harmonious societies they observed among the Pueblo Indians of the American Southwest. In subsequent studies, however, Esther Goldfrank, Dorothy Eggan, and others revealed the superficiality of this characterization. Discord was in fact ubiquitous among the Pueblos, both in their social relationships and in their attitude toward the spirit world. These twin hostilities stemmed in part from initiation ceremonies (apparently unknown to earlier investigators) in which adults dressed as gods scared the living daylights out of nine- and ten-year-old children while beating them severely. What held aggression in check in the adults these children became was not love but repression: the Pueblos' child-rearing methods were so harsh that social harmony was virtually ensured—as was quite a bit of personal unhappiness.

More than the Samoan and !Kung cases, this one is a matter of interpretation as well as of fact, but Shore's complex orchestration of contradictions would seem as applicable here as in Samoa, and would be about as close as the Hopi or Zuni will get to harmony.

The other example comes from the social behavior of the chimpanzee, *Pan troglodytes*, one of our closest nonhuman relatives. During the sixties and early seventies, the famed ethologist Jane Goodall published numerous reports describing the chimpanzees of Tanzania's Gombe Stream Reserve as perfectly gentle and cooperative creatures. According to

Goodall they exhibited lasting loyalty and love; were excep-
tionally kind and nurturing toward their offspring, and lived
in exquisite harmony with nature. It is clear from the tone of
these early writings that Goodall viewed the chimps not only
as scientific models for human evolution but, in some re-
spects, as ethical models for human action. She even claimed
to be raising her child according to their method.

In recent years, however, Goodall has compiled quite a
different picture of the chimpanzee, well documented—along
with more pleasant aspects of their lives—in her masterwork
The Chimpanzees of Gombe. Both directly and in the work of
others, she has seen evidence of deadly fights between males,
brutal beatings of females by much larger males, even the
killing of infants by two adult females working together.
Particularly startling was her discovery of conflicts in which a
group of adult males from one community systematically
assaulted and killed males in a neighboring band until it was
decimated and the survivors were forced to abandon their
territory. Although she was working on a major book,
Goodall felt it necessary to report these new findings not only
in the *National Geographic,* where she frequently writes, but
on the op-ed page of *The New York Times,* in an admirable
effort to redress the imbalance she herself had created. Of
course, the chimpanzee's fall from grace cannot be adduced as
evidence against the existence of a human version of Eden; but
it is evidence about how we behavioral scientists sometimes
think—or rather, allow our thoughts to stray.

Centaurs and dragons, miracles and prodigies. This, alas, is
the view we must take of the perfectly harmonious, perfectly
happy society, whether it is discovered among Samoan Islanders, !Kung hunter-gatherers, Pueblo Indians, or our nonhuman relatives. If people could live independently of one

another, the dream of nature without culture, of life without strife or conflict, might well be attainable. The catch, of course, is that we could not exist in such circumstances; people, like nearly all other primates, have by sheer biological necessity been highly social throughout their evolution. In social groups, the possibility of mutual aid arises, but so does the reality of conflicting interests. And once interests clash, paradise is lost. Getting by requires compromise and restraint—the stuff of culture.

Yet the fact that anthropologists, even good ones, should sometimes be smitten by an exotic people is not really so shocking. Anthropology is after all a kind of philosophy with data, and thus is unable to escape being in part about how we should live. So it is not surprising that it has also not escaped one of the major Western philosophic errors—the myth of Eden and the fall from grace. In the !Kung case, as in the Samoan and the others, the correct view is not one of an inspiring set of behaviors worthy of immediate emulation but, rather, one of magnificent human complexity worthy of ultimate comprehension. Such comprehension cannot be guided by any hidden agenda—neither a moral agenda insisting that the !Kung are somehow superior or inferior nor a scientific agenda insisting on the fundamental flexibility or inflexibility of human behavior. They are merely initial attempts to describe a portion of the natural (in this case human) world.

Anthropologists have taken justifiable pride in those descriptions, and pleasure in undermining the smug attitudes of Westerners whose cultural blinders give them a narrow vision of what is human. This effort, embodying the idea of cultural relativism, is anthropology's most important contribution to human thought. But some have used ethnological description as a sort of projection. Such phrases as "the gentle people," "the harmless people," or even "the fierce people"—the opposite kind of distortion—come to stand for whole cultures. These simplifications—a sort of philosophic reductionism as opposed to the more usual scientific kind—can abolish at one blow not only the creative variety of generations of a culture but also the individuality of its living members. These initial narrow accounts of a culture are likely to have wide appeal but to present puzzles that later investigators can solve only by working against them.

Perhaps it is not too optimistic to suggest that anthropology—after some recent methodological soul searching—may be entering a new, mature phase in which human nature will be viewed not as a bugaboo to be attacked but as a platform on which to build a human science. Such a science must begin with an account of the ethnological universe as rich with complexity, and even with contradiction, as is that universe itself. But the contradictions will not make the complexity lawless. Generalizations—laws of culture, society, behavior—are gradually emerging from the vast human complexity arrayed on the platform of ethnology, and those laws will be anthropology's second most important contribution.

THE GENDER

OPTION

During the eighteenth century, Japanese peasants had at least two uses for the word *mabiki*. Depending on the context, it could mean either to "thin out" a rice crop, by pulling up newly sprouted seedlings, or to "thin out" one's progeny, by killing unwanted newborns. Babies with congenital defects often were subject to *mabiki*, as were twins, with their burdensome material needs. But what most often marked an infant for suffocation or a blow to the head was its sex—or rather, *her* sex.

The Japanese, with their patrilineal traditions, had always prized male children for their unique ability to propagate surnames. For centuries, families managed to ensure their continuity by producing plenty of offspring, and thus plenty of boys. But during the eighteenth century, as the small island nation fell short of farmland with which to feed its burgeoning population, families with five and six children stopped making sense. Caught between their traditions and the threat of mass starvation, peasants resorted to *mabiki* to achieve the ideal combination of two sons and one daughter—a second son to ensure against the death of the first, and a daughter who could be married off in exchange for a wife for the heir.

Such a custom may seem barbaric, but the fact is, human societies have been manipulating their sex ratios since time immemorial, and little girls have generally borne the brunt.

Female infanticide has been documented among peoples as diverse as the Eskimo of the Canadian Arctic and the hunter-gatherers of the Australian bush. On the South Sea island of Tikopia, live baby girls have been buried in the earth and covered with stones. In India, they have been held to their mothers' poisoned nipples. In rural China, they have been drowned.

Even societies that forbid outright infanticide have long managed to manipulate their sex ratios through neglect. They may sanction weaning daughters at a younger age than sons and thus deprive them of adequate nutrition—a common practice among peasants in ninth-century France. Or they may underfeed and overwork females throughout childhood, as was the case in colonial America, where girls sometimes died at twice the rate of boys from ages one through nine. In Ireland, this pattern continued well into the twentieth century, and throughout much of Asia and the Middle East it remains a fact of modern life.

A survey by Susan Scrimshaw, an anthropologist at the University of California at Los Angeles, showed that in most present-day Asian nations, female infants and children die at much higher than their expected rates, while males are favored in the same mortality charts. For example, in Bangladesh the postneonatal infant mortality rate in 1974 was 98/1,000 for males and 126/1,000 for females, a difference that continued through age four. Similar excesses in female mortality before age four have been shown for Burma, India, Jordan, Pakistan, Sabah, Sarawak, Sri Lanka, and Thailand. In Japan and China, at least temporary excesses of female mortality have been documented in recent decades—some probably nonaccidental.

A related historical study by Sheila Ryan Johansson, of the University of California at Berkeley, brought these skewed

ratios back home. So common was excess female mortality in
rural populations in Europe during the nineteenth century
that among social historians it has both an acronym—EFM—
and a nickname—"deferred infanticide." Of five counties in
England classified as "very rural" and studied for the year
1837, four (all but Cambridge) had a marked excess of female
deaths in the age group 5–15.

All of which provides an unsettling context for thinking
about recent advances in reproductive technology. The first of
these was the development, during the late 1960s, of amniocentesis, a prenatal diagnostic test that involves withdrawing
fluid from the womb of a pregnant woman and cultivating
cells from it. By examining the chromosomes in the nuclei of
those cells, clinicians managed, for the first time, to discern
the genetic makeup of the developing fetus. If the cells
contained pairs of X chromosomes, the child would be a girl;
if the X chromosomes were paired with smaller, less impressive looking Ys, it would be a boy. Amniocentesis cannot be
initiated before the second trimester of pregnancy (only then
will the amniotic fluid produce cells). It is usually done at
around sixteen weeks, and since growing the cells in culture
takes three to four weeks, the analysis cannot be completed
until the fetus is close to five months old. Still, the development of this technique gave determined couples an option
they had never had before: they could, by way of legal
abortion, ensure that a child of the wrong sex never saw the
light of day.

Today, amniocentesis-cum-abortion is among the cruder
forms of sex control; improved methods of prenatal diagnosis
have allowed for much earlier intervention. With a newer,
though riskier, technique known as chorionic-villus sampling,
a clinician can, as early as the eighth week of gestation, snip a

tiny piece of tissue from the developing placenta. Since the tissue consists of actively growing and dividing cells, genetically identical to those of the fetus itself, there is no need for incubation; the chromosomes can be analyzed quickly and the sex revealed well within the first trimester of pregnancy, when abortion is an easier medical option.

Even earlier gender readings have been reported by a researchers at the University of Edinburgh's in vitro fertilization unit. Using commercially available DNA probes—molecules that bind selectively to male-determining DNA segments within the chromosome—the Edinburgh team managed to discern the sex of test-tube embryos just four to eight days old. This technique, like amniocentesis and chorionic-villus sampling, was developed as a tool for screening against various hereditary diseases, but it could make dictating an infant's sex as simple as selecting among artificially fertilized embryos for implantation in the womb. "It certainly wouldn't be ethical to use this method to choose the sex of a baby," John West, a member of the team, has said. "But we couldn't prevent the technique's being used that way."

Meanwhile, other researchers are working on techniques that would allow parents to settle on a gender before their child is even *conceived*. These techniques are based on a procedure, developed in 1973 by the American biochemist Ronald J. Ericsson, for segregating sperm cells according to the chromosomes that determine sex. Each sperm contains either an X or a Y chromosome, which combines with an X chromosome in the egg to produce either a girl or a boy. Ericsson found that Y-bearing sperm, possibly because they are smaller and more motile than X bearers, pass more readily through dense, viscous fluids, such as human serum albumin. He was thus able—by placing undifferentiated sperm cells atop a column of such liquid, and later harvesting them exclusively from the bottom—to generate samples in which as many as 85 percent of the sperm were male.

Since the late 1970s, a handful of physicians in the United States and Japan have been combining such sperm-sorting techniques with artificial insemination to let parents create embryos of a specified sex, and the results have been impressive. Teams at the University of Chicago's Pritzker School of Medicine, at the University of Pennsylvania School of Medicine, and at a private clinic in Berkeley, California, have reported 75 to 80 percent success rates. And in Japan (where physicians generally withhold amniocentesis results from their patients for fear that they will abort fetuses identified as female) some sixty gynecologists now offer the new sperm-sorting techniques in private clinics.

Clearly, we've come a long way since the days of *mabiki*; what we once accomplished by killing infants, and later by destroying fetuses or discarding embryos, we can now achieve by segregating sperm cells. But while the new gender-control technologies are undoubtedly less brutal than the old ones, they may have even graver implications. The reason, ironically, is that they make it so easy for us to get what we want. In a world where gender is a matter of choice, any popular preference for children of a particular sex will likely be mirrored by a distortion in the population. And the social effects of such distortions could be dire.

Analysis of the anthropological record suggests that a society's preference for children of a particular gender is often associated with specific demographic pressures. For example, boys seem to be favored in societies in which male labor is the basis of economic production. Johansson documented this correlation in her study, showing that the advent of commercial agriculture in nineteenth-century Europe was closely tied to excess mortality among young girls. When families lived directly off the land, Johansson explained, men and women participated jointly in the labor of subsistence. But as farming became a commercial activity, men and boys grew "disproportionately involved in production for the market," and the domestic labor performed by women and girls was "perceived as less and less valuable to the family economy." The result was that daughters received less care than sons, and their survival rates shifted accordingly.

Another common source of antifemale bias is the need to control population growth. The number of females always determines a society's capacity to expand, of course; a village of a hundred men and no more than seven women will still see only seven pregnancies in a given year. Communities threatened with overpopulation have long understood that principle, and many have exploited it—by doing away with potential mothers long before they reached reproductive age. On Tikopia, censuses conducted during the 1920s and the 1950s suggested that females were by far the more common victims of infanticide: in some age groups, male-to-female ratios were as high as 153:100 (the expected human ratio at birth, without interference, is 106:100).

A third type of society that tends to want sons is one engaged in warfare, as anthropologists William Divale and Marvin Harris showed in 1976. Divale and Harris analyzed data from 561 primitive social groups and found that those oriented to war were "heavily unbalanced in favor of male infants and children," apparently because girls were either killed at birth or neglected during childhood. Specifically, they found that groups currently at war had an average sex ratio of 128:100 for children under fifteen. For populations that had seen no war in five to twenty-five years, the average childhood sex ratio was a more balanced 113:100. And for groups that had been at peace for more than twenty-five years, it was 106:100. Divale and Harris theorized that in primitive societies, warfare and female infanticide serve as checks on population growth, each compensating for the distorting effect of the other. Indeed, they found that the groups with the most imbalanced childhood sex ratios managed, by sending young men into battle, to achieve *adult* ratios of almost perfect parity.

Male babies also tend to be favored in societies that practice hypergamy, a system in which the payment of dowries enables young women to marry into higher social classes. Mildred Dickemann, an anthropologist at California State University at Sonoma, has made a study of such systems in Darwinian perspective. In a hypergamous society, daughters can provide people of low social standing with valuable links to nobler families, but since each daughter requires a dowry, there is a strong incentive not to have many of them. And at the top of the social hierarchy, the incentive is to have no daughters at all, for they can provide no upward mobility. In fact, a *dearth* of daughters serves a positive purpose for these nobles: it keeps brides—and dowries—moving up the ladder. Northern India, with its caste system, has long felt the effects of these incentives. As recently as the nineteenth century, 30 to 100 percent of the daughters born into upper castes were killed in some provinces; sex ratios among higher castes in the Kangra district of Punjab averaged 302:100. In Mainpuri, the raja's family had allowed no girls to live for centuries.

Though British colonialism effectively ended the tradition of mass infanticide, the mania for sons remains very much alive in parts of India today. In fact, some Indian couples clearly are using amniocentesis and abortion to express it. A survey of seven hundred women who underwent amniocentesis at a hospital in Poona during 1976 and 1977 found that, of the four hundred fifty who learned they were carrying daughters, four hundred thirty—nearly 96 percent—opted for abortion. Of the two hundred fifty fetuses determined to be males, not one was aborted, even though some were identified as suffering genetic disorders. Another study, conducted in the Bijnor district in 1984, suggested that amniocentesis would be used to similar ends if it became available there. Recent laws have prohibited the use of amniocentesis in some parts of northern India, but the newer sex-control technologies would make it even easier to act on antifemale prejudices.

What about our own society? Given the power to choose the sex of our offspring, will we express a similar prejudice? We may not fall neatly into any of the four classic categories of male-biased societies, yet several features of our culture suggest that we are far from neutral in our gender preferences. Western traditions of male supremacy, though they may be dying, are dying hard. The defeat of the Equal Rights Amendment, the persistence of pay discrepancies between male- and female-dominated professions, the unequal domestic burdens borne by women in working couples, the dominance of males in government, industry, religion, and, of course, the military: all of this demonstrates clearly that males retain a favored status in our society. And there is no reason to assume it will stop at the gender-clinic door.

No one would argue that people in New York or Los Angeles crave sons with the fervor of, say, people in Poona. But, as the sociologist Amitai Etzioni demonstrated in a 1968 review of studies, the available data on American gender preferences suggest that the bias is substantial. In one survey, of fifty-five college students, the fifty-one who planned to have children expressed a 65 percent greater preference for boys. A second survey, conducted among parents in Indian-apolis, found that although half the respondents were indif-ferent to gender, and the women expressing a preference were about evenly split between boys and girls, the men who voiced preferences voted nearly five to one in favor of boys.

Still another study, this one of completed families, found that American couples often continued having children after giving birth to a girl but stopped after having a boy—a pattern suggesting a clear preference for the latter. The result, in fact, was a sex ratio of 117:100 in a sample of more than five thousand last-born children. A skewed ratio in last-borns does not, of course, change the ratio for completed families, but it does indicate a subjective preference that can have a demographic impact in other ways.

The studies Etzioni reviewed were conducted decades ago, but more recent ones provide similar results. For example, a 1984 survey of college students in Texas showed that 62 percent wanted their firstborn to be a boy, whereas only 6 percent preferred a firstborn daughter. And there doesn't seem to be much wariness of new sex-control technologies. In 1977, 66 percent of a random sample of California college students said such technologies should be available to all parents, and 45 percent said they would want to use the technologies themselves.

When having another child is the only way to get one of the desired gender, strong preferences cause only minor demo-graphic distortions; the law of averages serves as a check. But suppose the couples in the various preference surveys had been able to dictate their children's genders: their biases would have translated directly into babies. If a nation of fifty-four million married couples enjoyed that power of choice, even a 30 percent increase in the male birthrate (half the increase the fifty-one college students might have achieved) would add hundreds of thousands of surplus males to the population every year. And as long as such a trend continued, its effects would be cumulative.

Is the potential for such distortion anything really to worry about? In evolutionary terms—as shown decades ago by Sir Ronald Fisher, the British mathematician and biologist—probably not. Natural selection guarantees that neither sex will ever become so scarce as to threaten a population's survival, for the scarce sex always gains a selective advantage over the plentiful one. If a population becomes 70 percent male, for example, each female's chances of finding a mate and bearing offspring will be good. But since there will be more than enough males to go around, many of *them* will never get a chance to reproduce. As long as that is true, families that bear and raise daughters will enjoy better long-term survival rates than will those that invest in sons, for they will on average produce more grandchildren. And as such families come to dominate the population, the daughters they generate will redress the shortage of females. In short, a scarce sex is a valuable one, and a valuable one tends not to remain scarce forever. That is why in most species, sex ratios oscillate around equality.

But the fact that evolution will someday correct our mistakes hardly warrants complacency. Other societies have managed, by means far cruder than those now within our grasp, to maintain male-dominated populations for hundreds of years. And, as we've seen, many of those societies have tended toward violence and social stratification. A tradition of war or hypergamy or the denigration of women's work may precipitate a preference for male offspring—but so, in turn, may a predominance of males foster and perpetuate such traditions. In many of the primitive societies analyzed by Divale and Harris, not only did female babies end up being killed so that more warriors could be raised, but war became in turn a necessary tool for eliminating excess males.

Obviously, these cultures are different from ours, and the fact that they have used sex control in certain ways doesn't mean we would do the same. But the evidence suggests that we *would* use it to create a surplus of males. And there is no doubt that such a surplus would create social distortions. For example, it is well known that young men are responsible for the vast majority of violent crime; indeed, one of the clearest influences on any society's crime rate is the percentage of its population made up of males between the ages of fifteen and thirty-five. It is thus fairly easy to see how a boom in baby boys could become a later surge in murder, rape, and robbery.

It is also easy to see how a radical gender imbalance might affect our society's attitudes toward war. We know that males, for reasons at least partly biological, are more given to aggression than are females. It's hardly inconceivable that a modern nation with an excess of ten or fifteen million adult males could, through voting and other expressions of public opinion, turn more readily to military action. In 1968, polls indicated that American men approved of U.S. involvement in the Vietnam War by a margin of 20 percent, and that women *disapproved* by nearly the same margin. Similar gaps have since been documented repeatedly.

And if we failed to kill them off in some suitable war, what would life be like for the armies of surplus males we brought into the world? Obviously, many would never find female companions and some of these would end up alone. The consequences of loneliness can range from clinical depression to physical illness; studies have shown that single men suffer more depression than married men, and that mortality rates are higher among people with few social ties, regardless of sex.

Together, these possibilities should be enough to make us wonder about the wisdom, and the moral meaning, of manipulating the sex ratio. As individuals, we may sense nothing wrong with choosing our children's genders—and in ultimate, evolutionary terms, it may be a harmless pastime. But we live our lives, and cherish hopes for our grandchildren, on a time scale of, at most, centuries. There is no evidence as yet that a large change in the overall human sex ratio will result from the new prenatal technologies, but there are worrisome indications in some parts of the species. Considering the social and ethical risks, perhaps we should just resist the temptation.

IS ORGASM

ESSENTIAL?

The French call it *la petite morte*—the little death—a convention shared by Shakespeare and other Elizabethans. Its etymological ancestors include the Greek words *orgasmos* (to grow ripe, swell, be lustful) and *orge* (impulse, anger) and the Sanskrit *urj* (nourishment, power, strength). Some novelists have given it almost a sacred status. For one Hemingway hero, the key question was "Did the earth move for thee?" while D. H. Lawrence wrote of Lady Chatterley's lover: "He had drawn her close and with infinite delicate pleasure was stroking the full, soft, voluptuous curve of her loins. She did not know which was his hand and which was her body, it was like a full bright flame, sheer loveliness. Everything in her fused down in passion, nothing but that." It is surely one of the most fundamental of human satisfactions—a pleasure for which we are at times willing to pay, to take risks, to commit ourselves to lifetimes of unwanted responsibility, even to kill.

Different cultures have taken different views of orgasm and have come up with countless strategies for achieving, avoiding, enhancing, or delaying it. Among the Mundugumor, of New Guinea, Margaret Mead found that lovemaking is conducted "like the first round of a prizefight," with biting and scratching being important parts of foreplay. In Samoa, by contrast, couples work up to the peak event slowly and gently: the man is expected to prepare the woman's mind with songs and poetry and her body with playful, skillful hands. But orgasm is a goal in both cultures, as in most others. The Mundugomor, despite their rough play, expect women to derive the same satisfaction from sex as men do. And a !Kung hunter-gatherer woman, interviewed by Marjorie Shostak, said that a woman "wants to finish too. She'll have sex with a man until she is satisfied. Otherwise she could get sick."

Even among the Arapesh of highland New Guinea, Mead found that "in spite of most women's reporting no orgasm, and the phenomenon's being socially unnamed and unrecognized, a few women do feel very active sex desire that can be satisfied only by orgasm." In modern Western societies, some psychoanalysts formerly decreed that only a disturbed woman would pursue multiple orgasms, whereas others have defined sexual satisfaction as a vital aspect of physical and psychic health. Societies may range from those that denigrate women for having them to those that denigrate them for not having them, but the potential and the tendency are apparently universal. Only within the tradition of Tantric Buddhism has there been systematic avoidance; men have typically been contemptuous of orgasm and have used various stratagems to maintain for hours on end the blissful vertiginous state that immediately precedes it. Yet the difficulty of doing this is in itself a tribute to the power of the inclination. Indeed, orgasm may be an experience, or at least capacity, not only of humans but of primates generally. Male monkeys often let out a whoop at the moment of ejaculation, as if in honor of some triumph of good feeling. For the females, with no event that compares with ejaculation, the inferences have always been more conjectural, but numerous studies have suggested that they too experience a climax. Doris Zumpe and Richard P. Michael, both of the department of psychiatry at Emory University, have found that the female rhesus monkey typically reaches back toward her partner, arms flailing spasmodically, at the moment he ejaculates. Given the unlikelihood that these animals show a stylized expression of concern for their erupting companions, the inference of a whole-body reflex seems reasonable. Other studies by primatologists, including Francis Burton and David Goldfoot, have shown that female monkeys experience generalized physiological changes during apparent sexual climax that parallel the changes seen in humans.

For all the attention it has received, though, orgasm has remained something of a mystery. The riddles of how it works and why it exists have never been fully resolved, despite the best efforts of physicians, psychologists, and evolutionists. The renowned sex researchers William H. Masters and Virginia E. Johnson shattered a number of myths about the phenomenon with their major 1966 study, *Human Sexual Response*. Yet their work left crucial questions unanswered—questions that continue to spawn confusion and controversy. Is orgasm primarily a physical phenomenon, or is it psychological at root? Where within the female sexual organs is it centered: in the clitoris or in the walls of the vagina? Are the apparent differences between male and female orgasm basic to our biology, or are they mere epiphenomena of culture? And, most interesting, why did such a sensation evolve in the first place?

One of the first modern clinical descriptions of orgasm was ventured in 1855 by the French physician Felix Riboud, who, in one dramatic paragraph, identified most of the main elements of the phenomenon as it is now recognized:

> The pulse quickens, the eyes become dilated and unfocused. . . . With some the breath comes in gasps, others become breathless. . . . The nervous system, congested, is unable to provide the limbs with coherent messages: the powers of movement and feeling are thrown into disorder: the limbs, in the throes of convulsions and sometimes cramps, are either out of control or stretched and stiffened like bars of iron: with jaws clenched and teeth grinding together, some are so carried away by erotic frenzy that they forget the partner of their sexual ecstasy and bite the shoulder that is rashly exposed to them till they draw blood. This epileptic frenzy and delirium are usually rather brief, but they suffice to drain the body's strength, particularly when the man's over-excited state culminates in a more or less abundant emission of sperm.

That orgasm might also have a psychological dimension was first formally recognized by Sigmund Freud, whose psychoanalytic theory—in a radical departure from the conventional wisdom of the late nineteenth century—initially located the problems of neurotics in the blockage of sexual fulfillment. Through analysis of his patients' jokes, dreams, and psychological symptoms, he attempted to show that the fear of normal sexual feeling caused neurosis, and that only recognizing such fear could bring psychic health. In his case study of Frau Emmy von N., a forty-year-old woman he treated in 1889, Freud attributed severe phobias in part to "the fact that the patient had been living for years in a state of sexual abstinence," adding that "such circumstances are among the most frequent causes of a tendency to anxiety."

Yet, because he misunderstood a crucial aspect of female physiology, Freud ended up describing orgasm in a way that ultimately would prove harmful both to women and to the study of sex. Being something of an evolutionist, he suspected that so impressive an event must exist to assist in reproduction—and must therefore be tied to intercourse. The male peak of pleasure, coinciding almost exactly with ejaculation, seemed nicely attuned to the demands of insemination. Freud reasoned, by analogy, that the vagina should produce a corresponding feminine ecstasy when closed around the organ that so relentlessly seeks a berth in it. To account for the sexual sensitivity of the clitoris (which is entirely external to the vagina), Freud theorized that female orgasm comes in two varieties—one a mere adolescent thrill, the other a product of maturity. He explained the difference in 1920, in *A General Introduction to Psychoanalysis*:

> Of little girls we know that they feel themselves heavily handicapped by the absence of a large visible penis and envy the boy's possession of it; from this source primarily springs the wish to be a man which is resumed again later in the neurosis, owing to some maladjustment to a female development. The clitoris in the girl, moreover, is in every way equivalent during childhood to the penis; it is a region of especial excitability in which auto-erotic satisfaction is achieved. The transition to womanhood very much depends upon the early and complete relegation of this sensitivity from the clitoris over to the vaginal orifice. In those women who are sexually anesthetic, as it is called, the clitoris has stubbornly retained this sensitivity.

It was not until 1953, when the American sex researcher Alfred C. Kinsey published his ground-breaking *Sexual Behavior in the Human Female*, that scientists began to see just how far wrong Freud had been about this. Kinsey studied more than twenty-seven hundred women, interviewed throughout the United States, and the great majority said they did not typically attain orgasm through vaginal stimulation alone. When questioned about techniques of masturbation, 84 percent reported that they achieved "the little death" through massage of the clitoris and the labia. And when, in another part of the Kinsey study, gynecologists examined the genitals of more than five hundred women, 98 percent were found to be sensitive to light touch on the clitoris but only 14 percent to equivalent touch on the vaginal walls. In the light of these findings, Kinsey sensibly declared the supposed transfer of sensitivity from clitoris to vagina a "biologic impossibility." He expressed sympathy for the countless normal women who had been led to expect such a transfer and had imagined themselves dysfunctional when they failed to achieve it. "There is," he wrote, "no evidence that the vagina is ever the sole source of arousal or even the primary source of erotic arousal in any female."

But it was Masters and Johnson who—after studying how hundreds of people actually had sex—really pulled the rug out from under Freud's armchair. In a series of studies conducted between 1954 and 1965 at the Reproductive Biology Research Foundation in Saint Louis, they went beyond the interview to make the study of sex an empirical science. Equipped with electrodes to measure heart rate and breathing, sensors to gauge the strength of muscle contractions, even cameras to film the inside of the vagina, they set about to observe the act itself. The nearly seven hundred participants were observed not only in intercourse but also in masturbation, including, for women, directed vaginal masturbation with a plastic penis that doubled as a camera. Some of the subjects were elderly, some were pregnant, some homosexual. But most were just conventional folks in the prime of their lives, doing what came naturally.

Like Kinsey before them, Masters and Johnson did a lot of

debunking—and Freud was not their only target. Physicians who thought sex during pregnancy would harm the developing fetus were proved wrong, as were psychologists who thought pregnant women did not desire it. Pundits who believed that aging takes away both impulse and ability were hard pressed to explain reports of eager septuagenarians with lubricating jelly. And there were startling findings about the routine details of sexual physiology, many of which had never been properly studied. In what would come to be known as the EPOR model, Masters and Johnson defined four stages of normal sexual response—excitement, plateau, orgasm, and resolution—which involved almost every part of the body.

The excitement phase was described as one of gradual buildup—of increasing muscle tension, vaginal lubrication, and engorgement of blood vessels in the penis, the clitoris, and the nipples. Plateau was a sustained period of excitement, during which heart rate and respiration increase and the skin flushes. Orgasm, the discharge of the built-up tension, was marked by muscle contractions throughout the body (particularly in the genital area), disgorgement of the collected blood, ejaculation in the male, and intense pleasure in both sexes. Resolution was a period of diminishing tension, in which the body returns rapidly through the plateau and excitement levels to an unstimulated state.

Masters and Johnson reported a number of striking similarities in the sexual functioning of men and women, including parallel sensitivities in the penis and the clitoris, flushing of the chest during the plateau phase, and identical rhythmic contractions of the anal sphincter during orgasm—exactly 0.8 second apart. But they uncovered at least one critical difference: in men the resolution phase was accompanied by a complete loss of sexual responsiveness, lasting anywhere from a few minutes (in teenagers) to a day or more (in older fellows), whereas women appeared capable of "returning to another orgasmic experience from any point in the resolution phase." Indeed, women seemed at times to experience one orgasm after another, in uninterrupted succession. This finding, anticipated in Kinsey's interviews, made women seem veritable sexual athletes compared with men. It overturned the Victorian notion of poorer female responsiveness and helped pave the way for a new sort of sexual liberation.

Like Kinsey, Masters and Johnson found no evidence that sexual sensitivity is transferred from the clitoris to the vagina as a woman matures. In fact, they challenged the very distinctness of vaginal orgasm, leading some to suggest that any female climax achieved through intercourse alone might result from indirect stimulation of the clitoris and labia. (This possibility led the popular author Shere Hite, in her polemical 1976 book, *The Hite Report*, to characterize vaginal penetration as the "Rube Goldberg" route to sexual satisfaction.)

Most of Masters and Johnson's findings have held up remarkably well, and the clitoris is now recognized as the primary center of female sexual pleasure. Yet some sexologists—and more than a few women—remain firmly convinced that there *is* such a thing as vaginal orgasm. In fact, one research team, that of Alice K. Ladas, Beverly Whipple, and John D. Perry, reported in 1982 that they had traced the vaginal orgasm to a particular location—a spot on the innermost third of the front vaginal wall. In a widely read book, they dubbed this region the G spot, in honor of Ernest Grafenberg, a physician who had described it in 1950. Other studies have since suggested that some women do experience purely vaginal orgasms, distinct from the clitoral type. And surveys have found that, although women prefer clitoral to vaginal stimulation *if* asked to choose, most prefer a climax that blends the two. None of this suggests that the capacity for vaginal orgasm is anywhere near as common as that for clitoral orgasm. But Freud may have been right at least in the belief that it exists.

Freud was also right to think of orgasm as a partly psychological phenomenon. One curious aspect of the Masters and Johnson outlook was the notion that sexual pleasure—whether male or female—is merely muscular and cutaneous. They didn't come right out and say that, yet they managed to write hundreds of pages on the subject with almost no mention of its mental or emotional aspects. The racing heart, the flushed skin, and the gasps were real, they seemed to suggest, yet the profound emotion that sometimes accompanies those physiological events was as insubstantial as a shadow.

This aspect of Masters and Johnson's work seemed a throwback to the model of emotion advanced by the psychologists William James and Carl Lange around the turn of the century, a model that defined such experiences as joy and sorrow, affection and anger not as primary sensations but as secondary mental reactions to physiological events. Even as Masters and Johnson's work was in progress, however, their physiological bias was being undermined.

One of the first researchers to show definitively that sexual feeling originates above as well as below the neck was the neurologist Robert G. Heath, of Tulane University, who found that certain areas of the brain, when directly stimulated, produce the sensation of sexual pleasure. Heath's study, published in 1972 in the *Journal of Nervous and Mental Disease*, centered on two subjects (a mentally disturbed man of twenty-four and an epileptic woman of thirty-four) who, for therapeutic reasons, had already had electrodes implanted in their limbic systems, the part of the brain that mediates pleasurable emotion.

Not only did neural stimulation induce sexual pleasure, but sexual activity seemed to cause a great deal of neural activity. Heath found that when either patient was sexually stimulated, electrical waves generated within the septal region, a crossroads between the limbic system and the hypothalmus, resembled waves whose appearance in other parts of the brain suggests the onset of a seizure. But these subjects were not experiencing seizures—except to the extent that orgasm constitutes one. (Here, Felix Riboud's early characterization of orgasm as an "epileptic frenzy" seems prescient.) Moreover, the electrical changes in the septal area were discernible before the orgasm even began, suggesting that they are not just secondary responses to orgasmic muscle contractions but may play a part in inducing them. The orgasm, it now seemed, was in essence a function of the brain and no mere twitch of the sexual flesh.

Intrigued by such findings, the physiologist Julian Davidson, of Stanford University's School of Medicine, proposed in 1980 a "bipolar hypothesis" of orgasm, intended to integrate all the known physiological and psychological data. Davidson first undertook to demonstrate that orgasm has many of the features of an altered state of consciousness—that it requires an ability to let go of inhibitions and involves changed perceptions of time, space, and motion. For example, he cited studies showing that both men and women, when asked to write subjective descriptions of orgasm, used such phrases as "loss of contact with reality. All senses acute. Sight becomes patterns of color, but often very difficult to explain because words were made to fit in the real world."

Having established that orgasm occurs in the mind as well as the loins, Davidson posited a hypothetical "organ of orgasm" to mediate between the two. He speculated that this organ—presumably a portion of the nervous system that includes the limbic system and the septal area studied by Heath—interacts with the cerebral cortex to create an altered state of consciousness during sex. Because the cortex processes sensory data, Davidson reasoned that it must bombard the organ of orgasm with "cognitive input," in the form of sight, sound, and fantasy. Meanwhile, according to his model, the organ would continue to generate—and respond to—pelvic muscle contractions, in a dynamic, two-way interchange.

Davidson's model remains largely untested, but it has much to recommend it as a heuristic device. For one thing, it rescues sexual feeling from muscular marginality and puts it back in the center of our experience (and our nervous systems), where most of us sense it belongs. For another, it enables us to talk about the psychological and physical mechanics of orgasm without giving either precedence over the other. For all its virtues as a description of the phenomenon, however, Davidson's model leaves untouched the central question of why we are subject to orgasm in the first place. Is orgasm an adaptation—a tendency that took hold by bestowing reproductive advantages on creatures who exhibited it, and that has been tailored by natural selection to the contingencies of survival—or does it exist by sheer happenstance?

It seems clear that, in males, orgasm directly rewards behavior associated with ejaculation, with insemination, and thus with reproduction. Various hypotheses have been proposed to account for female orgasm; theorists have speculated that uterine contractions may promote the motility of sperm and thus assist in fertilization (weakly supported); that recovery from orgasm may serve to keep women at rest in a horizontal position while the sperm find their way (a plausible speculation); and that the sensation itself rewards sexual activity (undeniable). What makes the largely nonvaginal female orgasm problematic is that, as Alfred Kinsey noted in 1953, "the techniques of masturbation and of petting" induce it more readily than "the techniques of coitus itself." This fact has led some evolutionists, such as Stephen Jay Gould, of Harvard, to argue that female orgasm is not an adaptation at all but a by-product of human development.

Males and females are, of course, variations on a single form; we are indistinguishable at conception but acquire separate characteristics during later stages of development, as hormones act to suppress or exaggerate particular anatomical features. The result is that each sex ends up sporting homologues of the other's distinctive organs. That being the case, it makes no sense, in Gould's estimation, to puzzle over the presence of, say, male nipples; they exist not because they enhance fitness but because they are part of the anatomical tool kit that enables females to develop breasts. Gould applies the same reasoning to female orgasm: it exists not because it fosters reproduction but because the clitoris is the homologue of the penis—"the same organ, endowed with the same anatomical organization and capacity of response."

Gould may be right about male nipples, but the idea that clitoral orgasm is an adaptation, and not just the by-product of one, can't be cast aside so easily. For one thing, as Masters and Johnson demonstrated, male and female orgasms are *not* identical phenomena. If, as Gould contends, the clitoris has exactly the same "capacity of response" as the penis, why is female orgasm more gradual, more sustained, and more repeatable than male orgasm? One plausible answer is that male and female sensitivities have been shaped by different selective pressures. For the males in many species, reproduction can be as simple as inseminating a female. For females, on the other hand, reproduction inevitably entails gestation, labor, and nursing. So it stands to reason that males would be rewarded, in an evolutionary sense, for rough-and-ready copulation—the sort encouraged by prompt, final orgasms—whereas females would do best by choosing carefully among suitors and trying to sustain a bond with one. Female orgasm, with its slower onset and its greater capacity for repetition, would seem far more likely to result from such sustained encounters than from quick, perfunctory ones.

But why, if female orgasm evolved as an aid to reproduction, is it centered largely *outside* the vagina? This is indeed a puzzling fact, but it doesn't automatically negate the adaptationist view. Certainly, a sensation can encourage an activity without being a direct product of it. Our sense of taste, so basic to nutrition, is not confined to the orifice that receives food; gustatory pleasure originates to a significant degree in the nose. No one would argue, on that basis, that taste does not serve to encourage and regulate eating. By the same token, female orgasm may originate outside the vagina and still serve as an inducement to copulation.

Moreover, as we have seen, the vagina has never been convincingly desexed. The existence of the G spot has not been proved; but suppose there *is* a sensitive region located on the front vaginal wall. What sort of of behavior would this encourage? As devotees of the G spot have long been aware, sexual intercourse in the en face, or "missionary," position affords only minimal stimulation to that area, whereas "bestial" intercourse—in the front-to-back position characteristic of nonhuman mammals maximizes it. (That position, incidentally, also facilitates clitoral touching.) The argument seems to be ripening toward climax: if there is such a thing as vaginal orgasm, it seems well adapted to the activity by which our primate ancestors engendered us.

Nevertheless, we are human, and humans in various studies prefer face-to-face intercourse. Here, perhaps, the downward sweep of the limbic system's power to generate orgasm becomes critical. Then too, one of the most distinctive characteristics of our species is an inventive use of the hand under the fine control of the cerebral cortex. (The hand, after all, was the instrument of sublime satisfaction in that passage about Lady Chatterley's lover.) In a creature for whom culture has greatly augmented the power of biology, it would be a pity if sex were limited to the same tactics used by our evolutionary forebears. On the contrary, if we want the earth to move, we should use every available sort of anatomical and psychological earth-moving machinery.

TOO DESPERATE

A CURE?

In the film version of Ken Kesey's novel *One Flew Over the Cuckoo's Nest*, the hero, Randle Patrick McMurphy—a reasonably sane fellow who has been committed to a mental hospital for his rebellious and mildly erratic behavior—is so mercilessly oppressed by the tyrannical Nurse Ratched that he eventually loses his temper and assaults her. This is her triumphant moment, for it frees her to do what she has wanted to do all along: send him for brain surgery. The operation doesn't merely calm McMurphy down; it eliminates every distinctive aspect of his personality—indeed, everything that makes him human. His best friend, a kind but depressed American Indian with the physique of a polar bear, sizes up the situation by saying, "Mac wouldn't want this thing hanging around here for twenty years with his name on it." Accordingly, he smothers what's left of his friend with a pillow, an act we perceive as a wholly humane response to the hospital's official barbarism.

One Flew Over the Cuckoo's Nest was no mere horror fantasy. Thousands of American psychiatric patients had undergone the treatment known as frontal lobotomy during the 1940s and 1950s, and the results had been devastating. Some of those patients (as many as one in twenty) died from the surgery. Others experienced side effects ranging from incontinence to epilepsy or paralysis, and many suffered a permanent loss of intelligence or motor skills. But perhaps the most disturbing feature of the operation was its effect on personality. As the American Psychiatric Association's commission on psychiatric therapies would report in 1984, "many patients, depending on the extensiveness of the section, were transformed into individuals without initiative of any kind—not infrequently to a vegetative state requiring almost complete supervision."

If psychosurgery was a controversial treatment during the 1970s, it is virtually taboo today. Ken Kesey's vision of Randle Patrick McMurphy, rendered inhuman as punishment for the crime of getting angry, has become emblematic of our culture's response to the issue. Historians still ponder the rise and demise of psychosurgery (Elliot S. Valenstein, a distinguished psychologist, does so in his latest book, *Great and Desperate Cures*), but its actual use in the United States now consists of only a small number of extremely modest operations—many of those in the 1980s performed by a single surgeon: H. Thomas Ballantine, of the Massachusetts General Hospital and the Harvard Medical School. In a society that cannot quite come to terms with ECT—electroconvulsive, or shock, therapy, an excellent, proven, and basically safe treatment for severe, prolonged depression—the odds that psychiatric neurosurgery will ever make a comeback seem exceedingly slim. Yet Ballantine's pioneering work with a procedure known as cingulotomy raises important questions: Have we drawn the line in the wrong place? And if we have, what is the human cost of our forbearance?

Psychosurgery—brain surgery for psychiatric illnesses—has a long and mostly undistinguished history. Trepanation, the practice of some primitive and ancient peoples in which a hole is made in the skull to let bad humors out of the brain, may go as far back as 2000 B.C. Roger of Salerno, a twelfth-century surgeon, recommended skull perforation as a treatment for mania and melancholy, and Robert Burton's seventeenth-century classic, *Anatomy of Melancholy*, gave it guarded endorsement as well, claiming that sword wounds penetrating the skull sometimes cured insanity. In modern times, this type of surgery apparently began around 1891, when Gottlieb Burckhardt described six patients he had operated on in Switzerland (he had tried, unsuccessfully, to treat mental illness by destroying part of the cerebral cortex), but it was rare until the 1930s, when the Portuguese neurologist Egas Moniz developed the prefrontal leucotomy, or lobotomy. ("Leucotomy," the more precise term, meant cutting of the white matter, or nerve tracts; but *lobotomy*, or cutting of the lobes, was the term that took hold.) By the time the technique won Moniz a Nobel prize, in 1949, it had been performed on tens of thousands of people.

The procedure, as performed in this country by the neuropsychiatrist Walter J. Freeman and the neurosurgeon James W. Watts, was a drastic one. It involved inserting blades about a third of the way into each side of the brain, through holes drilled at the temples, and levering them up and down to sever major nerve fiber tracts in the frontal lobes. By thus interrupting the connection between the anatomical centers of thought (in the cerebral cortex) and those of emotion (in the limbic system), the lobotomy dimmed, or even eliminated, the patient's awareness of whatever feelings ailed him. Such radical cutting sometimes reduced or eliminated depression, obsessive compulsiveness, and intractable pain. But it came at a terrible cost.

While the lobotomy was losing favor as a treatment for common psychiatric disorders, neurosurgeons developed a different procedure, known as amygdalotomy, to subdue extremely violent patients. The amygdala—an almond-shaped structure located about an inch inside the skull near the top of each ear—is a part of the limbic system involved in aggression, arousal, and fear. By destroying it, surgeons found they could sometimes transform explosive patients into docile ones—and this without the extensive damage of McMurphy's frontal lobotomy.

During the 1950s, follow-up studies of lobotomy patients established with clinical certainty what should have been clear all along: that many had suffered unacceptable losses. In response, surgeons began developing less radical techniques to achieve the same ends, with the result that lobotomy gave way to an operation called cingulectomy. Whereas lobotomy severed the entire connection between the limbic system and the cerebral cortex, cingulectomy destroyed only a four-centimeter segment of the cingulum, a paired bundle of nerve fibers that runs along the main axis of the brain, traversing the two cerebral hemispheres like a set of railroad tracks.

Cingulectomy—still a highly invasive procedure—gave way in the early 1960s to cingulotomy, a much less radical interruption of the cingulum. This treatment, first reported on by Eldon L. Foltz and Lowell E. White in the *Journal of Neurosurgery* in 1962, was soon taken up by Ballantine and his colleagues in Boston. It involves the passage of an electrode wire through two small holes in the top front portion of the skull. Guided by X-ray images, the wire targets a tiny region of the bundle and destroys it—not by way of crude, mechanical cutting but by more precise electrical burning. Cingulotomy (which Ballantine still practices) posed fewer risks than its predecessors, and it showed promising results as a treatment for depression and intractable pain. It was the cruder measures—lobotomy, amygdalotomy, and cingulectomy—that became so controversial.

It wasn't just the intrusiveness of those more radical procedures that caused the outcry but also the applications that certain proponents seemed to favor. The neurosurgeons Vernon H. Mark and William H. Sweet and the psychiatrist Frank R. Ervin, for example, wrote a letter to the *Journal of the American Medical Association* in 1967 that implied that psychosurgery might help quell the urban riots then sweeping the nation: if, in each city, there were a handful of trouble-makers with abnormalities of the amygdala, the troubles might have a medical explanation. These physicians seemed ready to diagnose as surgically treatable derangements of the brain the violent outbursts that others viewed as a complex social problem.

Psychosurgery had become such a bitterly divisive issue by 1973 that when it was addressed at a meeting of the Society for Neuroscience, leaflets attacking both the practice and its practitioners were distributed. This cast an unusual chill over the scientific discussions. Any physician willing to perform an amygdalotomy was a butcher, the dissidents implied. It was no more a medical treatment than were the chains and dungeons to which the mentally ill were confined during the Dark Ages, and its cost was greater: chains and dungeons may have punished the body, but they didn't extinguish the soul. So went the arguments of many knowledgeable people—arguments that have by now become conventional wisdom.

During the sixties I, too, was insulted by the notion of damaging the brain to save the mind, and appalled by the overweening ambition with which many physicians had pursued the treatment. Pharmacology had produced other, truly effective treatments for severe mental illness—lithium for mania, chlorpromazine for schizophrenia, and a number of chemical remedies for depression. So why pursue surgical treatments with such potential for Orwellian abuse?

Then, during the seventies, I began to sense that the opponents of psychosurgery might be going too far. I was present at that meeting of the Society for Neuroscience in 1973, and the leafleters attacking psychosurgery began to seem shrill to me. Not content to debate the merits of particular forms of surgery, they resorted to distortion and intimidation to get their points across: they exaggerated the number of operations actually being performed, and they impugned the motives of physicians I knew to be well-meaning. The distinguished neuroanatomist Walle J. H. Nauta, who was president of the society, defended the importance of exploring treatments that could alleviate the suffering of people with severe mental illness. Those attacking psychosurgery most vigorously, he pointed out, were not always those who had witnessed the daily horror that mental illness can be.

That observation struck a chord in me. While in college, I had worked for a summer with a child whose autism cut him off completely from human contact; he went through life groaning to himself, a look of terror in his eyes, and modern medicine had nothing to offer him. This boy would not have been a candidate for psychosurgery, and I knew that emotional appeals to patients like him had prepared the way for lobotomy's abuses. But I wondered whether there was something specifically wrong in his brain—something that might someday be repaired surgically.

Another experience that changed my perspective was my realization, as a medical student during the early eighties, that nonsurgical treatments for mental illness are neither as harmless nor as effective as I had imagined. I sat for hours with a man who could talk of nothing but his inability to control his terrifying thoughts; years of drug treatment had brought him no relief. I got to know a lucid young woman who had suffered profound and irreversible nervous-system damage from antischizophrenic drugs—drugs she probably had never needed, since her symptoms were mainly of depression. Many of the patients I saw *had* been helped by drugs, or psychotherapy, or shock treatment. But it was clear that in other cases, none of these treatments was good enough.

As a student at the Massachusetts General Hospital, I met Ballantine and several of his patients. I talked with these patients before and after their cingulotomies, even took part in the operations, and I never witnessed anything remotely resembling the spiritual murder of Randle McMurphy. The patient would be lightly sedated, the tiny burr holes drilled into the skull, and the electrode wire introduced quickly and painlessly into the brain. Then, as images flashed on an X-ray screen, a current would be turned on for a minute or two and the wire withdrawn. Later the same day, the patient would be lucid and talkative—not noticeably changed, but at least more hopeful.

Like most of the psychosurgical procedures that have been tried in modern times, cingulotomy was designed to interrupt certain circuits in the limbic system, or emotional brain— which was first characterized in 1878 by the neuroanatomist Paul Broca. He called it "le grand lobe limbique," defining it as a series of structures in the limbus, or fringe, of the cerebral hemispheres around the corpus callosum. In 1937, just as Moniz was beginning to extend the use of his new procedure, James Papez, a Cornell University comparative neurologist, published a crucial analysis of these structures, which he called "the stream of feeling." Paul MacLean, a psychiatrist and neuroanatomist, explored them further in a 1949 paper, where he coined the term "limbic system," one that has stuck. He and Nauta made many contributions to the understanding of the structure and function of this system, one of which was to define the frontal lobes as the part of the cerebral cortex that interacts with the limbic system. Although neither of them was involved in the development of psychosurgery, their discoveries suggested that several procedures, including cingulotomy, could be characterized as diminishing that interaction.

But theory, like history and anecdote, cannot answer the question of whether we should be employing particular surgical procedures. Only good research can, and good research has not been plentiful in relation to psychosurgery. In the United States, the brightest spot has been a study of Ballantine's cingulotomy patients, over the past fifteen years, by an independent group at the Massachusetts Institute of Technology. In this study, initiated by the neuropsychologists Hans-Lukas Teuber and Suzanne Corkin, patients have undergone psychiatric, logical, and neuropsychological testing before, immediately following, and years after the cingulotomy procedure. All tests were done by experienced investigators who were completely independent of the neurosurgeon except as a source of referral.

In 1980 Corkin published preliminary results on a group of eighty-five patients—twenty-six suffering from intractable pain and fifty-nine from psychiatric disorders, the most common being depression. The mean duration of the illness or complaint was about eleven years for the pain patients and fifteen years for the psychiatric patients. Each patient had been given thirty standard tests: two of overall intelligence; seven that register frontal lobe function (for instance, the ability to sort the same cards by different principles); seven of memory; three of spatial ability; eight of sensory and motor activity; and three of personality. Each subject also underwent a thorough neurological examination. Although several patients developed postsurgical complications, the principal finding—one that was replicated in a later study, of more than a hundred eighty patients—was that cingulotomy is generally safe. In fact, in the initial study, the operation was followed by at least moderate short-term improvement in 75 percent of the pain patients and 61 percent of those suffering from depression.

Further analysis of the larger sample has since bolstered the conclusion that cingulotomy is a relatively harmless procedure, but Corkin has become skeptical about whether it brings any benefits. One reason is that not all the patients have made themselves available for follow-up study, and it is possible that those who benefited least from the surgery were the least likely to show up for reexamination. Moreover, the study necessarily lacked two key features of a controlled experiment—random assignment of similar patients to one treatment or another and the performance of sham, or placebo, operations—so it is possible that the benefits were partially psychological in origin.

Ballantine and his colleagues, meanwhile, have conducted their own study and are (not surprisingly) more optimistic. In a 1987 report in the journal *Biological Psychiatry*, they summarized the results of more than seven hundred cingulotomy procedures performed on some four hundred patients over a period of twenty years. Their data document not only a low level of risk (there were two cases of partial paralysis as well as a one-percent incidence of seizures, always a risk with brain surgery) but also, for many patients, a significant benefit. Ballantine found that some disorders were consistently more responsive to the treatment than were others; the operation was less effective for treating obsessive-compulsive illness or schizophrenia than for alleviating depression and anxiety. But, overall, 62 percent of the psychiatric patients experienced considerable improvement following cingulotomy. Some even went on to function normally without medication.

While these observations are not completely unbiased, that has been true in the early stages of much of clinical research throughout the history of modern medicine. And it must be noted that these were not run-of-the-mill patients with serious mental illnesses; each had been certified by a three-physician Institutional Review Board appointed by the hospital as extremely resistant cases. The board included the operative neurosurgeon but also a psychiatrist and a neurologist, and "cingulotomy was recommended only if the IRB concluded unanimously that all reasonable nonoperative treatments had failed." One patient wrote in 1986 that she celebrates the date of her cingulotomy operation yearly "as my re-birthday":

> For many, many years before this day, I was plagued with severe depression and was in and out of mental wards and hospitals many, many times. There was no apparent reason for my being depressed. I had taken many different kinds of medication, therapy and shock treatment—none of which had lasting good results. Many, many times I was not much more than a vegetable—merely existing—not really living—a burden to my family. During the eight and a half years since I had the cingulotomy operation, I have been able to lead an active, useful, productive, happy life . . .

She appended figures on her medical expenses for the eight months prior to the operation and for the first eight months of 1986: these were $18,494.80 and $588.00, respectively. She was one of thirty patients in the sample of 120 with mood disorders who were classified after operation as functioning normally but requiring medication; nineteen were rated higher—as functioning normally without medication. Such testimonials from individuals cannot bear scientific weight; they can only illustrate an optimal outcome. But they can also be viewed beside our vivid images of people whose personalities were destroyed by frontal lobotomy.

In the light of these studies, three things seem fair to say. First, cingulotomy, as practiced by Ballantine, appears to cause no significant cognitive or emotional harm. Second, the operation may be an effective treatment for chronic pain and it may alleviate chronic anxiety and depression. Third, our admittedly elementary science of the limbic system provides some theoretical basis for such positive effects. These effects could turn out to be temporary or to occur only in certain patients; the obvious way to find out is to amass more data on the procedure. But on that front, the news is not encouraging—at least not in this country.

Outside the United States, physicians are actively studying several forms of psychiatric neurosurgery. This is true in such countries as Spain and India, where less stringent systems of medical regulation might make us skeptical, as well as in England, where no such skepticism is warranted. Hundreds of British patients have had a promising operation called sub-caudate tractotomy, which involves a small interruption of fiber tracts leading to the frontal lobes under the head of the caudate nucleus, a large, arc-shaped paired structure located below the cingulum bundle. The technique, very similar to cingulotomy but with a different target, also attempts to reduce the volume of impulses traveling between the emotional and cognitive centers of the brain. Follow-up studies indicate that the operation may help alleviate both depression and obsessive-compulsive illness. Meanwhile, yearly advances in neurobiology, including a better understanding of the structure and function of the limbic system, promise to suggest other sorts of interventions that might be worth trying. These could be surgical, chemical, or even combined approaches that would introduce chemicals to specific parts of the brain.

In the United States, these approaches are receiving little attention. More than ten years ago, a federal commission—including leading physicians not involved with brain surgery, as well as lawyers and bioethics professors—concluded that "there are circumstances under which psychosurgical procedures may appropriately be performed" and recommended that the government "conduct and support studies" of specific procedures. Yet psychosurgery remains such a taboo that few physicians are willing to stake their careers on it. In the decade since that report was issued, Ballantine's and Corkin's studies have been the only ones undertaken in this country. Ballantine will retire in a few years, and when he does, patients who might benefit from cingulotomy may be deprived of it altogether. What's worse, the slowly advancing frontier of knowledge about psychosurgery may come to a halt.

I think of the patient I knew who was permanently harmed by a routinely misprescribed antischizophrenic drug. No one who has undergone Ballantine's surgery, with the exception of the very few who experienced hemorrhages or convulsions, has suffered *any* detectable nervous system damage, let alone the severe movement disorder and postural deformity she had to live with. She would almost certainly have been better off with the surgery—if not helped, at least less harmed. That cannot be said of many depressed patients, but those who have tried everything else should be offered the opportunity to take part in a properly supervised clinical trial.

Inappropriate timidity should not be allowed to undermine

the logic of our approach to severe mental suffering. If we believe, with Hippocrates, that "from the brain and from the brain only arise our pleasures, joys, laughter, and jests as well as our sorrows, pains, griefs, and tears"; that "it is the same thing which makes us mad or delirious, inspires us with dread and fear, whether by night or by day, brings sleeplessness, inopportune mistakes, aimless anxieties, absent mindedness and acts that are contrary to habit . . ."; then we must concede that brain surgery may someday be able to help alleviate the pain of some mental illness. One must look long into the eyes of the mentally ill, must really see something of their pain, before concluding that brain surgery will always be too desperate a cure.

EVERYMAN

Gathered together in front of their huts, during the days of leisure after harvest time, the Tiv, of Nigeria, had regaled Laura Bohannon with legends and folktales. It seemed only polite, then, that the anthropologist return the favor. So one day, over the customary bowls of beer, Bohannon recounted a tale whose appeal seemed so universal, it was sure to touch the hearts of the tribe's elders. But although they enjoyed the story, they were baffled by many parts. Hamlet, the young prince, objected to his mother's marriage to Claudius? Certainly the man was obligated to marry his brother's widow. The ghost of Hamlet's father had accused Claudius of murder? This must have been an omen sent by a witch! The prince's betrothed, Ophelia, had gone mad and drowned? What could be more conclusive proof of sorcery? And when Laertes had thrown himself on his sister's corpse in the open grave, hadn't he exposed himself as the witch? Bohannon, slightly inebriated and very confused, was forced to conclude that she had guessed wrong about the play's universal appeal.

Her experience has a familiar ring: an anthropologist encounters a way of thinking so unpredictable, it calls into question our basic assumptions about what people are like. There is the "semen belt" of New Guinea, a geographic strip in which pubescent boys practice homosexuality, believing they must imbibe semen to grow, and then abandon the behavior in adulthood—thus challenging virtually every theory of how sexual orientation develops. There are the grotesquely fat African queens and densely scarified Polynesian maidens who expose our own, Western ideal of beauty as parochial—and as arbitrary and ephemeral as the latest shade of lipstick or eyeliner. And on a more mundane level there are the American businessmen who have sabotaged their enterprises in Arab countries by sitting too close—at a distance that would be normal back home—to customers during conversation.

Finding exceptions to our assumptions about human nature has become the anthropologist's stock-in-trade. "Not among the people I study, they don't!"—the anthropological veto—is offered when anyone mentions standards of behavior thought to apply to everyone. Indeed, some people choose anthropology as a career specifically to combat ethnocentrism, that special brand of egocentricism shared by members of a society, who feel superior to nonmembers and are unable to see clearly beyond their own, narrow cultural perspective. Those who overgeneralize—psychologists with their grand sex-role theories, plastic surgeons with their so-called classic ideal of beauty, businessmen with their self-assured ploys—offend us.

For some of us the goal becomes *épater les bourgeois*—except that we want to shock not just the middle class but as large as possible a proportion of the population of the United States and Europe. Yet the motive has its serious side. In my own case the realization that there was an almost infinite variety of religious forms—whose practitioners all felt they were absolutely, uniquely right—played a role in my abandonment of the religiosity of my teenage years. Later, the lessons of Margaret Mead and others about the great cross-cultural variety of women's roles penetrated my dense Brooklyn male chauvinism and changed my views—as well as those of many in my generation. And still later, my children's lives were transformed by the experiences my wife and I had had among the !Kung San before the children were even born. The !Kung slept with their children, rarely punished them, and rarely weaned them before age three. These experiences opened a seam for us in the ethnocentric blinders with which almost all Americans approach parenthood, and the opening let in a different kind of light.

This is the meaning, in anthropology, of the term "cultural relativism." It does not mean, and never has meant, "anything goes" in terms of values; it is more about perception than about values. It means that our very vision of reality, especially social and psychological reality, is conditioned by culture to such an extent that without ethnological studies, we could go through life, and even through history, with blinders on. Unquestionably, anthropology's most important contribution to human knowledge so far has been to reveal the world's great cultural diversity, forcing us to see life as others see it.

Ironically, though, this penchant has led to a new sort of smugness. Anthropologists have become so obsessed with the mission of overturning generalizations about human behavior that they have obscured a separate reality. Beneath the vast array of cultural variations are features of behavior that do not vary. There is, in fact, a human nature, which all of us share. Philosophers have mused on it for millennia, but the only way to understand it fully is to find out exactly what it is made of, to know which behaviors are universal. The question is, Can anthropologists finally accept this challenge and, without sacrificing the glory of cultural relativism, identify the qualities that make us human?

An important first step toward understanding the basic similarities between cultures was taken, surprisingly, before anthropologists had gotten very far in their study of human diversity. In 1872, Charles Darwin wrote *The Expression of the Emotions in Man and Animals,* in which he compared the behavior of different animals as he had compared their physical traits in *The Origin of Species* thirteen years earlier—with a view toward understanding evolutionary relationships. Specifically, he compared the ways in which various mammals engage in nonverbal communication, the physical manifestations of such emotions as fear and anger. He presented vivid line drawings depicting dogs with their hackles raised, their eyes widened, their ears laid back, and the corners of their mouths drawn taut. Alongside these, he displayed realistic sketches of human faces with essentially the same fearful expressions. And to complete the picture, he gave written descriptions of primitive peoples—provided by missionaries and other travelers—whose facial expressions of fear were identical to those of the Europeans he had depicted. Darwin's conclusion: the similarities in emotional reaction displayed by different cultures, and different species, offer proof that they descended from common ancestors and thus share many traits.

Darwin's monograph inspired the science of ethology, the evolutionary study of behavior. But during the science's early years, speculations about the biological underpinnings of human behavior were widely misinterpreted as evidence that one sex, or one race, was superior to another. These misconceptions ultimately had grave political consequences, and as a result, ethologists limited themselves to studying animals, and anthropologists concentrated on the differences, not the similarities, between humans.

It was not until the 1960s that the German ethologist

Irenäus Eibl-Eibesfeldt, at the Max Planck Institute for Behavioral Physiology in Seewiesen, West Germany (the same place where Konrad Lorenz had studied his famous geese), carried forward the work that Darwin had begun a century earlier. Instead of comparing drawings, Eibl-Eibesfeldt looked at films of human behavior, which he shot among diverse cultures, including the Waika of Venezuela, the Eipo of New Guinea, the Balinese, the Trobriand Islanders, the Bushmen and the Himba of Namibia, as well as the Bavarians of Germany. Because his camera filmed sideways, through a mirror, so that the subjects could not tell when they were being watched, he was able to capture candid moments.

In reviewing the films, Eibl-Eibesfeldt found himself watching certain standard behaviors over and over. Toddlers in societies throughout the world engaged in hitting, kicking, biting, and spitting at one another. Adults, when embarrassed, hid their faces, and when disappointed, pouted— Indonesian, African, and European alike. And when two people met, anywhere, they usually raised and lowered their eyebrows abruptly. This gesture—called an eyebrow flash, because it takes no more than half a second—was typically accompanied by a brief, slight lift of the head and was often followed by a smile. Eyebrow flashes were used to signal parting, flirting, or agreement; if the eyebrows remained raised, disdain, or even threat. Many of these findings were confirmed in research by Paul Ekman, a psychologist at the University of California at San Francisco, and other investigators.

While Eibl-Eibesfeldt was collecting his films, linguistic anthropologists were beginning to recognize certain universals in human language. They demonstrated that despite the immense variety of tongues spoken by different peoples, any infant can be placed within any culture and learn to speak the language. That is, Chinese babies are no better at learning Chinese than Brazilian babies would be, and American babies are not inherently adept at learning English. This is true because all languages are basically alike. In the sixties, Charles F. Hockett, a professor of anthropology at Cornell University, identified eight key features that characterize them. These include displacement, the way in which words can be used to describe events in the past or in the future, or in some distant location; arbitrariness, the lack of any intrinsic ties between particular words and what they represent (languages often go through major changes in vocabulary and pronunciation); and duality of patterning, the way in which the order of sounds in one word can be rearranged to produce a wholly different word ("meat" and "team," for example). Thus, any human baby capable of learning to use the eight features is capable of learning any language.

Beyond these universals of facial expression and language, other uniformities of human behavior have been discovered, albeit unintentionally, by the very anthropologists whose mission has been to document diversity. Some behaviors, they have found, are not manifest in everyone but are merely tendencies that characterize a particular age group. Not all one-year-olds cry when their parents leave them with strangers, for example. But in all cultures, no matter what the child-rearing traditions, one-year-olds are much more likely to protest than are six-month-olds or four-year-olds. Other universals have been found among members of one sex or the other. Males of all ages, in every culture, exhibit more physical aggressiveness than do females (though there is great overlap in distributions: the most aggressive females are far more violent than the least aggressive males). Such patterns tell us as much about the underlying regularity of human nature as do the universals that apply to every one of us.

Anthropologists have also documented a *tendency,* in all human cultures, toward certain unusual, even antisocial behaviors. Some have gone to great lengths to find communities in which homicide does not occur, but this search has proved only that no such communities exist. And as Jane M. Murphy, of the Harvard School of Public Health, and others have shown, mental illnesses corresponding to schizophrenia, mania, and depression are recognized in all cultures. In some cases, one or another of these syndromes, when first manifest in an individual, may be mistaken for a culturally sanctioned hallucination, a shamanistic activity, or the like. But when the illness persists, it is ultimately recognized for what it is.

Universals of behavior often are reflected in the habits, rules, and institutions of whole societies. Charles Hockett, in his textbook of anthropology, took a lesson from his own work on language universals and applied it to the much more complex matter of universals of culture. He charted a large number of such features, including some that anthropologists have occasionally gotten quite hot under the collar about. (Getting hot under the collar, by the way, is a perfect example of a human universal, and is a component of anger that we share with other mammals. It has to do with the slow burn of the brown-fat energy store that sits between the shoulder blades.) Included are such mundane things as the draping and adornment of the body, the use of fire in cooking, and the forging of weapons but also such hoary anthropological collar warmers as marriage, the incest taboo, and the prohibition of homicide.

Hockett's generalizations were well grounded. In his book *Social Structure,* published in 1949, the anthropologist

George Peter Murdock, of the University of Pittsburgh, analyzed two hundred and fifty cultures and discovered that all have standards for determining who may have sex with whom. The most prevalent of these standards is the incest taboo. Murdock also found that one of the most important universals of culture is the nuclear family. "Either as the sole prevailing form of the family or as the basic unit from which more complex familial forms are compounded," he said, "it exists as a distinct and strongly functional group in every known society."

At the time that Murdock made this assertion, it contradicted the views of other anthropologists—for example, Ralph Linton, of Columbia University, a leader of the discipline in the thirties, who had said that the nuclear family has "an insignificant role in the lives of many societies." Linton cited the Nayar, a warrior caste in India, in which it was said to be common for newly married men to go off and live permanently among other soldiers, leaving their wives to take lovers at home. But examination of the culture revealed that this description was exaggerated and that the nuclear family is, in fact, important in Nayar society. Later, in 1954, Melford E. Spiro, now of the University of California at San Diego, cited the Israeli communal farm, the kibbutz, as an exception, because members collectively took on traditional family responsibilities. But by 1958, many kibbutzim had begun to back away from their strictly communal ideology, and Spiro was prepared to reinterpret his findings, saying that "the relationship between kibbutz parents and children satisfies Murdock's definition of family." Subsequently kibbutzim went on to allow families increasing responsibility for child rearing, meal preparation, and so on. Clearly, the attempt to do away with the nuclear family in these experimental cultures had failed.

This is but a brief sampling of the many similarities already observed between people in different cultures. If students of culture were to conduct a determined search, perhaps they could come up with a nearly complete accounting of the attributes all people share, no matter what their race, homeland, upbringing, or way of life. But most anthropologists are still inclined to disregard universals, arguing that the standard behaviors of mankind are only the dull foundation of the house of culture, which ends where all the interesting design features begin.

The great drawback of this way of thinking is that it prevents us from developing a science of human nature, for every science needs some framework of known principles with which to understand disparate phenomena. The science of biology could not advance until Linnaeus came up with a taxonomy that clarified and codified the relationships among various species. Physics could not move forward until Newton delineated the basic principles of gravitation and objects in motion. Similarly, anthropologists cannot fully appreciate the significance of human diversity until they grasp the fundamentals of human nature—until they establish a human "biogram," a list of the characteristics common to all cultures.

Beyond enabling us to construct a more complete picture of what it is to be human, a full accounting of human universals would help unify anthropology and biology. After all, there is strong reason to suspect that all uniformities of human culture are biologically based. Assuming that the Waika and the Trobrianders developed their own cultures in isolation from each other, why would members of each group raise their eyebrows in greeting, in the exact same manner, unless this behavior was a largely reflexive response somehow wired into their brains? And why would every culture in the world respect and rely on some form of nuclear family, unless humans had some inherent propensity to do so?

When Hockett identified the underlying similarities in languages, the suspicion arose that these features reflect similarities in all human brains. Displacement, arbitrariness, and duality of patterning, he suggested, must be fundamental skills embedded in our neurological pathways. Anthropologists initially responded to this insight by suggesting that it was only the large size of the human brain—its great capacity and flexibility—that, in a general way, provided the thinking power to enable people in all cultures to develop language. But that was before much was known about the brain. As our understanding of neurology advances, it becomes more and more obvious that, indeed, our brains contain many highly specialized-circuits, some of them designed to make possible the use of human language. Overall, specific circuits in the human brain provide tendencies, competencies, and constraints. They make universals both possible and necessary, and add up in the end to a rough definition of human nature—an image that, flexible though we seem, we can't quite remake ourselves out of.

It will be quite some time before anyone will be able to discern exactly which circuits correspond to such things as the eyebrow flash, the development of fear of separation among one-year-olds, and the propensity for homicidal violence. But, at least, by allowing that these behaviors are universal we can assume that they have a biological substrate—that we perform them because our brains are wired for them and that the pattern for this wiring is coded in our genes. Then, by exploring the full extent of universals, we can learn the degree to which attributes of culture are inherent and thus inflexible. None of this undermines efforts to investigate the great diversity of culture; it only reveals which aspects of different cultures are truly diverse.

Yet to ignore the unifying features would be tantamount, in human biology, to being intensely interested in population variations in blood pressure, while declining to learn the fundamental relationships among heart rate, cardiac output, and blood pressure; or to documenting elaborately the height difference between the Watusi and the Pygmies while denying any interest at all in the fundamental actions of growth hormone.

In other words, it is a scientifically inexcusable kind of nihilism. And, ironically, it is the product of ethnocentrism among anthropologists themselves; but here the "in-group" is anthropology, and the disdained, ignored out-groups are ethology, sociobiology, and neuropsychology, among other disciplines.

Nevertheless, the elucidation of universal features of human behavior and culture is increasingly being recognized as one of the central tasks of the discipline, and one likely to enhance, not hinder, the analysis of cultural variation. Recently the distinguished anthropological linguist Joseph Greenberg, of Stanford University, has said, "Whenever the cross-cultural distribution of linguistic forms is not random, that is evidence of an underlying causal principle subject to generalization." Of these, he goes on to point out, the simplest is that there is no variation at all—that the particular language feature is universal. This harks back to Hockett's earlier formulation, but has now resulted in a four-volume work edited by Greenberg and his colleague Charles Ferguson, *Universals of Language,* that makes Hockett's pioneering scheme of eight features all languages share seem modest indeed. Prominent among the new language universals are those delineated by Noam Chomsky and his disciples—the universals of grammatical function that go deeper than the observable features, and begin to point toward universals of mind.

Even some cultural anthropologists—most notably Claude Lévi-Strauss, the great French structuralist—have attempted to delineate universal elements in symbol systems and mental structures. Such characteristics link widely disparate surface manifestations in art, language, and ritual. One example is the duality Lévi-Strauss has recognized in the themes of many myths. This model provided new insight into the workings of the so-called savage mind—a category that, in Lévi-Strauss's view, includes our own culture's allegedly more complex mental functions.

Recent discoveries not only in neuropsychology but in genetics help to explain why all these universals exist. Using the latest methods of molecular biology, several different investigators have estimated the time and place of the point of origin of all current human populations. The method involves sequencing the DNA in mitochondria, which allows investigators to reconstruct the mutation events that have led to the current worldwide distribution. While the attempt by journalists to depict a single "Eve"—one woman from whom we all stem—is exaggerated, there is no doubt that a small population bottleneck occurred some time between a hundred thousand and two hundred thousand years ago.

This is amazingly recent, as human origins go. The famous Lucy, for instance, was an australopithecine ancestor of ours who made her mark more than three million years ago. Even the use of fire in cooking dates back at least three hundred thousand years—around the same as the documented age of *Homo sapiens,* our species. The mitochondrial DNA studies show conclusively that all existing human populations derived from a common point of origin at least a hundred thousand years after our species evolved. Some small—very small—minority of the human population of that time gave rise to all who inhabit the planet today.

Small wonder, then, that the search for human behavioral and cultural variation has tossed up a fair number of robust universals. We all of us have quite similar brains. Our small coterie of ancestors back in the bottleneck bequeathed us those brains in the form of the genes that guide brain development. The eyebrow flash in greeting, the displacement function of language, and even the horror of homicide depends on features of those brains—mostly still obscure— just as warmth under the collar depends on the stimulation of fat-burning by aroused sympathetic nerves.

It's only a matter of time before those brain functions are described by neuropsychologists. In fact, odd as it seems, cultural anthropology, by inadvertently unearthing universals of human behavior, continues to elucidate functions of the brain. After all, that organ's principal output is behavior. Look into the eyes of an Rwandan Pygmy hunter or a Tahitian princess and—after, of course, the requisite eyebrow flash—you will see into a brain that works more or less like yours does; that will show terror using the same facial muscles, or master your language and then tell you how terror feels. Biopsychologically, you are staring into a mirror.

In this light, we can reconsider Bohannon's exchange with the Tiv. Certainly, the elders' bewilderment reflected their own, unique cultural expectations. But one can discern, beneath their confusion, a foundation of common understanding. Despite their belief that it was Claudius's duty to marry Gertrude, the Tiv were still outraged by the possibility that Claudius might have murdered his brother. They understood perfectly Hamlet's conflict between revenge for his father's death and grief at the thought of murdering his own uncle. And although they thought witchcraft had muddied the waters (much as a Western reader would assume madness had), they still responded to much of the play as we do: throughout its telling, they were riveted, and at the end they said, as we have said, "That was a very good story."

GENES AND

THE SOUL

"Imagine the enormous differences that would be found in the personalities of twins with identical genetic endowments if they were raised apart in two different families," a psychology text urged in 1981. But since then research on the personalities, habits, and quirks of identical twins reared apart has suggested a surprising result for the exercise. Consider Jim Lewis and Jim Springer, separated at birth and brought together at age forty. Both had taken law-enforcement training. Both had blueprinting, drafting, and carpentry as hobbies. Lewis had been married three times, Springer twice. Both first wives were named Linda; both second wives, Betty. Each had given his first son the name James Allan. Each had a dog named Toy. Of their first meeting, Lewis remarked that "it was like looking in a mirror." When they enrolled in an ongoing twin study at the University of Minnesota, they were found to have similar IQs, personality scores, electroencephalograms, electrocardiograms, fingerprints, and handwriting. As Springer put it, "all the tests we took looked like one person had taken them twice."

These are chilling statements for anyone who cares about human individuality. Not surprisingly, identical twins reunited in adulthood have experienced strong emotions, ranging from disgust to what Susan Farber, a clinical psychologist at New York University, has called "a strange, boundary-blurring union." *Who am I?* is one of the most basic human questions, and the answer provided by meeting another person who is in effect a flesh-and-blood mirror-image can only be unsettling. The answer at that moment must be something like *No one very special.*

Given which, it is not exactly amazing that twin studies of personality—and human behavior genetics in general—have produced some of the bitterest controversies in all of twentieth-century science. The challenge to individual identity is only part of the threat. Even more important, perhaps, is the challenge to human potential: not just who we are but who we might become. It is this "predestination" part of the behavior genetic story—the surreptitious modern return of the ancient, classical Fates, which we thought we had abandoned in the eighteenth-century Enlightenment—that makes us irretrievably uneasy. If a few strings of nucleic acids tossed together in the heat of lust control our psychological lives, unfolding for most of a century, then what does this say about social programs? morals? education? psychotherapy? What of our hopes for ourselves, or even our children?

During the 1960s and 1970s, scientists exploring genetic answers to psychological questions evoked strong, even violent passions from well-meaning people disturbed by these implications. Sandra Scarr, the doyenne of developmental behavior genetics—a brilliant psychologist with a dignified, appealing personal style—was spat upon by demonstrators. E. O. Wilson, the respected intellectual leader of the new field of sociobiology, which attempted to find the evolutionary underpinnings of behavior, had water poured on his head as he sat on the podium at the annual meeting of the American Association for the Advancement of Science. Picketers and hecklers intimidated professors and students at many universities. It was not a noble passage in the story of science in America.

Most of the scientists who had come under attack held no brief for political applications of their discoveries, and gradually the controversy waned. But in the meanwhile, greatly improved twin studies, together with other data from adoption and family studies and, most recently, studies using DNA technologies, have relentlessly, step by step, removed any basis for doubt about the psychological impact of genes.

For instance, beyond the anecdotes like that of the Springer twins, there are the real results of the University of Minnesota Twin Study, published in the *Journal of Personality and Social Psychology* in June 1988. A team of investigators, including Auke Tellegen and David Lykken, administered a well-validated personality questionnaire to 402 pairs of twins. Two hundred sixty-one were identical—monozygotic, or one-egg, twins, sharing all the same genes; of these 44 pairs were reared apart. One hundred forty-one were nonidentical—dizygotic, or two-egg, sharing no more genes than ordinary siblings—of whom 27 were reared apart.

Sophisticated statistical methods were used to measure the forces—genes, shared family environment, nonshared individual environment, and interplay among these forces—that affect variation in personality. Subjects' replies to hundreds of questions about their inclinations and preferences were statistically summarized to produce scores on eleven primary scales, including well-being, achievement, social closeness, stress reaction, alienation, aggression, and even traditionalism. The estimated genetic contribution to individual differences ranged from 39 percent for achievement to 55 percent for harm avoidance.

These high proportions are important in their own right, but the investigators also combined the scales to produce three broader factors: *positive emotionality*, or active, pleasurable, effective interactions with surroundings; *negative emotionality*, or involvement in life in a negative way, with frequent stress, anxiety, and anger (this was not the opposite of positive emotionality, since one person at different times could be high on both); and *constraint*, or restrained, cautious, deferential, and conventional attitudes and behavior—avoiding danger or impulsive thrill seeking. These three factors were then analyzed, using twin similarities and differences: positive emotionality had a genetic contribution of 40 percent; negative emotionality, 55 percent, and constraint, 58 percent.

To the skeptical eye of a behavioral scientist, the results are stunning: "about 50 percent of measured personality diversity can be attributed to genetic diversity." This is already a much larger proportion than the zeitgeist of late-twentieth-century America—with our commitment to human potential, formative parenting, and psychotherapy—would lead us to expect. While this would seem to imply that the remaining 50 percent is explained by environmental effects, that is an oversimplification. In fact, at least 15 percent of that remainder is measurement error, inflating the estimate of the environmental contribution; thus, a clear majority of the accurately measured variation is genetic. The match between identical twins reared apart is "remarkably similar" to that of identical twins reared together. And the match between *non*identical twins, regardless of rearing condition, is much less impressive.

The inclusion of all four types of twins also made it possible to estimate just where the *environmental* influences came from, after the role of the genes was accounted for. The result—again, surprising to those who have not been following the research of the eighties—was that the great majority of the *non*genetic part comes from environmental effects *specific to the individual*, not from effects shared by children living in the same family. That is, they could be experiences with different friends or different schooling, or distinct family influences—parental favoritism toward one sibling, for example—but they would be much less likely to be things like a weak father or an ungenerous mother or a late bedtime or a prohibition of television, which would be experienced more or less equally by all siblings.

These two conclusions—that the main explanation for personality differences is genetic, and that the family environment shared by siblings contributes only a little to the remainder—so fly in the face of our modern beliefs about how we have come to be who we are, that we understandably find ourselves groping for flaws in the study. Although it is an unusually fine study, designed to avoid the weaknesses of earlier twin research, it can be criticized, of course. But it is only the most famous of several major studies and many minor ones, using not only twins but also natural and adoptive families. Of the two main conclusions of the Minnesota study, virtually all others support the first, and most support the second.

In fact, as early as 1976, a study of 850 twin pairs conducted by John Loehlin and Robert Nichols, psychologists at the University of Texas provided a first indication of the inadequacy of conventional wisdom. It was not just that the genetic contribution to personality was large; it was the then puzzling conclusion that little of the twins' parallels in personality could be attributed to parallels in their treatments while growing up. All twin pairs in this study were reared together, but the authors' review of previously published literature on twins reared apart led them to conclude that being separated permanently early in life does not give identical twins different personalities, and that being brought up in the same family "may even make them less alike."

In 1981 Susan Farber reached a similar conclusion. In her book *Identical Twins Reared Apart* she said, "The more separated the twins, the more similar they appeared to be on personality tests." In fact, the similarities were "so striking as to be unnerving"—and not just in realms such as mood and patterns of anxiety. "Why," Farber asked, "should most of these twins laugh alike, describe symptoms in the same way, smoke similar numbers of cigarettes, choose similar creative pursuits, and sometimes even marry the same number of times? . . . Someone will have to fathom why twins reared in different environments should so frequently bite their nails, grimace, snicker, tap their fingers, and even have 'neurotic' symptoms . . . in such similar ways." Her anguish in discussing the implications for psychotherapy, with its strong commitment to environmental influence, is palpable.

Meanwhile, others around the nation and the world were amassing new and better data. Hans J. Eysenck, Sybil Eysenck, and Michael Eysenck, along with others in the Institute of Psychiatry of the University of London, have worked for decades to understand the structure of personality and its genetic underpinnings. Three broad factors, usually called extraversion, neuroticism, and psychoticism, have been confirmed in study after study; these bear a strong similarity to positive emotionality, negative emotionality, and constraint, the factors in the Minnesota Twin Study. The dimensions have held up repeatedly, in tests of both sexes, and in a number of different countries, including England, Spain, Iceland, and Singapore.

People scoring high on extraversion are sociable, lively, active, assertive, sensation seeking, carefree, dominant, surgent, and venturesome; those high in neuroticism are anxious, depressed, guilt-ridden, low in self-esteem, tense, irrational, shy, moody, and emotional; and those with high psychoticism scores tend to be aggressive, cold, egocentric, impersonal, impulsive, antisocial, unempathic, creative, and tough-minded.

Clearly, different scales of personality with different emphases can sometimes produce other patterns. Some critics propose that psychoticism should be called psychopathy, to indicate antisocial behavior rather than mental illness, but this is a matter of labeling. Other heritable personality factors, such as sensation seeking, can be broken down so that they fit the Eysenck three-factor pattern. Many studies that have looked at the heritability of the three have found it to be substantial—of the same order of magnitude as the Minnesota study found for its three factors. About half the variation, possibly more, is genetic.

In two recent examples, unprecedentedly large—really massive—twin studies have been undertaken in Sweden and Finland, where systematic national records make such research possible. The Swedish study, led by Birgitta Floderus-Myrhed, included 12,898 twin pairs, 5,025 of which were identical pairs. A shorter form of the Eysenck inventory was used, but factors closely resembling extraversion and neuroticism were extracted. The identical twin correlations resembled those in the Eysenck and Minnesota studies, and were more than double the correlations for nonidentical same-sex twins, indicating once again that at least half the variation was genetic.

In Finland, a collaborative effort between Richard Rose, a psychologist at the University of Indiana, and a Finnish team led by Heimo Langinvainio examined 7,144 twin pairs, 2,320 of which were identical pairs. The correlations confirmed again the Eysenck finding showing inheritance of extraversion and neuroticism. Unlike the Swedish group, Rose and his colleagues were able to divide the sample according to the degree of social contact between adult twins. The more frequent the contact, they found, the more similar the twins were on personality measures. Since identical twins exhibit substantial differences as well as great similarities, they reasonably concluded that degree of contact influences the degree of difference. No one has claimed that environment is unimportant in the formation of personality; it's just that modern research has registered a stronger claim for genetic influence than has ever before been reasonable. Rose has also collaborated with psychologists Kay Phillips and David Fulker of the University of Colorado in a sophisticated study of common phobias in twins, nontwin siblings, and their parents. Fears of dangerous places, morbid settings, illness, heights, social criticism, and social responsibility were all shown to be partly heritable, in decreasing order of genetic influence—although not to the same extent as the major personality dimensions. And in a new study of 820 twin pairs followed from adolescence to young adulthood, Rose found six out of nine factors of the widely used Minnesota Multiphasic Personality Inventory—neuroticism, psychoticism, extraversion, somatic complaints, inadequacy, and cynicism—to be highly heritable, with values comparable to those found previously in older twins.

Alcohol use and abuse has also been a research interest of Rose's. Relying again on the Finnish sample, he collaborated with Jaako Kaprio, of the University of Helsinki, and others, studying 879 identical and 1940 nonidentical pairs of twin brothers. High heritabilities were found for measures of alcohol use, including frequency of beer consumption, frequency of spirit consumption, drinking a lot on one occasion, and overall quantity consumed. Teetotaling, studied separately, also showed a much higher rate of similarity for identical than for nonidentical twins. Only the experience of passing out while drinking showed no heritable component.

Such evidence for a genetic factor in alcoholism grows. C. Robert Cloninger, a psychiatrist at Washington University in Saint Louis, summarized his research and that of others in an article in *Science* in 1987: "The strong familial aggregation of alcohol abuse is one of the most robust observations in medical research." In more than one hundred studies alcoholism has been found to be three to five times as frequent in the parents, siblings, and children of alcoholics as it is among people in general. Being raised by alcoholics as an adopted child does not increase your risk, but having alcoholic biological parents certainly does, no matter who raises you. You can even inherit either of the two specific types of alcoholism: an early-onset, usually male type associated with fighting and arrests, or a late-onset type affecting both sexes, associated with guilt and depression. An environment that encourages drinking is important, especially for the late-onset type, but without a genetic predisposition it is rarely enough.

So far these are all statistical studies of adults. They show that something in people's genetic background is very important, but they do not show how. "Genes" alone don't amount to a theory of how these family and twin patterns manifest themselves in behavior. Such a theory requires research into the physiological underpinnings of the behavior; when and how the behavior emerges during the course of development; and, finally, direct studies of the genes themselves using modern DNA technology. These three steps carry behavior backward, through the body and brain's machinery, to the chemical materials that form the genetic foundation.

Physiological studies have begun to provide corroborating evidence for many of the statistics in twin and adoption studies. Sensation seeking has been proposed to be related to the activity of catecholamine neurotransmitter systems in the brain. Those at genetic risk for alcohol abuse have distinctive ways of metabolizing alcohol, and even distinctive electroencephalograms. Schizophrenia may well have something to do with abnormal receptors for the key neurotransmitter dopamine. Such hypotheses are at an early stage of their development, and in the past similar physiological theories have come and gone, leaving only embarrassment in their wake. (For example, one "promising" biochemical factor in schizophrenia turned out to be the result not of illness but of something in mental-hospital diets.) Yet the interplay between physiological theory and the behavior genetic research we have been tracing is one of the healthiest trends in modern psychology.

Second, behavior genetics has at last acquired a genuinely *developmental* dimension. Under the leadership of Sandra Scarr, Robert Plomin, Jerome Kagan, and others, psychologists have begun to address the mystery of how personality unfolds from infancy to adulthood as our genetic predispositions confront a succession of environments. Scarr has advanced a theory emphasizing the child's ability to organize around itself the psychological environment it needs because of the genes it has; in this view, environment is only the genes' handmaiden. Plomin has focused on the part of family life that is experienced differently by two different siblings rather than on the shared family environment. And Kagan has meticulously documented the stability of one temperamental dimension—timidity—in infants and young children, and tried to understand how this genetically influenced trait unfolds.

And finally there is that newly discovered continent, which we have just now set foot on: direct study of the "behavioral genes" themselves—the molecular genetics of the nervous system. Huntington's disease, a movement disorder whose first manifestations are often emotional, has been localized to a region on the short arm of chromosome 4. One form of Alzheimer's disease, with its devastating memory loss and consequent loss of identity, has been tentatively traced to chromosome 21. Manic-depressive illness, a disorder of catastrophic mood swings, has been linked, tentatively, to the X chromosome. Schizophrenia may be influenced by a gene on chromosome 5. With these tentative discoveries we have begun the genetic "dissection" of the human brain. As these genes are pinned down, the way they work will become apparent in a direct chemical sense, and the mystery of how genes could affect the mind will begin to dissolve before our eyes.

Already various laboratories are working out in animal models the structure of genes for key functional proteins of the nervous system: ion channels in the nerve cell membrane, which form the basis of all the brain's electrical activity; receptors for neurotransmitters, which make possible the conveying of specific messages from one brain center to another; enzymes for neurotransmitter manufacture and removal; and neuromodulators, hormonelike chains of amino acids that modify the responsiveness of brain cells. These lines of research will ultimately converge to provide a convincing physiological substrate for the conventional genetics of behavior.

Even the gap between sociobiological, or neo-Darwinian, theory and the data of behavioral genetics has begun to close. J. Phillippe Rushton, working with Eysenck's London group but grounded in evolutionary theory, has looked at the heritability of altruism and aggression—central behaviors for Darwinians—in an otherwise conventional 1986 personality study of 573 twin pairs. Items like "I have given directions to a stranger" and "I have donated blood" were part of the altruism rating form, while "Some people think I have a violent temper" was one of the items on the aggression form. As in more general studies of the genetics of personality, genes were found to account for at least half the spectrum of differences. One common criticism of sociobiology in the 1970s—that there was no evidence for heritability of its most important behaviors, altruism and aggression—is thus being laid to rest.

No one doubts that the environment is important—the genetic studies prove that as much as they prove the importance of the genes. Half the variation may be heritable, or perhaps a bit more than half; but the rest—a very large amount—is still environmental. Some of that environmental influence is undoubtedly prenatal—nutrition, hormones, maternal-fetal immune responses, even the process of birth itself—and child psychologists still underestimate the importance of such environmental forces. But however skeptical the hard-liners may be about the importance of human childhood experience, studies of early deprivation and stimulation in rats, dogs, and monkeys show decisively that such experience changes the personality. It's just that in humans, we don't know *how*; it is perhaps the crowning irony of current research that we need behavior genetics to help us find out.

We speak of a "timid" soul, a "troubled" soul, a "hearty" soul, an "inward" one; a "temperate" soul, a "vengeful," a "generous," a "venturesome" one. These and countless other phrases using words like "soul," "spirit," or "character"— and much more so, words like "personality"—are now being shaken by a biological revolution. Medieval, even ancient ideas about our constitutional predisposition to certain character types—choleric and quick to anger, say, or phlegmatic and unemotional—are rising up again, in altered form, with data to back them up.

Explosive advances in conventional behavior genetics—with immensely increased sample size and sophisticated new statistical methods—have occurred during the 1980s, but the sound has not yet been heard by many clinical psychologists or psychiatrists. The unsung heroes of this revolution—Sandra Scarr, Richard Rose, John Loehlin, Robert Plomin, Robert Cloninger, Irving Gottesman, and others—are all old enough to remember the sting of political opposition that made the debates about this subject so nasty during the sixties. One can't exactly blame them for lying a bit low. Some investigators in the field (not the ones mentioned) continue to rush to make policy inferences about race and social class from these data.

The data have no such implications; they relate to individual differences only. But in the circumstances it is not surprising that political opposition to behavior genetics continues, and that leaders in the field who interpret their data responsibly are loath to raise their heads above the trenches. They do solid research year after year and publish it in distinguished journals, but they are not the sorts of people who take to the hustings and let everyone in psychology know the facts in no uncertain terms: that many accepted ideas about the development of the psyche and the treatment of its disorders are wrong, and in a truthful world could not survive much longer.

But what can we do with this information, other than retreat to what Susan Farber, and Freud before her, called "hereditarian nihilism"?

A very great deal. First, we need to recognize that to no small extent we are who we are when we are conceived. To deny this is to deny the very essence of human individuality. We seek our environments and we determine them as much as they determine us. Of the fact that, as shown in some studies, identical twins become more dissimilar after contact, Farber asks, "Is there any more striking example of the need of each individual to be an individual?" Parents who subscribe to an extreme environmentalism often jettison it at the birth of a second child; in spite of their efforts to establish the same environment the child becomes different. Each human infant comes to us unique, and the illusion that we can mold our children exactly as we wish is both authoritarian in intent and hopeless in execution. Even behavior modification, if it is to work, must itself be modified for children with different temperaments.

The same is true of child or adult psychotherapy, which brings us to the second take-home lesson: the contribution of the environment is large and, ironically, increases the more genetic effects can be accounted for. Given a pair of identical twins, only the environment can make them different; and— also ironically—some of our greatest insights into how the environment works have come from studies using genetic paradigms. As a result of such studies, some investigators of personality development have deemphasized the search for causes of personality in the shared family environment and opened an almost uncharted developmental territory—the nonshared, or individualized, environment—the environment that presents itself to each child in a family in a unique and specific way. From intrauterine hormones to sibling jealousy, these effects will teach us much about how the psyche grows.

An ancient prayer asks that we be given the strength to change the things we can change and the wisdom to accept those we cannot; but in this, as in most things, we are left to our own human resources. Thanks to the courage and perseverance of a handful of scientists in the face of unfair criticism, we have in the past decade greatly increased those resources. As we pursue this "genetics of the soul," we can look forward both to greater sympathy for our human foibles and more deliberate influence over them. And we can at least hope for a steady increase in the requisite wisdom and strength.

ART OF

DARKNESS

Robert Lowell, regarded by many as the best American poet since World War II, was repeatedly hospitalized for mental illness—which afflicted him from early adulthood to his death, in 1977. Severe periodic mood swings dragged him from the abject depths of despair to the heights of flighty, unreasoning, and, paradoxically, often painful elation. In his haunting "Skunk Hour," composed in the early fifties, he wrote with characteristic confessional plainness, "My mind's not right," and went on to say,

> I hear
> My ill-spirit sob in each blood cell,
> as if my hand were at its throat. . . .
> I myself am hell . . .

He used similar imagery in his nonconfessional poetry, as in the powerful "After the Surprising Conversions," about a suicide and its aftermath in Puritan Concord. The poem takes the form of a letter from a clergyman to a colleague. The suicide, he writes, was "a man of some renown," but

> He came of melancholy parents; prone
> To secret spells, for years they kept alone—
> His uncle, I believe, was killed of it . . .

After becoming convinced, through a dream, that he is called to trumpet Judgment Day to Concord, the man kills himself inexplicably; the preacher imagines for him a voice saying, "My friend, / Cut your own throat. Cut your own throat. Now! Now!"

The trumpeting of Judgment Day was Lowell's ironic stand-in for his own poetic vision; and like the unfortunate Puritan, he felt his hand at his own throat. The imagery isn't pleasant. Yet the same poem could end, "the bough / cracks with the unpicked apples, and at dawn / The small-mouthed bass breaks water, gorged with spawn." This juxtaposition of the fear and despair of madness with a transcendent aesthetic contemplation and speech occurred beyond the poem as well. Lowell articulated the connection as well as anyone ever has, not only living it but writing both within it and about it; for, to repeat a cliché that has in the past few years been scientifically proven, it's often a fine line between genius and madness.

The nature of this line has been the subject of speculation since ancient times, and has frequently been close to the definition creative people have held for their own genius. In Aristotle's words, "All extraordinary men distinguished in philosophy, politics, poetry and the arts are evidently melancholic," and in Plato's, the poetry of sane men is "beaten all hollow by the poetry of madmen." Artist D. Jablow Hershman and psychiatrist Julian Lieb, writing in *The Key to Genius: Manic-Depression and the Creative Life*, list similar observations made by dozens of artists and thinkers throughout history. Some, like Anton Chekhov, bemoaned their *lack* of a little madness. This supported both the reality of the connection and its limitations: Chekhov's literary genius did not require madness. Still, there is evidence that diagnosable mood disorders did play a role in the creative lives of Newton, Beethoven, Dickens, and van Gogh, to name just a few.

Newton, for instance, spent most of his life alternating between periods of the most intense mental hyperactivity and abject depression. Socially, he swung between extreme isolation and irrational suspicions directed at his closest friends. Physiologically, insomnia and anorexia were intermittent lifelong problems. These features might be brushed aside as a genius's personality quirks, except that he had a full-blown breakdown at age fifty. He hallucinated conversations and experienced other symptoms, including confusion, memory loss, anorexia, insomnia, rage, and paranoia. These symptoms, consistent with the mental state psychiatrists call mania, gave way to a profound depression in which he broke relations with lifelong friends, accusing them of outrageous misdeeds against him.

Yet despite this and other well-known case histories suggesting a connection between creativity and madness, there has been no good research to support the link until very recently. Indeed, until the mid-1980s it was possible for some authorities on creativity to deny that the link exists. Albert Rothenberg, for example, a Harvard psychiatrist who has interviewed hundreds of leading American talents in many fields, found that most were of normal mental health, and challenged the whole concept of a relationship between creativity and madness. But five new studies, all confirming that relationship, should now lay most doubts to rest.

Three of the studies took the approach of identifying writers and artists of distinction and looking at their rates of mental illness. Nancy Andreasen, a biological psychiatrist who held a Ph.D. in English literature before going to medical school—she had written a thesis on John Donne—published the first of the studies, in the October 1987 issue of the *American Journal of Psychiatry*. Thirty faculty members (twenty-seven men and three women) in the Iowa Writers' Workshop—the nation's most distinguished writing program—were compared with a group of occupationally varied controls, including lawyers, hospital administrators, and social workers, who matched the writers in age, sex, and educational attainment. All sixty subjects participated in confidential structured interviews designed to reveal their patterns of both creativity and mental illness, as well as those of their closest relatives.

Andreasen had hypothesized that creativity would show some relation to schizophrenia. Many had likened the thought processes of this severe isolative mental disorder—often including hallucinations and delusions—to bursts of creative genius. The pioneering Swiss psychiatrist Carl Jung had been impressed, early in his psychiatric career—probably too impressed—with the *content* of the delusions of schizophrenic patients; he admired the creative power they often showed, and he embarked on a study of mythology because he believed that great and lasting myths had much in common with schizophrenic fantasies. Anthropologists have gone so far as to speculate—wrongly, it now seems—that schizophrenia might be a viable form of mental life in a culture that values the flights of imagination of its victims. Similar thinking led Andreasen to try to test the hypothesis of a connection between schizophrenia and certifiable writing talent.

But she found no such relationship. Instead, she identified an unexpectedly strong link between creativity and the other leading category of severe mental illness: affective disorder. This disorder includes a unipolar form, consisting of recurring depressions, and a less common, bipolar form—also known as manic-depressive illness—characterized by mood swings, often severe enough to be incapacitating at both extremes. In the depressions, despair can be so total as to prevent all action, and hospitalization may be required for treatment. In the manic phase of the bipolar form, elation may give way to extreme, even delusional risk taking—speeding violations, shopping sprees, petty thefts, compulsive sexual indiscretions, and grandiose, poorly planned business ventures. Thought patterns that are frankly psychotic—"The CIA is watching me through the television"—are not unusual. Drinking problems can go with either form, and the three disorders—depression, manic-depressive illness, and alcoholism—occur side by side in close relatives at a frequency much greater than chance.

Of the thirty writers, twenty-four (80 percent) had experienced one or another type of affective disorder at some time during their lives. Forty-three percent had had bipolar illness to some degree, and another 30 percent alcoholism. Of the thirty control subjects, only nine (30 percent) had had any affective illness; three had been bipolar, and two alcoholic. All three differences between the writers and the controls—a varied group of professionals, including hospital administrators, lawyers, and social workers—were statistically significant, and the overall difference in total affective disorders was highly so. But, as Andreasen notes sadly, "two of the 30 [writers] committed suicide during the 15 years of the study. Issues of statistical significance pale before the clinical implications of this fact."

Two other studies, both even more recent than Andreasen's in Iowa, provide strong support for her conclusions. Kay Jamison, a psychologist at the Johns Hopkins Hospital, studied forty-seven eminent British writers and artists. Nine of the eighteen poets in the sample were already represented in

The Oxford Book of Twentieth-Century English Verse. The other writers studied included eight novelists, eight playwrights, and five biographers. Six of the eight playwrights had won the New York Drama Critics Circle Award, the Evening Standard (London) Drama Award, and/or a Tony Award. Other literary prizes in the group included the Queen's Gold Medal for Poetry and the Hawthornden, Booker, and James Tait Black Memorial prizes. All eight visual artists (painters and sculptors) were either full members or associates of the Royal Academy. Eighty-seven percent were male, and their average age was fifty-three.

Open-ended clinical interviews and questionnaires showed that 38 percent of these outstandingly creative Britons reported having been *treated* for affective disorder, three-fourths of these with medication or even hospitalization. The poets had been most seriously ill; 55 percent had received some treatment for affective disorder, of which all but 5 percent received medication, electric shock, or hospitalization as treatment—not just psychotherapy. Poets in Jamison's sample were also uniquely vulnerable to manic-depressive illness, Lowell's problem. Three (17 percent) of the eighteen poets had been treated for this severe subtype of affective disorder. Playwrights had a higher total proportion of past treatment—63 percent—but mostly with psychotherapy alone. Two of the eight novelists had received medication for depression, as had one of the five biographers and one of the eight artists. Apart from this history of formal psychiatric treatment, 30 percent of the total sample reported having experienced severe mood swings.

Kareen and Hagop Akiskal, working in the department of psychiatry at the University of Tennessee in Memphis, have conducted similar studies—in Paris, of twenty painters, sculptors, and writers, and back in Memphis, of twenty-five blues musicians born in the southeastern United States. Each person in both groups is an established and recognized artist. In contrast to the Iowa and British studies, though, the Akiskals found no history of full manic episodes in any of their forty-five subjects. But what they did find was that about two-thirds of each group had one of two disturbances representing what the investigators call "the soft end of the affective disorder spectrum." These disturbances are hyperthymia, characterized by intermittent periods of agitated activity, and cyclothymia, distinguished by marked mood swings—each in the absence of more severe classic manic-depressive illness.

If, as these three studies show, the creative are more likely than others to suffer affective disorders, is the converse true? Are people with affective disorders abnormally predisposed toward creativity? That is the question the Akiskals next set out to answer, in an ongoing study of seven hundred fifty psychiatric patients in Tennessee. They found no evidence of heightened creativity in several major subgroups of these patients, including those with schizophrenia, combined schizophrenic and affective disorders, unipolar depressions, and, surprisingly, classic manic-depressive, or bipolar, illness with its full-blown manic episodes. The Akiskals did find, however, that bipolar disorders of moderate or mild intensity are more likely—8 percent likely, in fact—to be associated with proven and recognized artistic creativity, creativity at a level of accomplishment not reached by anything like 8 percent of the general population.

From the Akiskals' standpoint, these findings suggest that although mania and depression are not creative states per se, mild to moderate forms of the same states, together with alternations between them, can actually enhance the creativity of individuals suffering from them. They do not deny that some prominent artists have been classic manic-depressives, but argue that these artists' creative work was done in periods of relative health between major episodes of illness—in a sense, at times when their mental states approached the "soft end" of the bipolar spectrum.

Psychologist Ruth Richards and her colleagues at the Harvard Medical School's MacLean Psychiatric Hospital carried the same idea a step farther in a study in Denmark of bipolar patients *and their relatives*. Their August 1988 report in the *Journal of Abnormal Psychology* advanced a formal hypothesis of balanced polymorphism to explain the maintenance of genes for manic-depressive illness in human populations. They drew an analogy to sickle-cell anemia, the best-known example of balanced polymorphism: homozygotes, who carry a double dose of the gene for this hereditary disorder, have a fatal illness, while their heterozygote relatives, carrying only one sickling gene, have little impairment but also have a greater resistance to malaria. Thus in malarial areas the advantaged heterozygotes keep the sickling gene, deadly in homozygotes, in evolutionary play.

Since it is well established not only that manic-depressive illness runs in families but that milder mood disorders—including severe mood swings, depression, and even alcoholism—are linked with classic bipolar illness in the same kin groups, a rough analogy seems valid. If close relatives of patients with affective illness were advantaged in creativity, this could help explain the maintenance of these debilitating mood disorders in the human population over the long course of evolution.

The investigators examined an index group consisting of seventeen manic-depressives in the classic sense, sixteen cyclothymes—patients with milder but still marked mood swings—and eleven normal close relatives of these two groups of patients. Their control group consisted of fifteen normal individuals and eighteen others with psychiatric problems, but *excluding* major affective illness, cyclothymic mood swings, and schizophrenia. Each subject was interviewed for several hours and then blindly rated using Richards's Lifetime Creativity Scales, a paper-and-pencil instrument designed to assess the creativity—vocational or avocational—of people who have not achieved public recognition. Peak lifetime creativity is assessed on a scale from zero to five. A former dancer and choreographer who had directed many productions but subsequently worked for years as a hotel clerk received a vocational rating of four, while a man who had designed in his spare time a complex apparatus to help his handicapped son, and later taught other children to use it, was assigned a rating of four for avocational creativity.

The results supported the hypothesis. Mean peak lifetime creativity was significantly higher in the index group than in the controls, with the highest levels of creativity being not in the manic-depressives but in the cyclothymes and in the normal relatives of people with mood disorders. In interpreting the findings, Richards and her colleagues suggest that some of the normal relatives in question may have been hyperthymic, or otherwise mildly affected with mood problems at the soft end of the bipolar spectrum. Not normalcy alone, but normalcy in the relatives of bipolar patients, predicted greater creativity. The authors aptly suggest that this relationship "may have been overlooked because of a medical-model orientation that focused on dysfunction rather than positive characteristics. . . . Such a compensatory advantage among the relatives of a disorder affecting at least 1 percent of the population could affect a relatively large group of people." Large enough, in other words, to carry the genes forward.

Thus, whether starting with creative genius and seeking affective disorder or starting with affective disorder and looking for creativity, modern research provides support for what Plato and Aristotle suspected. It's not that you have to be crazy to be creative; most creative people are not, and most of the mentally ill—the seriously mentally ill—do not function well enough to do important sustained creative work. But there is now no doubt that the percentage of overlap between the two categories is too high to be explained by chance; it must be explained, instead, by some intrinsic causal linkages.

A few hypotheses have been advanced: the brooding solitude and hypersensitivity of depression leads to special insight; the transforming energy of mania or hyperthymia leads out of that depressed state to a productive one—and those afflicted often experience flights of imagination, together with just that degree of grandiosity needed to push forward an innovative and ambitious project. But at present, reasonable though they may seem, such explanations await investigation.

Meanwhile, in addition to systematic psychiatric research, more conventional historical and biographical studies continue to illuminate the links between mood and creativity. In her summary of Western civilization's great creative past, Jamison lists the names of twenty-six poets and writers unquestionably in the long-term literary canon who were "greatly impaired by their mood disorders," including Blake, Byron, Coleridge, Poe, Shelley, Hart Crane, Goethe, Balzac, Virginia Woolf, and Ernest Hemingway. Similar illnesses affected at least twelve major composers, including Handel, Schumann, Berlioz, Mahler, Rossini, and Tchaikovsky.

Casting an intriguing sidelight on the issue is the work of Donald Goodwin, a psychiatrist who is an authority on alcoholism. Like Nancy Andreasen, he was a literary scholar before going to medical school—in fact, he had studied with Lionel Trilling. Returning to his first pursuit and combining it with his psychiatric expertise, he has, in his 1988 book, *Alcohol and the Writer*, identified what he calls an epidemic of alcoholism among prominent American writers during the first half of the twentieth century. The group includes F. Scott Fitzgerald, William Faulkner, Ernest Hemingway, Eugene O'Neill, John Steinbeck, Malcolm Lowry, Tennessee Williams, Jack London, Truman Capote, Thomas Wolfe, Wallace Stevens, and Robert Lowell, among many others. Goodwin estimates that at least a third of twentieth-century American writers of stature were or are alcoholics by current reasonable definition, and that over seventy percent of American Nobel laureates in literature have been alcoholic as well.

The point is not merely to suggest another way in which creative people can be psychiatrically impaired. Like the soft end of the bipolar spectrum, alcoholism tends to run in families with major affective illness. Although Goodwin sees the phenomenon as an epidemic transmitted largely through cultural means, it likely that there is an underlying biological foundation. Some psychiatrists view alcoholism as being on a continuum with affective disorder, and indeed there is much evidence that many people become alcoholics because they are using this over-the-counter drug to medicate themselves for troubling moods or mood swings. If so, the disproportionate amount of alcoholism among writers provides further evidence of the link between affective illness and the creative life.

In all likelihood, this link is in essence a genetic one. Consider the Memphis Slim song "Born with the Blues," which the Akiskals cite:

My mama had them, her mama had them
Now I've got them too . . .
You just got to inherit the blues.
When I'm sad and lonely, even when I am happy too
All of a sudden, I find myself singing the blues
That's why I know I was born with them.

Slim goes on to name ten other famous singers affected by "the blues." And, as the Akiskals point out, in recognizing their inherited component, and its relationship to singing itself, Slim "demonstrates an insight deeper than that of many psychiatrists."

Today, affective disorders can be successfully treated. Major depression responds to antidepressant drugs, psychotherapy, and electroconvulsive shock, while the decisive treatment for mania is usually lithium, which also helps prevent recurrences. Some patients have reported that lithium dampens their creativity, and current psychiatric research is testing that possibility. But it is more likely that lithium's main effect—like the effect of other mood-stabilizing treatments—is to push a classic manic-depressive toward the soft end of the bipolar spectrum. In contrast to the outcome in Peter Shaffer's frequently cited play *Equus*—in which a psychiatrist cures a psychotic youth only by robbing him of his brilliant and beautiful fantasy life—the probable outcome of the treatment of manic-depressive illness is to make such a fantasy life usable. Lowell himself is a case in point.

Unlike his friend the poet John Berryman, who jumped smilingly off a bridge into the Mississippi River, Robert Lowell did not die by his own hand. He died of a heart attack while on the way to see someone he loved but from whom he had been estranged. "Nobody's here," he had written forlornly in "Skunk Hour," but really he was not alone all that much—someone was usually there. As he says in another poem, his first wife "faced the kingdom of the mad" with him four times, "and dragged me home alive." He was married twice, had children, many friends, students—and doctors. Far from erasing his creativity, the spectrum of modern psychiatric therapies—psychotherapy, drugs such as antidepressants and lithium, hospitalization, and electric shock—kept him well enough, often enough and long enough, so that he was able to create a large body of poetry. Some of his poems, critics believe, will last.

One of these, "Waking in the Blue," describes early morning in Bowditch Hall—a residential unit of the MacLean Psychiatric Hospital in Belmont, Massachusetts, where Lowell usually stayed—with a strange blend of irony and affection. Today the poem hangs in the nurses' station at Bowditch, where it inspires the staff to remember that mental illness can coexist with the greatest creative achievements. Another poem, "Waking Early Sunday Morning," echoed, twenty years later, his imagery of the small-mouthed bass in Concord:

> *O to break loose, like the chinook*
> *salmon jumping and falling back,*
> *nosing up to the impossible*
> *stone and bone-crushing waterfall—*

But the salmon manages "to clear the top on the last try, / alive enough to spawn and die." As he watches it break water, the poet's own body "wakes / to feel the unpolluted joy / and criminal leisure of a boy."

Lowell's courage "to clear the top" and his "unpolluted joy" probably owe something to manic-depressive illness. But the "criminal leisure" in which he created so many fine poems owes much as well to the modern treatments that prevented his illness from being incapacitating and deadly—as it has been to so many artists in the past. One might speculate, in fact, that modern treatment can take a classic manic-depressive and push him toward the soft end of the bipolar spectrum—the range in which artistry is enhanced rather than damaged. In the future, sensitive psychiatrists, working together with their creative patients, will learn to titrate mood swings by varying treatment regimens, in an attempt to optimize creative energy even while they try to minimize psychic pain. As we refine those treatments, fully recognizing at last the partial connection between art and madness, we may release newer, purer, more sustained wellsprings of human creativity.

NERVOUS

ENERGY

A male college student sits in front of a table holding a strange apparatus called a pursuit rotor. A rotating disc about fifteen centimeters in diameter—the size of a small plate—lies before him. On the disc is a small square of light, spinning around with the disc at varying speeds. The young man's job is to try to track the light using a stylus with a photocell in its tip. It requires a certain amount of concentration, and he enjoys the challenge.

Near the disc on the table are dishes holding Chinese noodles and carrot sticks, and also a can of soda. The young man has been told that there happened to have been a party in the room a short while ago, to celebrate the graduation of new Ph.D.s; he should feel free to avail himself of the leftovers. The rotor turns, he tracks it with the stylus, and pretty soon his free hand shoots out to the nibbles, almost as if it had a mind of its own.

Surprising as it seems, some complex theories of how the mind works have come from studies of fidgeting—ordinary, embarrassing, nervous fidgeting. Nail biting, nose scratching, beard pulling, and desk tapping are some of the adult versions. Readjusting yourself in your chair, smoothing your skirt, getting up and pacing, and twirling a pencil are other fidget-favorites. Children extend the list to thumb sucking, nose picking, genital scratching, and other such banes of parental sensibility and dinner-table decorum.

But as our student nibbler showed, the list doesn't end with these more or less empty "spillover" behaviors—repetitive movements with no apparent function. Actions that are clearly purposeful (though not necessarily adaptive)—such as reaching for a potato chip, lighting up a cigarette, sucking at coffee, and pouring a splash of some ethanol-bearing nectar—all, in a way, qualify. (I can still remember the late night when, working on a graduate-school paper instead of a pursuit rotor, I began smoking again after three months away from it. Eventually, I replaced it with safer habits like pencil flipping.)

It's not that those of us who take off our glasses and chomp on the temples are psychological replicas of the inveterate boozer. The alcoholic, like the compulsive smoker or cocaine sniffer, has experienced brain changes due to chronic excess, and the chemical state induced by a drug cannot be compared to what happens when we merely shrug our shoulders aimlessly or twist our own noses between finger and thumb. Nevertheless, what the two categories of behavior have in common turns out not to be trivial.

What we know about all this comes about as much from research on animals as on people. Animals, like humans, have their fidget-favorites. Stressed monkeys hug or bite themselves or rock, while stir-crazy rats lick the cage bars or turn in a circle, and tethered sows being fattened for the slaughterer's blade repetitively bite the bars of the pen, wave their heads, or chew the air.

Some of these behaviors in monkeys and rats have been intensively studied as animal models for aspects of human psychosis. I once did a series of experiments in which stimulant drugs such as amphetamine were injected into caged white rats. Activity was elevated, but not in a random fashion. The animals seemed to concentrate intensely on their aimless activities—gnawing a chip of sawdust, rearing up and down scores of times in one place, or sniffing each of the four corners of the cage in seemingly endless succession. Some of the same behaviors can be induced in animals by means of behavioral stress. Many investigators have seen in these repetitive physical acts an analog of compulsive human behavior, such as hand washing, or of the endlessly repeated verbal musings that plague some schizophrenic patients.

"It made me nervous" or "It's getting on my nerves"—we often say such things of a test, a game, a meeting, a noise, or even a period of waiting. But the phrase contains a folk theory· that the fidgets, including the nibbles, strike us becaus⌐ of some spillover of energy built up in our nerves. This kind of thinking about the brain—sometimes called "hydraulic" because of its analogy to the build up of water pressure in physics—was common a century ago, before the mass of bioelectricity in the nervous system began to be delineated in terms of circuits and chemistry. The concept seems almost meaningless in the light of modern brain science; yet this bit of folk wisdom was due for a revival. The behavior seems unimportant, but an exploration of what the brain does during fidgeting may come close to the core of all behavior.

Like many new paths in science, this line of research began serendipitously. In 1961 John Falk, a Skinnerian psychologist at Rutgers University, was doing a standard experiment on a typical platoon of white rats. The idea was to feed them unpredictably. They could get a pellet of chow by pressing a bar, but the bar was geared to a frustrating timer. The interval between pellets could and did vary randomly from three seconds to two minutes. The rats pressed at a slow, steady rate and were rewarded with an occasional pellet. They got the job done: as in many another psychological experiment, they learned enough about the task to keep themselves satisfactorily fed.

But, unexpectedly, they also drank enormous amounts of water. As another investigator was to recall much later, "A 200-gram rat would drink half its body weight in water in three hours. He'd balloon out practically to a football shape. Turn him over and water would pour out of him. The cage would be awash with water."

At first the finding seemed a mere laboratory curio; the largest implication announced in the abstract of the paper published in *Science* was that "it might serve as a useful tool in the study of renal function." Yet this behavior had nothing to do with real bodily needs. On the contrary, it seemed "crazy": useless, eccentric, excessive. It happened to be harmless. But could it have implications for other useless, troubling, even damaging eccentricities?

As Falk and other investigators began to explore it further, the phenomenon proved limited neither to rats nor to drinking. Schedules of reinforcement, it turned out, could produce excessive behavior that was as varied as it was pointless. Chewing inedible substances, attacking without cause, running in an activity wheel, and licking air were among the behaviors pursued to pointless excess by species as varied as guinea pigs, gerbils, rhesus monkeys, and pigeons. Nevertheless, the phenomenon—which began to be called "off-task" or "adjunctive" behavior, since it appeared as an adjunct to reinforcement schedules for *other* behaviors—remained a relatively minor laboratory curiosity. Then, in the late 1970s, Michael Cantor, a psychologist then at Columbia University, was struck by Falk's discovery (it was he who compared the ballooned rat to a football) and explored it systematically.

Cantor knew that rats would eat or gnaw the cage bars, as well as drink water to excess, under Falk's condition of a feeding schedule with widely varying intervals between the pellets. But he noticed other research reports in the literature showing that a ninety-decibel noise or a not-really-painful pinch on the tail would also make a full rat eat. Evidently, then, it was not something particular about the reinforcement schedule. Rather, there seemed to be a general frustration effect, caused by the schedule in one experiment and the noise or tail-pinch in others.

Cantor and his colleagues began to explore the parallels. They reproduced Falk's drinking experiment with food, and then showed a certain interchangeability between noise-induced and tail-pinch eating: animals that had had the tail-pinch experience could be induced to eat excessively by noise alone, but ordinary animals couldn't. Furthermore, there were individual differences apparently based on genetic background. All rats would show tail-pinch-induced excessive behavior, but they differed in the amounts, and even in the type of behavior, with one group mainly eating in excess and another mainly licking the cage floor. Either way, these were *satiated* animals; all had had plenty to eat and had in fact eaten their fill for days. It seemed as if anxious eating had found its rat counterpart. And if the human analogy were not clear enough, Cantor's group even induced well-fed male rats to overeat enormously by interrupting them in mid copulation.

Cantor began human experiments—although he did resist repeating the last-mentioned rat study, nor did he try the human equivalent of tail-pinching. The tactic used instead to induce human arousal was the more seemly pursuit rotor in the nibbling experiment described earlier.

Not only eating and drinking but "grooming" (hair pulling, nail biting, mouth wiping, and head scratching, among other behaviors) and "fiddling" (touching or handling objects on the table) were carefully scored. In general, the faster the rotor turned, the more spillover behavior there was in all four categories. There were also individual differences: the better trackers were those who tended to eat more, while worse trackers tended to groom or fiddle. (So much for our social prejudice against inveterate nibblers—they seem to function better, not worse, with their habit.) But in any case, the excessive behaviors that went along with the challenging task were just as predictable in human subjects as they had been for years in rats.

People, like rats, could be made to eat, drink, shuffle, and fidget when engaged in a challenging task. Furthermore, as Cantor puts it, "Everyone has an adjunctive behavior signature"—a pattern that balances eating and foot tapping, say, or drinking and pencil twirling. One subject—call him Roger—produced a distinctive balance of self-grooming and eating, never drinking. His and other "signatures" could be recognized immediately from charts showing the relative frequency of the different categories of adjunctive behavior during a session.

Other psychologists showed that a timed reinforcement schedule in children could produce excessive eating, drinking, grooming, and movement—suggesting that childhood hyperactivity might belong in the fidget continuum. And even hospitalized mental patients would pace or drink under similar schedules. In papers called "Bad Habits" and "Feeding the Face," Cantor attempted to draw together all these separate threads of animal and human spillover or excess. All had in common that they were pointless behaviors caused by arousal, which in turn was caused by mild pain, or even just by uncertainty about reward.

Meanwhile, independently, a parallel course was being followed by *physiological* psychologists. These are the kind who explicitly reject Skinner's attempt to treat the brain as an impenetrable "black box." Skinner argued that animal and human behavior must be understood from the study of observable externals—hence the term "behaviorism" as a description of the approach. But physiological psychologists, in contrast, want to know what the devil is going on inside the box. They believe—correctly, it now seems—that studies of brain function and behavior must inform and support each other.

By the 1970s Elliot Valenstein, one of the most distinguished practitioners of the discipline, had discovered that the concept of brain "centers" for the control of certain behaviors had been widely oversold. In particular, the hypothalamus—a key processing center for the emotions and motivation, and for information exchange between the body and the brain—had been prematurely divided up into a center for satiety and one for hunger. This division had been based on brain-stimulation studies in rats. Electrodes were introduced into specified parts of the hypothalamus, and when a small current was turned on, eating of available food would either increase or stop.

Using rats much like the ones studied in the hunger experiments, Valenstein and his colleagues aimed stimulating electrodes at the "hunger center," which was believed to be in the lateral, or side, part of this brain region. But instead of running the current into the brain only when the rat had food in the cage, as in prior studies, they varied the kinds of objects available. This area—the lateral hypothalamus—proved to be a general pathway for activation, not a specific center for anything.

The rat stimulated with food around ate; with water, drank; with sawdust, gnawed; with objects to retrieve and carry, hoarded; with a member of the opposite sex, copulated; and with a potential enemy, attacked. The same rats could be made to switch from one type of response to another, although the same electrode in the same position was used for stimulation. There were no cases in which switching could not be accomplished. "We are not suggesting," the authors concluded, "that any elicited consummatory response may substitute for any other, but rather that the states induced by hypothalamic stimulation are not sufficiently specified to exclude the possibility of response substitution."

The similarity to Falk's and Cantor's interchangeable arousal behaviors was remarkable, and in the mid-eighties the two lines of research converged. Valenstein, together with Guy Mittleman—both were working at the University of Michigan—wanted to know if the behaviors elicited by brain stimulation were fundamentally similar to adjunctive behavior. They studied electrical stimulation of the lateral hypothalamus and schedule-induced drinking in the same individual rats. The result was that the same rats that drank or ate to excess when their brains were stimulated also imbibed intemperately when a reward pattern resembling Falk's was applied.

There was thus a clear crossover in susceptibility. This implied that schedule-induced excessive behavior might make use of the same neural pathway in which electrical stimulation produced eating and drinking. Furthermore, there were consistent individual differences. Some rats tended to drink excessively under either condition and others under neither. This suggested that individual differences in the tendency to excess might eventually be explained by neurological differences. A possible brain basis of bad habits had been found.

In trying to develop a theory to account for these surprising findings, Valenstein reasoned that the discharge of nervous excitation built up in the hypothalamus could in itself be rewarding. This, he knew, harked back not only to folk wisdom but to long neglected instinct theories of animal behavior. It was also reminiscent of the theory of Sigmund Freud, who thought that pleasure consisted of the discharge of pent-up nervous energy in the brain. Falk, in regard to "the psychopathology of everyday life"—slips of the tongue, pointed instances of forgetfulness, and the like—and Cantor, in regard to jokes and laughter, both explained adjunctive behavior in a way that recalled the Freudian notion of overflow. Trying to stay "on task" in the face of uncertainty—for Cantor's human subjects, the effort to track the rotating light—led to nervous eating or fidgeting, just as the uncertainty of a schedule or the mild stress of a tail-pinch have driven many rats to drink.

But we can't avoid activation and arousal; these states are life itself. They keep us moving—"us" meaning all creatures, including the white rat—through a complex, dangerous world in which sitting still is often maladaptive. And even when we do sit still, there is plenty to be aroused about; the one who would make a meal of us is just around the corner. As for frustration, uncertainty, stress—only the dead can escape them. We are locked in to events, internal or external, that constantly charge and recharge the arousal mechanisms in our brains.

Suppressed anger spills over into eating, failure into nail

biting, prolonged hunger into cigarette smoking, thwarted lust into violence. The deadly, hopeless environment of the ghetto turns a person into an alcohol abuser or a mainliner of crack, just as the milder stresses and uncertainties of bourgeois life cause us to cling to cigarettes or lose the battle of the bulge. And the chief executive or armed forces officer famous for grace under pressure—the man on whose brow a bead of sweat never appears, who never gains a pound or raises his hand in public to scratch his head—may discharge his surplus nervous tension with irrational acts, monetary or military, far more dangerous than fidgeting.

The hero of Saul Bellow's novel *Henderson the Rain King*—a man with immense gustatory as well as sexual appetites—says at the outset that his chronic mental state is best described as "I want! I want!" This odd, intransitive use of the verb is not so funny when we realize that all of us share the state to some degree. The psychology textbooks endow us with highly specific motives—we're hungry, we eat, we are satisfied; or we are thirsty, or lustful, or full of rage. But the facts of brain function are otherwise, endowing us instead with a sloppy system of partly interchangeable, indeterminate wantings. Is it any wonder we are so rarely satisfied? That we pursue all sorts of things we don't really need? Perhaps it's God's cleverest joke. Or perhaps it's only the white rat's revenge.

MINDING

THE PAIN

In David Lean's film *Lawrence of Arabia*, the hero is shown playing a boyish game—Lawrence, with almost incredible slowness, twists a burning match head between his thumb and finger until the flame is out. A companion tries it, burns himself, and shouts, "Oh! It damn well hurts!" "Certainly it hurts," Lawrence replies calmly. "Well, what's the trick then?" asks the other, bewildered. "The trick, William Potter, is not minding that it hurts." Lawrence, of course, goes on to become the great and original leader who helps save the British position in the Middle East, while William Potter is lost in the mists of history.

We humans have a bit of a love affair with pain, and with our ability to stand up to it. It is fundamental to our conceptions of our bodies, and also of the minds that live in them. Tolerance for pain in a sense sets our boundaries. In dreadful fantasies of terrorism and persecution, capture and torture, we ask ourselves: How much could I take? When would I give in? Whom would I betray? We don't have to descend to the level of games to puzzle these questions out with an eerie, almost perverse fascination.

Most of us, fortunately, will miss out on the chance to answer them in anything like the imagined situations. But almost all of us have had or will get the chance to experience the pain of illness and injury. The stabbing sensation of a kidney stone, the searing agony of migraine, the explosive pressure of childbirth, the long dull ache of nausea, the chest-crushing weight caused by an oxygen-starved heart, the ever-worsening, seemingly endless, soul-destroying hurt of some terminal cancers—all of these can bring a vivid sense of how much we can stand (and how we can manage it) as real as any we might get from torture, and much more real than that of the match game.

Doctors' ability to deal with these pains is the mark of their profession, and has been since time immemorial. According to some philosophers, the experience of pain is so subjective that none of us can ever be sure that another is in the midst of it. But doctors have resolved this the way the wag resolved Zeno's paradox: confronted with the claim that he could not leave the room because he would first have to go half the way, then half of the remainder, then half of that, and so on, he simply left the room. Similarly, doctors have most often simply treated the pain as if it were real; and as a result of successfully battling this "inscrutable" condition, they have become the most revered of professionals.

Pain is real. But this is not to say that some people do not fake it, or exaggerate it, or use it. Nor, stepping back from these moral questions, can we ignore critical differences in the way individuals, and even cultures, feel, face, and interpret it. How much do these differences matter? And what lessons can we learn from them about how the mind—and beyond it, the cultural framework of language and symbol—can alter the subjective reality of bodily anguish?

Anthropologists have not taken a special interest in pain, but it has often forced itself on their consciousness, and they have documented customs far stranger than the match game. Among some North American Plains Indians, captive fighters were expected to die well under torture, and their public display of courage was as much a source of pride to them as the ingenuity of the torture was to their gloating enemies. For the Pawnee, natives of what is now Nebraska, self-inflicted pain was crucial to a religious ceremony that has become known as the Sun Dance. A man would dig bone shafts into the skin of his chest and, having tied them to a fixed pole with leather thongs, dance away until the bone tore his flesh. When someone survived serious trouble, the Sun Dance expressed gratitude to the gods.

For the Australian aborigines, the ability to bear pain is an essential rite of passage through puberty. Slicing open the underside of a teenage boy's penis is their way of testing his mettle and making him a man. And in any number of African societies, to blithely suffer transformations of the body ranging from facial scarification to removal of the clitoris is considered a sign of manhood or womanhood, as the case might be.

From the standpoint of the Judaeo-Christian tradition— both branches of which have included a cult of martyrdom as well as traditions of self-mortification—we should not be too surprised. That this cross-cultural tendency to toy with pain is not just about machismo is shown by cosmetic scarification of women, by clitoridectomy, and indeed by our own saying "Beauty knows no pain," which has been used to justify cultural practices ranging from suffocating girdles to toe-crushing high-heeled shoes.

In fact, it could be argued that the human ability to tolerate pain evolved precisely in the most feminine possible context: that of childbirth. As we rose from our ape ancestor, the need for a pelvis sturdy enough to bear us walking upright ran counter to the bulging of our brains. This led to what anthro-pologists know as the great evolutionary squeeze—a big baby's head shoving its way out through a stubborn pelvis.

One of the more unusual ways of handling it, among the !Kung San of Botswana, is for a woman to go it alone. As documented by Marjorie Shostak, most women attain this ideal after their second birth. Feeling the labor pains, they leave the village quietly, calling for help if they need it, but preferably *after* the birth; the ultimate ideal is simply to walk back with the baby. And the women are explicit about it being a matter of courage. They also say that fear makes for disastrous births. This is getting close to being a theory of the evolution of courage, and of the ability to tolerate pain, that leaves men far out of the picture.

There is no doubt that !Kung women endure the pain of childbirth with more equanimity than do most Americans, despite running much greater risks. They probably owe this equanimity to their cultural framework for managing fear. This involves extensive social support in the first birth, followed by a gradual transfer of responsibility—and of empowerment—in subsequent births, to the laboring mother herself. Women give birth alone during the later births, having experienced a process of adult development of pain tolerance in a uniquely encouraging cultural setting.

Similarly, a study of Nepalese mountain porters with a lifetime of experience trekking through hard terrain showed that they are just not as distressed as Westerners by the same level of physical pain. Experimental analysis showed that the porters recognized the electrical stimuli to the same extent at all levels, but were much more stoical than Westerners in reacting, whether the stimulus was described as "faint pain" or "very painful." Overall, the degree of disturbance caused by the pain was well correlated with the individual's past exposure to uncomfortable or even harsh living conditions. In the case of the porters, this included being "accustomed to carrying seventy-seven-pound packs at high altitudes wearing only light clothing, even at freezing temperatures."

Even American subcultures differ systematically in pain tolerance and reactions. A classic study by cultural anthropologist Mark Zborowski on patients in a Bronx hospital compared ethnic Italians and Jews with "Old Americans"—mainly WASPs. Both Italian-Americans and Jewish-Americans complained, even cried about their pain, while the Old Americans kept a stiff upper lip. But the Italians believed in their doctors, and once the pain was dealt with, were satisfied. The Jews and the Old Americans were skeptical of doctors; and the Jews were so anxious about the significance of the pain that they sometimes wanted to keep it—miserable as it made them—so as not to be lulled into a false sense of security about the underlying disease.

These findings, along with extensive psychological research in laboratory settings, show that learning and mental factors in general exert a powerful influence on the degree of pain experienced for a given injury. Even within one subculture, soldiers wounded at the front were shown to have experienced less pain than others who suffered similar wounds in peacetime. Hypnosis, suggestion, preparedness, biofeedback—all have been proven to moderate pain in a large proportion of victims. Yet much remains to be understood about how the body and brain process pain, and we are even farther from an explanation of how the "top-down," or psychological, factors may work.

But what we do know comes largely from analyzing the impact of drugs that have been used by various cultures to fight pain, and then refined by Western pharmacology. They constitute a systematic approach to understanding how the body delivers a painful sensation from the site of injury to the core of the self. And, interestingly, they have origins that are as geographically wide and historically deep as are the cultural methods of pain management already described. The attempt to manage pain with natural plant-derived remedies is probably as old as our species. Doctors like to think that we have invented most important drugs based on knowledge of how the body works. But as far as drugs for pain go, something like the reverse has been true.

Aspirin, for instance, stems from a compound found in the bark of the willow tree, which was used traditionally by the Cherokee and other Indians of the eastern woodlands of North America. The Reverend Edmund Stone reported to the Royal Society of London in 1763 that he had tasted it, presumed it was medicinal, and given it to about fifty people suffering from rheumatoid arthritis; he claimed benefit to all of them. Two centuries of clinical experience, billions of doses, and thousands of modern experiments finally showed how this remarkable substance works. Prostaglandins—chemicals produced in the skin and some other organs upon injury—cause local nagging pain by irritating nerve endings; aspirin (like other similar drugs) inhibits a key enzyme called cyclo-oxygenase, and thus keeps prostaglandins from being made.

This is the first way station of pain delivery, and the only one that does not (just yet) involve the nervous system. Whether it is a persistent, nagging ache or the instantaneous stab caused by burning or cutting, the next link in the pain chain is the nerves that lead toward the spinal cord. One reason we can be sure that these nerves carry the message of pain is thanks to another drug that began as a folk remedy: cocaine, purified in 1860 from the coca plant traditionally chewed by the Indians of Peru. German scientists (Sigmund Freud among them) adapted cocaine for dulling the pain of surgery, by local application to the skin or eye—not by the systemic effect for which it is known on the street. Modern drugs such as Novocain and Xylocaine resemble it, and all such drugs work by blocking the electrical discharge of the nerve. It is the long tubular membrane of the nerve cell that carries electricity, and when the discharge gets to the spinal cord, a pain-signaling chemical known as "substance P" (actually a chain of eleven amino acids) is released there. But the local anesthetic makes the membrane unresponsive by making it less permeable to sodium ions; no substance P is released, and no painful message is sent to the brain. Blockade of the release of substance P has also been shown to result from stimulation of certain higher brain regions; this has helped to provide a basis for understanding the psychological modulation of pain—if the brain can affect chemicals in the spinal cord, then maybe the mind can.

Still, the most exciting discoveries have been about the brain itself—the supervising organ that *notices* the pain, and that sends messages down to the spinal cord to regulate incoming pain traffic. Here too, as with aspirin and cocaine, the story began with drugs known for centuries. Opium, and its derivatives heroin and morphine—named for Morpheus, the Greek god of dreams—came originally from the poppy plant. Its seeds have been found by archaeologists in excavations of Swiss lake dwellings six thousand years old, and over three thousand years ago its use was reported in Egypt. Yet it was not until the early 1970s that experiments began to reveal how it works. From evidence about the timing and nature of morphine's action, Lars Turenius, Avram Goldstein, Candace Pert, Solomon Snyder, and other brain chemists reasoned that there must be receptors—locks fit by a chemical key—for morphine in the brain. Having found and mapped them using radioactively tagged forms of the drug, they speculated that the brain wouldn't *have* receptors for morphine unless it also had a similar substance of its own; and within a few years, "the brain's own morphine"—the now famous *endorphins,* short for "endogenous morphines"—had been accurately described.

These endorphins (like substance P, each is a small chain of amino acids) have provided more insights into pain in the past decade than we have gained in all the previous history of science. And they may also help to explain many individual and cultural differences in response to pain. As is now well known, when our brains release endorphins it is a bit like having a shot of morphine. But people must differ in their ability to produce endorphins. And a variety of activities and conditions can produce them temporarily—conditions that have begun to form a pattern. For example, acupuncture releases endorphins, and its pain-blocking effect—proven in countless major operations in modern China, as well as in experiments in the West—depends on them. (Another drug, naloxone, which blocks endorphin receptors, also prevents the anesthetic effect of acupuncture.) Electrical stimulation of a central region of the brain stem can be used to help people with severe chronic pain—such stimulation releases endorphins into the fluid bathing the brain. Endorphins have also been implicated in long-distance running and in pregnancy and labor. Even prolonged stress makes us produce more endorphins.

But hypnosis blocks pain *without* releasing them, and so do certain kinds of brain damage. This means that the brain, and the mind that lives in it, can reduce pain—or worsen it—through at least two different mechanisms, one using endorphins, one not. The deservedly maligned frontal lobotomy did help pain patients, but they said they still felt the pain—they just didn't care about it anymore. Much safer present-day brain operations such as cingulotomy seem to help with chronic pain, although we don't know how they do it. A few individuals who have come to the attention of physicians are incapable of experiencing pain, and this tragic defect can lead to fatal injury. But investigations of their brains have yielded few clues as to what the defect is.

Finally, there is the fascinating fact that many patients with intractable chronic pain—for example, phantom-limb pain, the bizarre persistence of often debilitating pain in an arm or leg that is no longer there—have been helped by standard antidepressant drugs, while in other patients depression can make a minor pain seem major. This further underscores the importance of central-nervous-system states in either intensifying or dampening pain. It is not clear that phantom-limb patients must be depressed to be helped by these drugs, but it does seem that the two states—depression and pain—have more in common chemically than we previously understood.

All these factors—cultural differences, hypnosis, brain surgery, depression—reveal a "top-down" component of pain that is very powerful. Pain is not in any sense located in the spot where the injury is, or for that matter in any place in the nerves or brain. Rather, it is "located" in the vastly complex interacting circuitry of the various components of the system. Thoughts and feelings are reverberations of neural circuits, so in the largest sense it is not a mystery to find that they participate in this intricate interaction. Why, after all, do studies of pain-killing drugs need a placebo control, without which they are not considered really valid? Because the administration of a pill is such a strong symbol that it alone can reduce pain for many people, even when the pill is made of sugar. Something similar may be said about the symbols used to treat pain in primitive cultures—or for that matter, in modern religions. Psychological experiments have proven the efficacy of beliefs and symbols in affecting pain perception. Some people gain relief by imagining themselves, pain-free, on a tropical beach; others by thinking of themselves as wounded soldiers.

The power of simple knowledge was once brought home to me by a particularly noxious stomach virus. I lay in bed for a day doubled up in a fetal position, in a feverish sweat, clutching my belly pathetically, wondering if perhaps what I had was not the typical stomach ailment but some exotic illness I had carried back from Africa, or some mundane but possibly deadly form of food poisoning. I was in agony until my wife called the doctor on duty at the university health services. She—someone I didn't know—listened to my wife's description of the symptoms and said, "Yes, that's going around." Her simple words, transmitted through my wife, reduced my pain drastically and almost immediately.

How does a hurt quarterback sprint through his pain, or a ballerina pirouette magnificently on bloody feet? Why do wounded soldiers need less morphine than civilians recovering from similar surgical wounds? How does prepared childbirth, or the presence of a supportive friend, reduce a woman's pain in labor? The ultimate answers have to do with adaptation— we evolved in situations where we couldn't always afford to stop and lick our wounds. But the much more complex questions about how the machinery works—and how we can learn to make it work in the anguished situations when it doesn't—are only beginning to be answered.

Modern pain clinics often involve psychiatrists at the beginning of the treatment plan—not just after other, physical means of treatment have failed. Pains may be perfectly physical in origin and still respond dramatically to psychological conditions—as Pawnee youths and !Kung laboring women might attest. Blocking pain with hypnosis or placebo is only the tip of an iceberg. Meditation, suggestion, guided imagery, and a positive emotional state all help reduce pain while giving the sufferer some sense of self-control. Formal interventions to provide external support—such as biofeedback, massage, and physical therapy—can work to reduce the sense of loneliness that, along with physical tension, can exacerbate pain. Religion serves a similar function for many patients, who see in it evidence of order in the world, order that makes pain more tolerable.

For predictable pain like that of childbirth, mental preparedness alone can make all the difference—and that applies to the pain of many scheduled medical interventions. And the idea of courage itself has pain-reducing power. Suppression and denial are wonderful mental strategies. We could not have evolved in the past, and we cannot survive in the future, without them. So what if we are kidding ourselves a little? Sometimes we can pretend it doesn't hurt so much, and the pretense can begin to come true.

Of course, we must not deny pain that is trying to tell us something about a serious medical illness. But frequently, after everything that can be done for that illness is done, pain lingers. It may be an inexplicable ache for which the doctor has said, "I can't find anything wrong with you." Or it may be a chronic or recurring pain—arthritis, say, or migraine—which has produced the words "We've done everything we can—you're just going to have to learn to live with it." Or it may be the tragic, desperate pain of advanced cancer, where nothing hopeful can be said and the pain goes on and on. In all these very different cases judicious combinations of drugs, and in extreme cases surgery, will do much to bring relief.

But these tactics alone are not the answer. Ultimately there must also be some element of will, some attempt on the part of the victim to exercise control, some decisive assertion of individual freedom in the face of a restricting, sometimes terrifying pain. And among the relaxation techniques and the biofeedback, the physical therapy and the emotional support, the childbirth-preparation classes and the encounter-group discussions, there must be something at the center—deep within the person who experiences the particular hurt—that can only be described as courage.

THE "I" OF

THE STORM

When I heard that Wade Boggs, the famous Boston Red Sox third baseman, had publicly declared himself a sex addict, it set me to brooding about responsibility.

Now, I admit I'm inherently lazy—not enough to avoid thought altogether, but enough to keep it within certain channels. Boggs got me thinking about some questions I had not taken an interest in since college. For twenty-five years or so I've been thinking about human behavior scientifically—first in anthropology, later in medicine. I was interested in the *causes* of behavior—normal or abnormal—since these could lead to the option of changing it with some sort of treatment.

But the notion of a sex addict—especially a male one—brought me up short. I knew about sex addiction, but (like most health professionals, including most psychiatrists) I was dubious about the category. In a world where the risk of sex is so much greater for women, and where men typically have more power, my natural impulse didn't lean toward medicalized sympathy for fellows who exploited the imbalance.

I thought back on others who have come, at a certain point in life, to regret the sexual excesses of their youth—Saint Augustine, for instance, and Leo Tolstoy. But here something was missing. *They* were saying words like *I did something very wrong. I repent of it now. You should think ill of me, and you probably should punish me—with censure, if noth-*

ing worse—but please, ultimately, forgive me. Present-day "sex addicts," though, are saying something more like *I am a sick man. My sickness did it, not I; right and wrong are not involved. Pity me, help me, take care of me; but whatever you do, don't blame me.* I tried to understand why this bothered me so much; it was not just the spectacle of a powerful man abusing his power and then requesting sympathy. It was the medical question at the heart of the spectacle: how much can the concept of illness expand at the expense of the idea of responsibility?

Although the question ranges far beyond that of illegal acts into the realm of moral dilemmas, most Americans have had this issue brought to their attention in the 1980s by two celebrated criminal cases. First John Hinckley, who attempted to assassinate President Reagan, was determined by some court psychiatrists to be mentally ill—and more important, to be mentally ill in a way that meant he was not guilty as charged. Interestingly, a then-new technique known as computerized axial tomography—CAT scanning—was used to study his brain, and it showed what some experts called an abnormal shape. This testimony suggested a greatly expanded future—even futuristic—role for technology in answering moral questions. Second, Dan White, who had killed the mayor of San Francisco and one of his aides, claimed in his defense that he had eaten a junk-food diet high in refined sugar, and that this diet had diminished his ability to restrain his violent impulses—the celebrated "Twinkie defense." This suggested that almost any medical fad, however poorly supported by evidence, could influence the judicial process.

Both defenses convinced the courts. These strategies are part of a framework of legal reasoning that emerged in the nineteenth century, often referred to as the M'Naghten Rules (pronounced "Mik-NAW-tn"). Daniel M'Naghten had attempted to kill the English prime minister in 1843. M'Naghten had been in the grip of paranoid delusions, but his exculpation, like Hinckley's, produced a public outcry—despite the fact that he had been committed permanently to an asylum. A panel convened by Queen Victoria arrived at the first formal rules for an insanity plea: the accused had to not know either "the nature and quality of the act" or the fact that "he was doing what was wrong." Later an emotion-based defense was added to the essentially knowledge-based approach of the M'Naghten Rules. Although it is usually called "irresistible impulse," the emotion does not have to be sudden for this defense to work. The main point has to do with the loss, due to "mental disease or defect," of the power to choose.

Together these rules made it possible for mental illness to bring a person under the protection of two ancient legal concepts: ignorance and coercion, either of which, in certain circumstances, have always had the power to limit guilt for crime. In the legal tradition that has come down to us today, mental derangement—temporary or long-term—can be used as evidence that the defendant was in the grip of an "irresistible impulse," or that the illness so clouded his judgment that he was ignorant of the moral meaning of what he did as he did it—in the common phrase, "he couldn't tell right from wrong."

"Sex addiction" is no crime, but a wide spectrum of acts of questionable morality—whether legal or not—are now falling under the rubric of "illness." Even as certain categories of human behavior—homosexuality in America, for instance, and perhaps now political nonconformity in the Soviet Union—are being "delisted" from the ranks of psychiatric categories, new diagnoses are being added. Increasingly, doctors—rather than pastors or prosecutors—are taking charge of certain acts by labeling them with a new kind of language. And with these labels they are shaping our emotional reactions to deeds that we once would have said, quite simply, were wrong.

Consider three cases. Once, in a medical-school psychiatry clerkship, I attended a hearing in which the state was trying to show that a man convicted of homicide but found to be mentally ill should continue to be kept in a prison-hospital for the criminally insane. His family retained a lawyer who presented a theory of why the young man had gone on a rampage assaulting a series of people with an ax. The lawyer had read some studies claiming to show that too much copper was a cause of irrational violence. Now, the young man was said to have drunk enormous amounts of milk as a child. According to other studies, milk reduced the absorption of copper. Since, went the theory, an excess of copper could cause violence, probably a deficiency of copper could too.

This argument was not successful—indeed, it was difficult to see its purpose, since the young man was already deemed mentally ill and was being given treatment rather than (merely) being imprisoned. Yet I was stunned: a completely baseless and self-contradictory "scientific" argument was politely heard by all concerned, with no form of reprimand to the lawyer, who had no basis for a claim of expertise.

A year later, returning to the same prison hospital with a psychiatrist-teacher, I helped him interview a young man who had confessed to killing a woman when she reprimanded him for urinating on her lawn. He had been working for a lawn-care company and was apparently exposed to large quantities of organic phosphates, which he was required to handle as fertilizer. The psychiatrist was preparing a case based on the notion that the organic phosphates in the fertilizer had given the man an uncharacteristic violent impulse. I pored through the doctor's stack of photocopied research papers. Organic phosphates in large doses certainly could cause nerve damage, which the young man did not have. Rarely, they had apparently caused brain damage too, but almost always in association with nerve damage. Nowhere in the literature was there a case of brain damage caused by organic phosphates and resulting in violence.

Thirty years earlier a psychiatrist with a Freudian orientation would have seized on the interpersonal situation—a young man urinating in the wrong place is surprised and reprimanded by an older woman—and related the violent outburst to deep problems stemming from his childhood, complete with Oedipus complex and castration anxiety. Now, in the eighties—the era of biological psychiatry—we had instead an equally tortuous, and equally unsupported, biochemical theory.

The third case came closest to home. *I* was approached by a criminal-defense lawyer and asked to testify on behalf of his client. This was a man who, under supposedly extreme provocation, had killed his lover in a fit of jealousy. The lawyer had read a book of mine about human nature, in which I described (among many other things) situations similar to his client's as occurring in cultures throughout the world, and indeed as having parallels in many animal societies. He wanted me to testify to these facts of anthropology, which he would then argue diminished his client's responsibility for the homicide. This was not an insanity defense, but intended instead to show that the man did not have "mens rea"—the criminal intent needed for complete guilt.

While I was wrestling with the ethics of this gambit— Would I be wrong to lend myself to it? Or, in our advocacy system of justice, would I be wrong to refuse to state what I knew?—I was let off the hook by the lawyer, who had found another defense. This too was instructive: his client had taken barbiturates by prescription before the crime, and they had found a psychiatrist who would testify that this could have impaired his capacity to act in accord with the law. The lawyer did not want to confuse the jury by invoking two sorts of exonerating expert testimony, and he was more comfortable with a psychiatric theory of an abnormal state of mind than with an anthropological theory of a passionate, predictable one.

Either way, and in every one of these cases, only the common sense exercised by the jury and the common law interpreted by the judge should count, not the expert testimony. But in reality judges and juries are influenced by experts—including those who go far beyond scientific knowledge in their testimony. And in noncriminal questions of moral judgment, we as a society—including even ethical advisers like ministers, priests, rabbis, and teachers—are inevitably influenced by changing cultural concepts of illness and responsibility.

The extremes in this controversy were staked out many years ago. Karl Menninger, a distinguished psychiatrist, wrote as early as 1928, "The time will come when stealing and murder will be thought of as a symptom, indicating the presence of a disease, a personality disease," and almost a half-century later, in response to the notion that wicked people exist, he said, "I don't believe in such a thing as the 'criminal mind.' Everyone's mind is 'criminal'; we're all *capable* of criminal fantasies and thoughts."

By the late 1950s psychiatry—especially in its Freudian form—was at the peak of its power, and the courts were showing signs of accepting Menninger's thesis. The clergy, for its part, was mastering the art and science of psychotherapy.

We seemed, as a culture, to have gone well down a path toward defining—medicalizing—wickedness out of existence, and with it, punishment. There would only be illness, treatment, and ultimate reintegration of the normalized individual into society. The courts and the churches alike were scrambling to avoid being left behind as the new science led the community in a race out of the sphere of moral judgment, having jettisoned outmoded concepts like responsibility.

In 1961 Thomas Szasz—a psychiatrist—challenged, in his book *The Myth of Mental Illness*, almost every aspect of psychiatry and publicly declared its legal authority to be illegitimate. The book's subtitle, "Foundations of a Theory of Personal Conduct," was significant. "Human behavior," he wrote, "is fundamentally moral behavior." He argued that individuals must be allowed to take drugs, commit suicide, and do harm to others without prior restraint and take the consequences of their acts—addiction, death, or the full force of the law—regardless of psychological conditions. "The concept of mental illness," he wrote elsewhere, "is a betrayal of common sense and of an ethical view of man."

A summary added to the book in 1974 stated, "Psychiatric diagnoses are stigmatizing labels, phrased to resemble medical diagnoses and applied to persons whose behavior annoys or offends others"; and "The introduction of psychiatric considerations into the administration of the criminal law—for example, the insanity plea and verdict, diagnoses of mental incompetence to stand trial, and so forth—corrupt the law and victimize the subject on whose behalf they are ostensibly employed." The title of one of his articles, in the leading British medical journal, *The Lancet*, summarized the viewpoint he has maintained for three decades: "Bad Habits Are Not Diseases."

Partly under his goad, and further stimulated in the eighties by the Hinckley case and the "Twinkie defense," a public outcry has altered the insanity plea. The Model Penal Code of the prestigious American Law Institute had helped codify the common law traditions, but its influence has weakened since Hinckley. The American Bar Association and the American Psychiatric Association both proposed an elimination of the "irresistible impulse" rule. In 1984 the Federal Criminal Code adopted this suggestion, and also abandoned the wording "substantial incapacity" in favor of "complete incapacity." In practical terms very few cases were affected—most crimes are tried under state law—but the message is influential. More than half the states, including especially California, have followed suit on "irresistible impulse." In addition, several states have adopted a new verdict: "guilty but mentally ill," which defense lawyers feel destroys the insanity plea, undermining a traditional pillar of justice.

This public reaction was based in part on major misconceptions. First—contrary to Menninger's sweeping prediction, and despite the famous cases—only a fraction of criminal defenses invoke the insanity plea, and only a fraction of that fraction succeed. Also, studies of arrests show that few crimes, and even fewer violent crimes—under 5 percent—are accounted for by former mental patients. Popular fears aside, very few mental patients are dangerous. Second, experts are not in charge of the decision—a jury and judge are in charge. They review the evidence, hear the expert testimony on both sides, and make the kind of judgment that courts have made for centuries before psychiatry was invented. Third, a successful insanity defense need not "get the guy off the hook and out on the street" promptly. On the contrary, this outcome is rare. In almost all states a verdict of "not guilty by reason of insanity" requires at least the consideration of commitment, and in some states commitment is mandatory.

The near-release of Arthur Jackson in a Los Angeles jurisdiction in 1989 shows what can happen if a sick criminal is *not* medically labeled. Although he assaulted actress Theresa Saldana with exceptional brutality—stabbing her so hard and so many times that his hunting knife bent—and then, while in prison, repeatedly threatened to kill her upon release, he was about to be released early from an ordinary criminal sentence, for good behavior. He had a long history of mental illness before the assault. Ironically, if he had been found not guilty by reason of insanity, his continuing psychosis would have allowed him to be kept behind bars in a prison mental hospital indefinitely. And psychiatric labeling appears to be the best way to prevent his release now.

The idea of using the concept of illness to lengthen detention is anathema to civil libertarians, yet it was narrowly supported by the Supreme Court in 1983, and it may be the most appropriate response in many cases. Some violent crime is the result of mental illness. If detention and deterrence are two of the goals of justice, then they may sometimes be attained more effectively through a medicalized approach. In the heyday of psychiatric exoneration, psychiatrists claimed to know more than they knew. They claimed to be able to predict future behavior and to be able to cure the mental illnesses that cause crime. As pointed out by Szasz and by Jonas Robitscher, who was doubly trained in psychiatry and law, these claims were greatly exaggerated. Robitscher's 1980 book, *The Powers of Psychiatry,* showed some of the limits of the claims, and studies over the past decade have proven him right. Prediction is almost impossible, cure is always partial at best, and even diagnosis cannot be agreed upon by experts in conflict. In Robitscher's words, "The medical basis for psychiatric authority must continue to be questioned."

Yet such authority must also continue to be considered. If

cures for most mental illnesses elude us, diagnosis is in a more advanced state—much better, in fact, than it was even in 1980. Judgments must somehow be both moral and medical. If a jury identifies a crime, it can, with the consultation of experts, also identify an illness. Whether the illness is treatable, resulting in a shorter period of incarceration than simple imprisonment, or untreatable, resulting in longer detention, a fair approach to wrongdoers cannot omit this consideration. Still, medical labeling must not result in the elimination of punishment. Even a hospitalized psychotic is capable of responding to some extent to the threat of punishment. This threat must enter the mind—however diseased—of every person who contemplates a wrongful act. In a world of uncertainties, only capital punishment seems unacceptable; it obviously differs from institutionalization in a way that imprisonment does not. In fact, our frequent inability to rule out mental illness is one of the best arguments against the death penalty. That penalty aside, the decision as to who shall be incarcerated for detention and punishment, and who for detention and treatment, can tolerate a certain amount of ambiguity.

Two stories, one true and one apocryphal, give glimpses of the balance between impulse and blame as it may have appeared at the dawn of human consciousness.

The true one comes from observations by anthropologist Richard Lee of the !Kung San of Botswana. These are people without lawyers or judges—without any legal forms or authority—and certainly without psychiatry. Lee showed that homicides occur among them in a frequency not very different from our own; there is sometimes revenge but there is no legal recourse. However, in one case of a man who had killed three times, the community concluded that he was incurably violent. This, in a sense, was a primitive psychiatric diagnosis, but the response in this society without police or prisons, hospitals or psychiatrists could not be incarceration or medical treatment. With no other choice open to them, three men premeditated his homicide, lay in ambush for him, and killed him.

The second story comes from a midrash—a rabbinic legend—about the conversation between Cain and God in Genesis, regarding Cain's crime of fratricide. According to the midrash, the argument goes on for some time after Cain asks insolently, "Am I my brother's keeper?" His final challenge to God is the most intriguing one: "You made me as I am. You put the evil inclination in me. Therefore I am not responsible." Thus, without mentioning mental illness, an ancient legend raised the same philosophical problem: if evil is built into some personalities, how can we confront them with blame? But the rabbis were not much impressed by Cain's challenge. The Talmud says, "Who is strong? He who conquers his inclination." Cain, they conceded, was—like the rest of us—endowed with an evil inclination, but also with a good one, and with a rational ethical faculty designed to set and keep the balance tipped against evil.

As we move through the 1990s, we as a society will have to accept more and more the evidence that a large part of what we call wickedness is *also* mental illness. Not only psychoses and depressions with delusional features but also certain impulse control disorders, adjustment disorders, sexual disorders, and personality disorders are legitimate psychiatric diagnoses that might tend to cause wrongdoing. And the frontier of diagnosis is moving fast.

Consider an instance of sexual harassment of a female employee by her male boss while he is under the influence of alcohol. He may blame the alcohol, and this tactic would work if he were involuntarily intoxicated. But we expect him to know that drinking may lead to such wrongs, and so we hold him accountable. Now suppose he is an alcoholic. He has a diagnosable substance-abuse disorder. Do we exonerate him because of this illness? Probably not; he should have known better than to drink himself into it. But now we have one last, new twist: in the eighties was decisively shown that some individuals are genetically predisposed to the development of alcoholism. Our man turns out to be one of them (in a few years' time, a test of his DNA may be available to prove it). What do we say now? Do we blame him for an immoral act at the end of a chain of events that began with a hereditary defect? I suspect that the answer is still yes—that we help him and blame him both—but clearly the judgment is not easy.

In the realm of crime, a substantial minority of criminals have what in the past was called psychopathy or sociopathy and is currently called antisocial personality disorder. Such personalities have been extensively studied by psychologists, whether or not they are criminals. Compared to average people, they are sensation seekers whose attachments to others are shallow, who experience little guilt, and who are relatively unresponsive to the threat of punishment. Strictly speaking, such people have a diagnosable mental illness. But the courts have been properly reluctant to accept an insanity plea from someone whose main symptom is repetitive antisocial behavior. Along the same line, the short-lived Durham rule, or "product test," of insanity was applied in the District of Columbia for a decade beginning in 1954. It stated that the insanity plea was valid if the crime was the *product* of the person's mental illness. This rule was dropped because it threatened to widen the insanity plea to encompass most crimes. The courts have thus essentially rejected Menninger's

view in *The Crime of Punishment* that all crime is evidence of
mental illness. "Blame and punishment," says one recent law
textbook, "are central to the criminal law." They are also
central to the moral fabric of society.

There are limits to punishment; a society as complex and
capable as ours only humiliates itself when it resorts to the
same tactic—removal by death—that the otherwise helpless
!Kung were forced to apply. Yet neither can we pretend that
we have advanced very far toward curing the illnesses that
partly cause crime. And if we can't cure mentally ill criminals,
then we need to separate them from potential victims. To
refuse to grant them treatment while they are incarcerated is
simply inhumane to them; but to release them in essentially
the same disordered state of mind in which they committed
crimes before is inhumane both to them and to their victims—
past and future.

In the realm of the moral, addictions to substances like
alcohol or habits like promiscuity do plenty of damage within
the bounds of the law. Say what we like about the people with
these problems—they certainly may have diagnosable mental
illnesses—there must, as in criminal cases, be some sense of
accountability. Even if these individuals have weaknesses that
are greater than average, or impulses stronger than average,
or rational ethical faculties less capable than average, we as a
society must strengthen their self-control—and our own—by
insisting that we all give an account of ourselves as moral
agents. No amount of explanation can be allowed to stand in
the way of this accounting. It is true, as Menninger said, that
we are all capable of criminal fantasies and thoughts; but
only some of us carry them out.

Whether we are talking about a presidential assassin, a
child abuser, a streetwise crack addict, a compulsively promiscuous man, or an alcoholic celebrity drying out at a

famous clinic, some expectation of moral restraint is always applicable. The tension between these two views of unwanted behavior is far from new. Aristotle's *Ethics* includes the observation that "foolish people whose folly arises from disease, e.g., from epilepsy, or from insanity, are in a morbid state," and implies that they are not responsible for their acts; yet he speculates that "it is perhaps wrong to say that actions which are due to passion or desire are involuntary." The Mishnah, which contains much of the foundation of Jewish ethics, observes, "An encounter with a deaf-mute, an idiot, or a minor is bad, for you are liable and they are not"; but it also says, "Man is always responsible, whether his act is intentional or inadvertent, whether he is awake or asleep." And James M. Gustafson, one of the leading Christian ethicists of our time, although widely known for his compassionate liberal theology, said recently, "If all actions for which we might be held responsible are classified as addictions or illnesses, then we totally surrender the sense of moral accountability."

A famous phrase of Freud's is usually translated as "Where id was, there ego shall be," implying a rendering of our irrational impulses to make them accessible to reality. But the passage may really mean "Where 'it' was, there 'I' shall be." This message, something like the opposite of psychological exculpation, is a far superior legacy for Freud to have left us. We would all like to point at an illness—a psychiatric label—and say of our weak or bad actions, "That thing, the illness, *it* did it—not me, it." But at some point we must draw ourselves up to our full height and say in a clear voice what we have done and why it was wrong. And we must use the word "I," not "it" or "illness." I did it. *I. I.*

REFERENCES AND

SUGGESTIONS FOR

FURTHER READING

Introduction

The following background references to the introduction also constitute a basic library of work on the emerging science of human nature.

American Psychiatric Association, *Diagnostic and Statistical Manual of Mental Disorders,* third ed., rev. (Washington, D.C.: American Psychiatric Association, 1987).

Bowlby, John, *Attachment and Loss,* 3 vols. (London: Hogarth, 1969–77).

Changeux, Jean-Pierre, *Neuronal Man: The Biology of Mind* (New York: Oxford University Press, 1985).

Eibl-Eibesfeldt, Irenäus, *Human Ethology* (New York: Aldine de Gruyter, 1989).

Eysenck, Hans, and Michael Eysenck, *Personality and Individual Differences: A Natural Science Approach* (New York: Plenum Press, 1985).

Gardner, Howard, *Frames of Mind: The Theory of Multiple Intelligences* (New York: Basic Books, 1983).

Goodwin, Donald, and Samuel Guze, *Psychiatric Diagnosis,* fourth ed. (New York: Oxford University Press, 1988).

Harris, Marvin, *Culture, People, Nature: An Introduction to General Anthropology,* fifth ed. (New York: Harper & Row, 1988).

———, *Our Kind* (New York: Harper & Row, 1989).

Hume, David, *An Enquiry Concerning Human Understanding*

(Indianapolis: Hackett, 1977). (Originally published in 1748.)

Johnson, Allen, and Timothy Earle, *The Evolution of Human Societies: From Foraging Group to Agrarian State* (Stanford, Calif.: Stanford University Press, 1987).

Kagan, Jerome, *The Nature of the Child* (New York: Basic Books, 1984).

Katchadourian, Herant, *Fundamentals of Human Sexuality,* fourth ed. (New York: Holt, Rinehart & Winston, 1985).

Konner, Melvin, "Anthropology and Psychiatry," in Kaplan, Harold, and Benjamin Sadock, *Comprehensive Textbook of Psychiatry,* fifth ed. (Baltimore: Williams and Wilkins, 1989), pp. 283–99.

———, *The Tangled Wing: Biological Constraints on the Human Spirit* (New York: Henry Holt, 1982).

Lee, Richard, and Irven DeVore, *Man the Hunter* (Chicago: Aldine, 1968).

Lenneberg, Eric, *Biological Foundations of Language* (New York: John Wiley, 1967). Despite its age, the argument of this classic remains valid.

Martin, Joseph, "Molecular Genetics: Applications to the Clinical Neurosciences," *Science* 238 (1987): 765–72.

Mesulam, M-Marsel, *Principles of Behavioral Neurology* (Philadelphia: F. A. Davis, 1985).

Moore, Barrington, Jr., *Reflections on the Causes of Human Misery, and Upon Certain Proposals to Eliminate Them* (Boston: Beacon Press, 1972).

———, *Social Origins of Dictatorship and Democracy: Lord and Peasant in the Making of the Modern World* (Boston: Beacon Press, 1966).

Moyer, K. E., *Violence and Aggression: A Physiological Perspective* (New York: Paragon, 1987).

Person, Ethel, *Dreams of Love and Fateful Encounters: The Power of Romantic Love* (New York: W. W. Norton, 1989).

Plomin, Robert, *Development, Genetics, and Psychology* (Hillsdale, N.J.: Lawrence Erlbaum Associates, 1986).

Storr, Anthony, *Solitude: A Return to the Self* (New York: Free Press, 1988).

Trigg, Roger, *Ideas of Human Nature: An Historical Introduction* (Oxford: Basil Blackwell, 1988).

Trivers, Robert, *Social Evolution* (Menlo Park, Calif.: Benjamin/Cummings, 1985).

Waltz, Kenneth, *Man, the State, and War: A Theoretical Analysis* (New York: Columbia University Press, 1959).

Wilson, James Q., and Richard Herrnstein, *Crime and Human Nature* (New York: Simon & Schuster, 1985).

Wong, Normund, "Classical Psychoanalysis," in Kaplan, Harold, and Benjamin Sadock, *Comprehensive Textbook of Psychiatry,* fifth ed. (Baltimore: Williams and Wilkins, 1989), pp. 356–403. A body of theory that, despite many flaws, remains centrally important.

Transcendental Medication

Gorman, James, and Steven Locke, "Neural, Endocrine, and Immune Interactions," in Kaplan, Harold, and Benjamin Sadock, *Comprehensive Textbook of Psychiatry*, fifth ed. (Baltimore: Williams and Wilkins, 1989), pp. 111–25.

Katz, Richard, *Boiling Energy: Community Healing Among the Kalahari Kung* (Cambridge, Mass.: Harvard University Press, 1982).

Lee, Richard, "The Sociology of !Kung Bushman Trance Performances," in Prince, R., ed., *Trance and Possession States* (Montreal: Bucke Memorial Society, 1968).

Locke, Steven, and James Gorman, "Behavior and Immunity," in Kaplan, Harold, and Benjamin Sadock, *Comprehensive Textbook of Psychiatry,* fifth ed. (Baltimore: Williams and Wilkins, 1989), pp. 1240–49.

Marshall, Lorna, "The Medicine Dance of the !Kung Bushmen," *Africa* 39 (1981): 347–81.

Hands and Mind

Geschwind, Norman, *Selected Papers on Language and the Brain* (Boston: D. Reidel, 1974).

Geschwind, Norman, and Albert Galaburda, *Cerebral Lateralization* (Cambridge, Mass.: MIT Press, 1987).

———, "Cerebral Lateralization: Biological Mechanisms, Associations, and Pathology," *Archives of Neurology* 42 (1985): 428–459, 521–52, 634–54.

Hertz, Robert, "The Pre-eminence of the Right Hand: A Study in Religious Polarity," in *Death and the Right Hand* (Glencoe, Ill.: Free Press, [1909], 1960).

Maybury-Lewis, David, and Uri Almagor, eds., *The Attraction of*

Opposites: Thought and Society in the Dualistic Mode (Ann Arbor: University of Michigan Press, 1989).

Needham, Rodney, *Right and Left: Essays on Dual Symbolic Classification* (Chicago: University of Chicago Press, 1973).

Cuisine Sauvage

Eaton, S. Boyd, and Melvin Konner, "Paleolithic Nutrition: A Consideration of Its Nature and Current Implications," *New England Journal of Medicine* 312 (1985):283–89.

Eaton, S. Boyd, Melvin Konner, and Marjorie Shostak, "Stone Agers in the Fast Lane: Chronic Degenerative Disease in Evolutionary Perspective," *The American Journal of Medicine* 84 (1988): 739–49.

Eaton, S. Boyd, Marjorie Shostak, and Melvin Konner, *The Paleolithic Prescription: A Program of Diet and Exercise and a Design for Living* (New York: Harper & Row, 1988).

Leaf, Alexander, and Peter Weber, "A New Era for Science in Nutrition," *American Journal of Clinical Nutrition* 45 (1987): 1048–53.

Roberts, William, "Stone Agers in the Atomic Age: Lessons from the Paleolithic Lifestyle for Modern Man," *American Journal of Cardiology*, June 1, 1988, pp. 1365–66.

The Nursing Knot

Blurton Jones, Nicholas, "Comparative Aspects of Mother-Child Contact," in Blurton Jones, Nicholas, ed., *Ethological Studies of Child Behavior* (Cambridge, England: Cambridge University Press, 1972).

Bowlby, John, *Attachment and Loss,* vol. I: *Attachment* (London: Hogarth, 1969).

Konner, Melvin, and Marjorie Shostak, "Timing and Management of Birth among the !Kung: Biocultural Interaction in Reproductive Adaptation," *Cultural Anthropology* 2 (1987):11–28.

Konner, Melvin, and Carol Worthman, "Nursing Frequency, Gonadal Function and Birth Spacing Among !Kung Hunter-Gatherers," *Science* 207 (1980):788–91.

Lawrence, Ruth A., *Breastfeeding: A Guide for the Medical Profession,* third ed. (St. Louis: C. V. Mosby, 1989).

MacLean, Paul, "Brain Evolution Relating to Family, Play, and the Separation Call," *Archives of General Psychiatry* 42 (1985): 405–17.

Not to Be

Alvarez, A., *The Savage God* (New York: Random House, 1972).

Asberg, Marie, and Lil Traskman, "Studies of CSF 5-HIAA in Depression and Suicidal Behavior," *Advances in Experimental Medicine and Biology* 133 (1981):739–52.

Goodwin, F. K., and R. M. Post, "5-Hydroxytryptamine and Depression: A Model for the Interaction of Normal Variance with Pathology," *British Journal of Clinical Pharmacology* 15 (1983):393S–405S.

Roy, Alec, "Suicide," in Kaplan, Harold, and Benjamin Sadock, *Comprehensive Textbook of Psychiatry*, fifth ed. (Baltimore: Williams and Wilkins, 1989), pp. 1414–27.

Van Praag, Herman M., "Biological Suicide Research: Outcome and Limitations," *Biological Psychiatry* 21 (1986):1305–23.

The Stranger

Bowlby, John, *Attachment and Loss,* vol. I: *Attachment* (London: Hogarth, 1969), pp. 327–30.

Evans-Pritchard, E. E., *The Nuer* (New York: Oxford University Press, 1940), p. 183.

Konner, Melvin, "Biology of the Mother-Infant Bond," in Emde, Robert, and Robert Harmon, *The Development of Attachment and Affiliative Systems* (New York: Plenum Press, 1982).

———, "Universals of Behavioral Development in Relation to Brain Myelination," in Gibson, K., and A. Petersen, eds., *Brain Maturation and Cognitive Development* (New York: Aldine de Gruyter, 1991).

Lewis, Michael, and Leonard Rosenblum, eds., *The Origins of Fear* (New York: Wiley, 1974).

Maybury-Lewis, David, and Uri Almagor, eds., *The Attraction of Opposites: Thought and Society in the Dualistic Mode* (Ann Arbor: University of Michigan Press, 1989).

Toynbee, Arnold, *A Study of History*, one-volume ed. (New York: Oxford University Press, 1972), p. 34.

In the Sisterhood of Seduction

Aries, Philippe, and Andre Bejin, *Western Sexuality: Practice and Precept in Past and Present Times* (Oxford: Blackwell, 1985).

Basserman, Lujo, *The Oldest Profession: A History of Prostitution* (New York: Dorset, 1967).

Dalby, Liza Crihfield, *Geisha* (Berkeley: University of California Press, 1983).

Katchadourian, Herant, *Fundamentals of Human Sexuality,* fourth ed. (New York: Holt, Rinehart & Winston, 1985).

Kinsey, Alfred, Wardell Pomeroy, and Clyde Martin, *Sexual Behavior in the Human Male* (Philadelphia: W. B. Saunders, 1948).

Lewis, Flora, "Now Turn to Women; What's Next for Japan and Miss Doi," *The New York Times*, July 26, 1989, op-ed page.

Murphy, Emmett, *Great Bordellos of the World* (New York: Quartet, 1983).

Sanger, David, "Reports that Premier Might Quit Plunge Tokyo into Renewed Crisis; Leader Denies Saying He Wants to Resign Over Geisha Scandal," *The New York Times*, June 29, 1989, p. 1.

The Riddle of the Smile

Eibl-Eibesfeldt, Irenäus, *Human Ethology* (New York: Aldine de Gruyter, 1989).

Haith, Marshall, John Watson, Robert McCall, and Philip Zelazo, symposium: "The Meaning of Smiling and Vocalizing in Infancy," *Merrill-Palmer Quarterly: Behavior and Development* 18 (1972):321–65.

Konner, Melvin, "Biology of the Mother-Infant Bond," in Emde, Robert, and Robert Harmon, *The Development of Attachment and Affiliative Systems* (New York: Plenum Press, 1982).

———, "Universals of Behavioral Development in Relation to Brain Myelination," in Gibson, K., and A. Petersen, eds., *Brain Maturation and Cognitive Development* (New York: Aldine de Gruyter, 1991).

Rinn, W. E., "The Neuropsychology of Facial Expression," *Psychological Bulletin* 95 (1985):52–77.

Van Hooff, J. A. R. A. M., "A Comparative Approach to the Phylogeny of Laughter and Smiling," in Hinde, Robert, ed., *Non-verbal Communication* (Cambridge, England: Cambridge University Press, 1972).

Birth Rites

Armstrong, E., and D. Falk, eds., *Primate Brain Evolution* (New York: Plenum Press, 1982), chapters by Walter Leutenneger and George Sachar.

Hobel, Calvin J., et al., "Prenatal and Intrapartum High-Risk

Screening," *American Journal of Obstetrics and Gynecology* 117 (1973):1–9.

Konner, Melvin, and Marjorie Shostak, "Timing and Management of Birth among the !Kung: Biocultural Interaction in Reproductive Adaptation," *Cultural Anthropology* 2 (1987):11–28.

Pritchard, Jack, Paul MacDonald, and Norman Gant, *Williams Obstetrics,* seventeenth ed. (New York: Appleton-Century-Crofts, 1985).

Schultz, A. H., *The Life of Primates* (London: Weidenfeld and Nicolson, 1969).

Wertz, Richard, and Dorothy Wertz, *Lying In: A History of Childbirth in America* (New York: Free Press, 1977).

Love Among the Robots

Aleksander, Igor, and Piers Burnett, *Reinventing Man: The Robot Becomes Reality* (New York: Holt, Rinehart & Winston, 1983).

Dreyfus, Hubert, and Stuart Dreyfus, "Mindless Machines: Computers Don't Think Like Experts, and Never Will," *The Sciences* 24 (1984):18–22.

Hofstadter, Douglas, and Daniel Dennett, *The Mind's I: Fantasies and Reflections on Self and Soul* (New York: Basic Books, 1981).

Searle, John, "Minds, Brains, and Programs," *The Behavioral and Brain Sciences* 3 (1980):417–57; with commentaries by various other authors and a reply by Searle.

Turkle, Sherry, *The Second Self: Computers and the Human Spirit* (New York: Simon & Schuster, 1984).

Weizenbaum, Joseph, *Computer Power and Human Reason* (San Francisco: W. H. Freeman, 1976).

Why the Reckless Survive

Benfari, R. C., E. Eaker, and J. G. Stoll, "Behavioral Interventions and Compliance to Treatment Regimes," *Annual Review of Public Health* 2 (1981):431–71.

Daly, Martin, and Margo Wilson, *Homicide* (New York: Aldine de Gruyter, 1988).

Douglas, Mary, and Aaron Wildavsky, *Risk and Culture: An Essay on the Selection of Technical and Environmental Dangers* (Berkeley: University of California Press, 1982).

Eaton, S. Boyd, and Melvin Konner, "Paleolithic Nutrition: A Consideration of Its Nature and Current Implications," *The*

New England Journal of Medicine 312 (1985):283–89.

Farley, Frank, "The Big T in Personality," *Psychology Today* 20 (1986):44–52.

Harris, Louis, and associates, "Risk in a Complex Society" (Marsh & McLennan Companies, 1980).

Istvan, Joseph, and Joseph D. Matarazzo, "Tobacco, Alcohol and Caffeine Use: A Review of Their Interrelationships," *Psychological Bulletin* 95 (1987):301–26.

Kahnemann, Daniel, and Amos Tversky, "Choices, Values, and Frames," *American Psychologist* 39 (1984):341–50.

Lewis, Oscar, *The Children of Sanchez* (New York: Random House, 1961).

Liebow, Eliot, *Tally's Corner: A Study of Negro Streetcorner Men* (Boston: Little, Brown, 1967).

Lopes, Lola L., "Risk and Distributional Inequality," *Journal of Experimental Psychology: Human Perception and Performance* 10 (1984):465–85.

———, "Some Thoughts on the Psychological Concept of Risk," *Journal of Experimental Psychology: Human Perception and Performance* 9 (1983):137–44.

Luker, Kristin, *Taking Chances: Abortion and the Decision Not to Contracept* (Berkeley: University of California Press, 1975).

Peck, Cecil P., "Risk-Taking Behavior and Compulsive Gambling," *American Psychologist* 41 (1987):461–65.

Perloff, Linda S., and Barbara A. Fetzer, "Self-Other Judgments and Perceived Vulnerability to Victimization," *Journal of Personality and Social Psychology* 50 (1986):502–10.

Simon, Herbert, "Rationality as Process and Product of Thought," *American Economic Review* 68 (1978):1–16.

———, *Reason in Human Affairs* (Stanford, Calif.: Stanford University Press, 1983).

Slovic, Paul, "Perception of Risk," *Science* 236 (1987):280–85. See also other articles on risk assessment in the same issue.

Tversky, Amos, and Daniel Kahnemann, "The Framing of Decisions and the Psychology of Choice," *Science* 211 (1981):453–58.

Urquhart, John, and Klaus Heilmann, *Risk Watch: The Odds of Life* (New York: Facts on File Publications, 1984).

Zuckerman, Marvin, Monte S. Buchsbaum, and Dennis L. Murphy, "Sensation Seeking and Its Biological Correlates," *Psychological Bulletin* 88 (1980): 187–214.

The Many Faces of Madness

Abrams, R., and M. Taylor, "The Genetics of Schizophrenia: A Reassessment Using Modern Criteria," *American Journal of Psychiatry* 140 (1983):171

Abrams, R., M. Taylor, and S. Kety, "Drs. Abrams and Taylor on Dr. Kety's Review" and "Dr. Kety Replies" [letters], *American Journal of Psychiatry* 140 (1983):1111–12.

Abrams, Taylor, McGuffin et al. [letters], *American Journal of Psychiatry* 42 (1985):422; 43 (1986):295; Hayward and Kendler, 43 (1986):714.

Akiskal, Hagop, "The Classification of Mental Disorders," in Kaplan, Henry, and Benjamin Sadock, *Comprehensive Textbook of Psychiatry,* fifth ed. (Baltimore: Williams and Wilkins, 1989), chapter 11, pp. 583–98. See also chapters 14 and 17.

Barnes, Deborah, and Constance Holden, "Biological Issues in Schizophrenia," *Science* 235 (1977):430–33.

Cade, John, "Lithium Salts in the Treatment of Psychotic Excitement," *Medical Journal of Australia* 36 (1949):349.

Goodwin, Donald, and Samuel Guze, *Psychiatric Diagnosis,* fourth ed. (New York: Oxford University Press, 1988).

Gottesman, Irving, and James Shields, *Schizophrenia: The Epigenetic Puzzle* (New York: Cambridge University Press, 1982).

Guze, S., R. Cloninger, R. Martin, and P. Clayton, "A Follow-up and Family Study of Schizophrenia," *Archives of General Psychiatry* 40 (1983):1273.

Kendler, K., "Heritability and Schizophrenia," *American Journal of Psychiatry* 140 (1983):131.

Kendler, K., A. Gruenberg, and M. Tsuang, "Psychiatric Illness in First-Degree Relatives of Schizophrenic and Surgical Control Patients," *Archives of General Psychiatry* 42 (1985):770.

Kety, Seymour, "Mental Illness in the Biological and Adoptive Relatives of Schizophrenic Adoptees: Findings Relevant to Genetic and Environmental Factors in Etiology," *American Journal of Psychiatry* 140 (1983):720.

Pope, Harrison, and Joseph Lipinski, "Diagnosis in Schizophrenia and Manic-Depressive Illness," *Archives of General Psychiatry* 35 (1978):811.

Pope, H., J. Lipinski, B. Cohen, and D. Axelrod, "Schizoaffective Disorder," *American Journal of Psychiatry* 137 (1980):921.

Pope, H., J. Jonas, B. Cohen, J. Lipinski, "Failure to Find Evidence of Schizophrenia in First-Degree Relatives of Schizophrenia Probands," *American Journal of Psychiatry* 139 (1982):826.

Taylor, Michael, "Schneiderian First Rank Symptoms and Clinical Prognostic Features in Schizophrenia," *Archives of General Psychiatry* 26 (1972):64.

Taylor, M., and R. Abrams, "The Phenomenology of Mania," *Archives of General Psychiatry* 29 (1973):520.

———, "Acute Mania: Clinical and Genetic Study of Respondents and Non-Respondents to Treatments," *Archives of General Psychiatry* 32 (1975):863; "A Critique of the St. Louis Psychiatric Research Criteria for Schizophrenia," 132 (1975):1276; "Mania and Schizophrenic Disorder, Manic Type: A Comparison," 133 (1976):1445; "The Prevalance of Schizophrenia: A Reassessment Using Modern Diagnostic Criteria," 135 (1978):945; "The Genetics of Schizophrenia: A Reassessment Using Modern Criteria," 140 (1983):171.

Taylor, M., P. Gaztanaga, and R. Abrams, "Manic-Depressive Illness and Acute Schizophrenia: A Clinical, Family History, and Treatment-Response Study," *American Journal of Psychiatry* 131 (1974):678.

False Idylls

Benedict, Ruth, *Patterns of Culture* (Boston: Houghton Mifflin, 1934).

Bennett, John, "Interpretation of Pueblo Culture: A Question of Values," *Southwestern Journal of Anthropology* 2 (1946): 361–74.

Eggan, Dorothy, "The General Problem of Hopi Adjustment," *American Anthropologist* 45 (1943):357–73.

Freeman, Derek, *Margaret Mead and Samoa: The Making and Unmaking of an Anthropological Myth* (Cambridge, Mass.: Harvard University Press, 1983).

Goldfrank, Esther, "Socialization, Personality, and the Structure of Pueblo Society," *American Anthropologist* 47 (1945):516–39.

Goodall, Jane, *The Chimpanzees of Gombe: Patterns of Behavior* (Cambridge, Mass.: Harvard University Press, 1986).

———, *In the Shadow of Man* (Boston: Houghton Mifflin, 1971).

Holmes, Lowell, *Quest for the Real Samoa: The Mead-Freeman Controversy and Beyond* (South Hadley, Mass.: Bergin and Garvey, 1987).

Lee, Richard, *The !Kung San: Men, Women, and Work in a Foraging Society* (New York: Cambridge University Press, 1979).

McDonald, Christie, "Jacques Derrida's Reading of Rousseau," *The Eighteenth Century* 20 (1979):82–95.

Marshall, Lorna, *The !Kung of Nyae Nyae* (Cambridge, Mass.: Harvard University Press, 1976).

Mead, Margaret, *Coming of Age in Samoa* (New York: William Morrow, 1928).

Montagu, Ashley, *The Nature of Human Aggression* (New York: Oxford University Press, 1976).

Sahlins, Marshall, "Notes on the Original Affluent Society," in Lee, Richard, and Irven DeVore, *Man the Hunter* (Chicago: Aldine, 1968), pp. 85–89.

Shankman, Paul, "The Samoan Conundrum," *Canberra Anthropology* 6 (1983):38–57.

Shore, Bradd, *Sala'ilua, A Samoan Mystery* (New York: Columbia University Press, 1982).

Shostak, Marjorie, *Nisa: The Life and Words of a !Kung Woman* (Cambridge, Mass.: Harvard University Press, 1981).

Thompson, Laura, "Logico-Aesthetic Integration in Hopi Culture," *American Anthropologist* 47 (1945):540–53.

The Gender Option

Chira, Susan, "Is Any Choice Right in Sex Selection?," *The New York Times*, October 26, 1986.

Corea, Gena, et al., *Man-Made Women: How New Reproductive Technologies Affect Women* (Bloomington, Ind.: Midland Books, 1987).

Corson, Stephen, et al., "Sex Selection by Sperm Separation and Insemination," *Fertility and Sterility* 42 (1984):756–60.

Dickeman, Mildred, "Demographic Consequences of Infanticide in Man," *Annual Review of Ecology and Systematics* 6 (1975): 107–37.

Divale, William, and Marvin Harris, "Population, Warfare, and the Male Supremacist Complex," *American Anthropologist* 78 (1976):521–38.

Etzioni, Amitai, "Sex Control, Science, and Society," *Science* 161 (1968):1107–12.

Finnell, Rebecca, "Daughters or Sons," *Natural History,* April 1988, pp. 63–83.

Fisher, Ronald, *The Genetical Theory of Natural Selection* (New York: Oxford University Press, 1930), pp. 141–45.

Jeffery, Roger, Patricia Jeffery, and Andrew Lyon, "Female Infanticide and Amniocentesis," *Social Science and Medicine* 19 (1984):1207–12.

Johansson, Sheila Ryan, "Deferred Infanticide: Excess Female Mortality During Childhood," in Hausfater, Glenn, and Sarah Blaffer Hrdy, eds., *Infanticide: Comparative and Evolutionary Perspectives* (New York: Aldine, 1984), pp. 463–85.

Johnston, Kathy, "Sex of New Embryos Known," *Nature* 327 (1987):547.

Miller, Barbara, "Female Infanticide and Child Neglect in Rural India," in Scheper-Hughes, Nancy, ed., *Child Survival: Anthropological Perspectives on the Treatment and Maltreatment of Children* (Boston: D. Reidel, 1987).

Ramanamma, A., and Usha Bambawale, "The Mania for Sons: An Analysis of Social Values in South Asia," *Social Science and Medicine* 14B (1980):107–10.

Scrimshaw, Susan, "Infanticide in Human Populations: Societal and Individual Concerns," in Hausfater, Glenn, and Sarah Blaffer Hrdy, eds., *Infanticide: Comparative and Evolutionary Perspectives* (New York: Aldine, 1984), pp. 439–62.

Is Orgasm Essential?

Alzate, Heli, "Vaginal Eroticism and Female Orgasm: A Current Appraisal," *Journal of Sex and Marital Therapy* 11 (1985):271–84.

Alzate, Heli, and Zwi Hoch, "The 'G Spot' and 'Female Ejaculation': A Current Appraisal," *Journal of Sex and Marital Therapy* 12 (1986):211–20.

Anderson, Barbara L., "Primary Orgasmic Dysfunction: Diagnostic Considerations and Review of Treatment," *Psychological Bulletin* 95 (1983):105–36.

Aries, Philippe, and Andre Bejin, *Western Sexuality Practice and Precept in Past and Present Times* (Oxford: Blackwell, 1985), chapter 15.

Chevalier-Skolnikoff, Suzanne, "Male-Female, Female-Female, and Male-Male Sexual Behavior in the Stumptail Monkey, with Special Attention to Female Orgasm," *Archives of Sexual Behavior* 3 (1974):95–116.

Davidson, Julian M., "The Psychobiology of Sexual Experience," in Davidson, J. M., and R. J. Davidson, eds., *The Psychobiology of Conciousness* (New York: Plenum Press, 1980).

Freud, Sigmund, *A General Introduction to Psychoanalysis* (New York: Washington Square Press, 1963), p. 327.

Goldfoot, D. A., H. Westerborg-Van Loon, W. Groeneveld, and A. Koos Slob, "Behavioral and Physiological Evidence of Sexual Climax in the Female Stump-Tailed Macaque (*Macaca arctoides*)," *Science* 208 (1980):1477–78.

Gould, Stephen J., "Freudian Slip," *Natural History*, February 1987, pp. 15–21.

Heath, Robert G., "Pleasure and Brain Activity in Man," *The Journal of Nervous and Mental Disease* 154 (1972):3–31.

Kinsey, Alfred C., Wardell B. Pomeroy, Clyde E. Martin, Paul H. Gebhard, et al., *Sexual Behavior in the Human Female* (Philadelphia and London: W. B. Saunders, 1953).

Masters, William H., and Virginia E. Johnson, *Human Sexual Response* (Boston: Little, Brown, 1966).

Mead, Margaret, *Male and Female: A Study of the Sexes in a Changing World* (New York: William Morrow, 1967). (Originally published in 1949.)

Nathan, Sharon G., "The Epidemiology of the DSM-III Psychosexual Dysfunctions," *Journal of Sex and Marital Therapy* 12 (1986):267–81.

Riboud, Felix, quoted in Aries, Philippe, and Andre Bejin, *Western Sexuality Practice and Precept in Past and Present Times* (Oxford: Blackwell, 1985), p. 182.

Sholty, MaryJo, Paul H. Ephross, S. Michael Plaut, Susan H. Fischman, Jane F. Charnas, and Carol A. Cody, "Female Orgasmic Experience: A Subjective Study," *Archives of Sexual Behavior* 13 (1984):155–64.

Vance, Ellen Belle, and Nathaniel N. Wagner, "Written Descriptions of Orgasm: A Study of Sex Differences," *Archives of Sexual Behavior* 5 (1976):87–98.

Too Desperate a Cure?

American Psychiatric Association Commission on Psychiatric Therapies, chaired by Toksoz B. Karasu, "Psychosurgery," in *The Psychiatric Therapies* (Washington, D.C.: American Psychiatric Association, 1984).

Ballantine, H. Thomas, Jr., "A Critical Assessment of Psychiatric

Surgery: Past, Present, and Future," in *American Handbook of Psychiatry*, second ed., vol. 8: *Biological Psychiatry*, Berger, Philip A., and Keith H. Brodie, eds. (New York: Basic Books, 1986), pp. 1029–47.

———, "Neurosurgery for Behavior Disorders," in Wilkins, Robert H., and Setti S. Rengachary, eds., *Neurosurgery* (New York: McGraw-Hill, 1985), pp. 2527–37.

Ballantine, H. Thomas, Jr., Anthony J. Bouckoms, Elizabeth K. Thomas, and Ida E. Giriunas, "Treatment of Psychiatric Illness by Stereotactic Cingulotomy," *Biological Psychiatry* 22 (1987): 807–19.

Burton, Robert, *The Anatomy of Melancholy. What It Is, with All the Kinds, Causes, Symptomes, Prognostickes & Several Cures of It*, Jackson, Holbrook, ed. (New York: Vintage Books, 1977), p. 242. (Originally published in 1621.)

Kalinowsky, Lothar B., Hanns Hippius, and Helmfried E. Klein, "Psychosurgery," in *Biological Treatments in Psychiatry* (New York: Grune & Stratton, 1982), pp. 272–93.

Sweet, W. H., "Neurosurgical Aspects of Primary Affective Disorders," in Youmans, Julian R., ed., *Neurological Surgery*, vol. 6 (Philadelphia: W. B. Saunders, 1982), pp. 3927–46.

Valenstein, Elliot, *Great and Desperate Cures: The Rise and Decline of Psychosurgery and Other Radical Treatments for Mental Illness* (New York: Basic Books, 1986).

Everyman

Bohannon, Laura, "Shakespeare in the Bush," *Natural History*, August–September 1966.

Darwin, Charles, *The Expression of the Emotions in Man and Animals* (Chicago: University of Chicago, 1965). (Originally published in 1872.)

Eibl-Eibesfeldt, Irenäus, *Human Ethology* (New York: Aldine de Gruyter, 1989).

Hackett, Charles, "The Origin of Speech," *Scientific American* 203 (1960):88–111.

Linton, Ralph, *The Study of Man: An Introduction* (New York: Appleton-Century-Crofts, 1936).

Murdock, George Peter, *Social Structure* (New York: Free Press, 1949).

Murphy, Jane, "Psychiatric Labeling in Cross-Cultural Perspective," *Science* 191 (1976):1019.

Spiro, Melford, "Is the Family Universal?," *American Anthropologist* 56 (1954):839–46. Reprinted, with addendum changing the answer, in Hunter, David, and Phillip Whitten, eds., *Anthropology:Contemporary Perspectives*, third ed. (Boston: Little, Brown, 1982), pp. 154–60.

Genes and the Soul

Cloninger, C. Robert, "Neurogenetic Adaptive Mechanisms in Alcoholism," *Science* 236 (1987):410–16.

Farber, Susan, *Identical Twins Reared Apart: A Reanalysis* (New York: Basic Books, 1981).

Floderus-Myrhed, Birgitta, Nancy Pedersen, and Ingrid Rasmuson, "Assessment of Heritability for Personality, Based on a Short-Form of the Eysenck Personality Inventory: A Study of 12,898 Twin Pairs," *Behavior Genetics* 10 (1980):153–62.

Kaprio, Jaakko, Markku Koskenvuo, Heimo Langinvainio, Kalle Romanov, Seppo Sarnov, and Richard J. Rose, "Genetic Influences on Use and Abuse of Alcohol: A Study of 5638 Adult Finnish Twin Brothers," *Alcoholism: Clinical and Experimental Research* 11 (1987):349–55.

Loehlin, John C., "Heredity, Environment, and the Thurstone Temperament Schedule," *Behavior Genetics* 16 (1986):61–73.

Phillips, Kay, David W. Fulker, and Richard J. Rose, "Path Analysis of Seven Fear Factors in Adult Twin and Sibling Pairs and Their Parents," *Genetic Epidemiology* 4 (1987):345–55.

Plomin, Robert, and Denise Daniels, "Why Are Children in the Same Family So Different from One Another?," *Behavioral and Brain Sciences* 10 (1987):1–60.

Pogue-Geile, Michael F., and Richard J. Rose, "Developmental Genetic Studies of Adult Personality," *Developmental Psychology* 21 (1985):547–57.

Rose, Richard J., Markku Koskenvuo, Jaakko Kaprio, Seppo Sarnov, and Heimo Langinvainio, "Shared Genes, Shared Experiences, and Similarity of Personality: Data from 14,288 Adult Finnish Co-Twins," *Journal of Personality and Social Psychology* 54 (1988):161–71.

Rushton, J. Phillippe, David W. Fulker, Michael C. Neale, David K. B. Nias, and Hans J. Eysenck, "Altruism and Aggression: The Heritability of Individual Differences," *Journal of Personality and Social Psychology* 50 (1986):1192–98.

Tellegen, Auke, David T. Lykken, Thomas J. Bouchard, Jr., Kimerly

J. Wilcox, Nancy L. Segal, and Stephen Rich, "Personality Similarity in Twins Reared Apart and Together," *Journal of Personality and Social Psychology* 54 (1988):1031–39.

Art of Darkness

Akiskal, H. S., and K. Akiskal, "Reassessing the Prevalence of Bipolar Disorders: Clinical Significance and Artistic Creativity," *Psychiatry and Psychobiology* 3 (1988):29S–36S.

Andreasen, Nancy C., "Creativity and Mental Illness: Prevalence Rates in Writers and Their First-Degree Relatives," *American Journal of Psychiatry* 144 (1987):1288–92.

Hamilton, Ian, *Robert Lowell: A Biography* (New York: Random House, 1982).

Hershman, D. Jablow, and Julian Lieb, *The Key to Genius: Manic-Depression and the Creative Life* (Buffalo: Prometheus Books, 1988).

Jamison, Kay Redfield, "Mood Disorders and Patterns of Creativity in British Writers and Artists," in Goodwin, Fredrick, and Kay Redfield Jamison, *Manic Depressive Illness* (New York: Oxford University Press, 1990).

Jamison, Kay Redfield, and Robert Winter, *Moods and Music*. Program produced for a concert featuring the works of Handel, Schumann, Wolf, Berlioz, and Mahler; sponsored by the University of California at Los Angeles Neuropsychiatric Institute and the Department of Music, featuring the Los Angeles Philharmonic Orchestra (Los Angeles: UCLA Publication Services, 1985).

Lowell, Robert, *Selected Poems*, rev. ed. (New York: Farrar, Straus & Giroux, 1977).

Richards, Ruth, and Dennis K. Kinney, Inge Lunde, Maria Benet, and Ann P. C. Merzel, "Creativity in Manic-Depressives, Cyclothymes, Their Normal Relatives, and Control Subjects," *Journal of Abnormal Psychology* 97 (1988):281–88.

Nervous Energy

Cantor, Michael B., "Bad Habits: Models of Induced Ingestion in Satiated Rats and People," in Miller, S. A., ed., *Behavior and Nutrition* (Philadelphia: Franklin Institute Press, 1981), pp. 31–49.

Cantor, Michael B., Stephen E. Smith, and Bonita R. Bryan, "Induced Bad Habits: Adjunctive Ingestion and Grooming in Human Subjects," *Appetite: Journal for Intake Research* 3 (1982):1–12.

Cantor, Michael B., and Josephine F. Wilson, "Feeding the Face: New Directions in Adjunctive Behavior Research," in Miller, S. A., ed., *Behavior and Nutrition* (Philadelphia: Franklin Institute Press, 1981), pp. 299–312.

Falk, John L., "Production of Polydipsia in Normal Rats by an Intermittent Food Schedule," *Science* 133 (1961):195–96.

Granger, R. Gray, Joseph H. Porter, and Nita L. Christoph, "Schedule-Induced Behavior in Children as a Function of Interreinforcement Interval Length," *Physiology and Behavior* 33 (1984):153–57.

Mittleman, Guy, and Elliot S. Valenstein, "Ingestive Behavior Evoked by Hypothalamic Stimulation and Schedule-Induced Polydipsia Are Related," *Science* 224 (1984):415–17.

Valenstein, Elliot S., Verne C. Cox, and Jan W. Kakolewski, "Modification of Motivated Behavior Elicited by Electrical Stimulation of the Hypothalamus," *Science* 159 (1968):1119–21.

———, "Reexamination of the Role of the Hypothalamus in Motivation," *Psychological Review* 77 (1970):16–31.

Wilson, Josephine F., and Michael B. Cantor, "An Animal Model of Excessive Eating: Schedule-Induced Hyperphagia in Food-Satiated Rats," *Journal of the Experimental Analysis of Behavior* 47(1987):335–46.

Minding the Pain

Clark, W. Crawford, and Susanne Bennett Clark, "Pain Responses in Nepalese Porters," *Science* 209 (1980):410–12.

Gilman, Alfred, and Louis S. Goodman, eds., *The Pharmacological Basis of Therapeutics*, sixth ed. (New York: Macmillan, 1980), chapters 15, 22, and 29.

Gintzler, Alan R., "Endorphin-Medicated Increases in Pain Threshold During Pregnancy," *Science* 210 (1980):193–95.

Hoffert, Marvin Jay, "The Neurophysiology of Pain," *Neurologic Clinics* 7 (1989):183.

Melzack, Ronald, and Patrick D. Wall, *The Challenge of Pain*, second rev. ed. (New York: Penguin, 1988).

Portency, Russel K., "Mechanisms of Clinical Pain: Observations and Speculations," *Neurologic Clinics* 7 (1989):205.

Rossier, Jean, Floyd E. Bloom, and Roger Guillemin, "Stimulation of Human Periaqueductal Gray for Pain Relief Increases Immunoreactive Beta-Endorphin in Ventricular Fluid," *Science* 203 (1979):279–81.

The "I" of the Storm

Aristotle, *The Nicomachean Ethics*, translated by J. E. C. Weldon (Buffalo: Prometheus Books, 1987).

Bacon, Doris, "Vicious Crime, Double Jeopardy," *People*, June 5, 1989.

Barth, Robert, and Bill Kinder, "The Mislabeling of Sexual Impulsivity," *Journal of Sex and Marital Therapy* 13 (1987):15–23.

Emanuel, Steven, *Criminal Law*, second ed. (Larchmont, N.Y.: Emanuel Law Outlines, 1987), pp. 60–90.

Ermutlu, Ilhan, and Jimmy Canady, "Mental Illness, Substance Abuse, and Criminal Behavior," *Journal of the Medical Association of Georgia* 78 (1989):213–17.

Gutheil, Thomas, "Legal Issues in Psychiatry," in Kaplan, Harold, and Benjamin Sadock, eds., *Comprehensive Textbook of Psychiatry*, fifth ed. (Baltimore: Williams and Wilkins, 1989), pp.2107–24.

Lee, Richard, *The !Kung San: Men, Women, and Work in a Foraging Society* (New York: Cambridge University Press, 1979).

Low, Peter, *Criminal Law* (St. Paul, Minn.: West Publishing Company, 1984). Includes Model Penal Code; quotation on "blame and punishment," p. 203.

Menninger, Karl, *The Crime of Punishment* (New York: Viking, 1968).

Robitscher, Jonas, *The Powers of Psychiatry* (Boston: Houghton Mifflin, 1980).

Siegel, Larry, *Criminology*, third ed. (St. Paul, Minn.: West Publishing Company, 1989).

Szasz, Thomas, "Bad Habits Are Not Diseases," *Lancet*, July 8, 1972, pp. 83–84.

———, "Getting It Backward on Crack Patients," letter to *The New York Times,* June 13, 1989.

———, *The Myth of Mental Illness: Foundations of a Theory of Personal Conduct*, second ed. (New York: Harper & Row, 1974).

Teplin, Linda, "The Criminality of the Mentally Ill: A Dangerous Misconception," *American Journal of Psychiatry* 142 (1985): 593–99.

Wilson, James Q., and Richard Herrnstein, *Crime and Human Nature: The Definitive Study of the Causes of Crime* (New York: Simon & Schuster, 1985).

Weissman, Moshe, ed., *The Midrash Says: The Book of Beraishis* (Brooklyn, N.Y.: Benei Yakov, 1980), pp. 64–65.